The champions of the crown

Lucy Sealy

THE CHAMPIONS OF THE CROWN

KING CHARLES 1 IN THREE POSITIONS

THE CHAMPIONS
OF THE CROWN

BY

LUCY SEALY

WITH TWELVE ILLUSTRATIONS

METHUEN & CO. LTD.
36 ESSEX STREET W.C.
LONDON

First Published in 1911

PREFACE

IT is to be feared that to many people the term "Cavalier" is still one of reproach. It calls up a vision of godless, roystering soldiers, fighting solely for the retention of power, wealth, or licence.

As the leaders, so the followers; and if this attempt to place before the public a simple record of the lives of some of the more prominent Royalists should serve to remove this popular misconception from the minds of any, the main purpose of the writer will be accomplished.

Another object has been the analysis of the motives which led men of such varying characters and ideals to adopt the Royalists' cause, and thus to form a veritable "Cloud of Witnesses" attesting the good faith of the King.

In conclusion, I should wish to express my deep sense of gratitude to Mr. Armstrong, of Queen's College, Oxford, without the stimulus of whose advice and encouragement the work would not have been attempted.

L. S.

NEWPORT, MON.

CONTENTS

LIST OF ILLUSTRATIONS

WILLIAM CAVENDISH, DUKE OF NEWCASTLE

FROM AN ENGRAVING BY G. VERTUE AFTER THE PAINTING BY VAN DYCK

THE
CHAMPIONS OF THE CROWN

TWO CHAMPIONS OF THE NORTH

THE MARQUIS OF NEWCASTLE

THE Marquis of Newcastle was born in the year 1592; he was the second son of Sir Charles Cavendish, but his elder brother died in infancy, so he became his father's heir. Sir Charles was younger brother of the first Earl of Devonshire, and had married Catherine, second of the two daughters and co-heirs of Cuthbert, Lord Ogle. As a child William Cavendish was educated at home, but was later entered at St. John's College, Cambridge. Here, apparently, his interests centred more in horses and sport than in books, for his father is said to have " suffered him to follow his own genius, and had him instructed by the best Masters in the Arts of Horsemanship and Weapons, which he was most inclined to, and soon became master of them." At the age of eighteen he was made a Knight of the Bath on the creation of Henry, Prince of Wales. Then for a time, in accordance with the custom of the age, he travelled to see the world. Sir Henry Wotton was going as Ambassador Extraordinary to the Duke of Savoy, and the youth was placed in his care. He speedily won the

I

favour and good opinion, not only of his fellow-countryman, but also of the Duke of Savoy, who offered him office in his service. His guardian would not, however, leave him without the consent of his parents, and he returned to England, having received handsome gifts from the Duke on his departure.

In 1617 Sir Charles Cavendish died, and William succeeded to the title and estates. In accordance with his mother's wish the young nobleman now married, his choice falling upon the daughter and heiress of William Basset, of Blore, in Staffordshire, with whom he received considerable estates and a good dowry in money. Although he was in high favour at Court, he never seems to have pursued office. At this period he spent most of his time in the country on his estates, and so had no special position at Court. In the year 1620 he was advanced to the peerage by James I with the title of Lord Ogle of Bothal and Viscount Mansfield, the former by right of his mother. This honour was conferred after the King's visit to Welbeck, in 1619, where he had been most royally entertained.

The death of James I put no period to Newcastle's advancement, for, though the favourite Buckingham hated and was jealous of him, the affection of Charles was strong enough to protect him. He was at once made Lord-Lieutenant of Nottinghamshire, and showed in that position those qualities of loyalty and integrity which distinguished him throughout his career. In 1627 the King advanced him to the dignity of Baron Cavendish of Bolsover and Earl of Newcastle-upon-Tyne. His conduct in these early years of the reign brought him to the notice of Wentworth; they had some correspondence, and it was probably due to the great statesman's advice that in 1638 Charles decided to make Newcastle Governor of the Prince of Wales. He certainly had many qualities which fitted him for the post. He was a man of considerable culture, with knowledge of the world, attractive in manner, irreproachable in his private as in public life, of intense loyalty and shrewd common sense. Pacific in disposition, he was at the same time manly in tastes well-fitted to win the affection and respect of his charge. His letter of instruction to the Prince on taking up his duties is remarkable for its wit and knowledge of the world. The Prince must study languages, " though I confess I would rather have you study things than words, matter than language." History is of special importance, " for men have the same passions now as then, and thus you shall see the excellency and errors both of kings and subjects." The Arts are to be studied, especially those most suitable for " war and use." Concerning religion the young Prince is warned against too much devotion, " how many will history represent to you that in seeming to gain the Kingdom of Heaven have lost their own." On the other hand, irreligion must be avoided; the Prince must be an example in religion, if not people will have no obedience to God and then none to the King. On the other side, " if any be Bible madd, over much burn't with fiery zeal, they may think it a service to God to destroy you and say the Spirit moved them and bring some example of a King with a hard name in the Old Testament." Men rather than books are to be studied, for no bookworms have ever been great statesmen; " the reason's plain, for divinity teaches what we should be, not what we are; so doth moral philosophy, and many philosophical worlds and Utopias scholars have made, and fancied to themselves such worlds as never was, is, or shall be ; and then I dare say if they govern themselves by those rules what men should be, and not what they are, they will miss the cushion very much."

Twice the pupil to-be is warned against becoming too studious. " You cannot be a good contemplative man and a good commonwealth's man." The lack of necessity for this injunction seems to have struck Newcastle, for he goes on to say, " But, sir, you are in your own disposition religious and not yery apt to your book, so you need no great labour to persuade you for the one, or long discussions to dissuade you from the other." He is advised also not to set aside state or lose dignity ; " you cannot put upon you too much King," yet " civility cannot unprince you, but much advantage you." " Temper yourself by remembrance that you are but mortal, so as to be a brave, noble, and just King, and make your name immortal by your brave acts abroad and your unspotted justice at home, qualified by your well temper and mercy."

The following epistle from the Prince to his preceptor is written entirely in his own hand, in lines ruled by a pencil above and below. It shows the affection that existed between pupil and governor, and also illustrates the fact that children of the seventeenth century were much like those of to-day.

· " MY LORD,

        " I would not have you take too much physic for it doth always make me worse, and I think it will do the like with you. I ride every day, and am ready to follow any other directions from you. Make haste to return to him that loves you.

" CHARLES P."

In the year 1639 the King sent an expedition against the Scots, under the joint command of Essex, Holland, and Arundel. The Earl of Newcastle gave ten thousand pounds towards the cost of this expedition and also raised a body of two hundred gentlemen, who served under him at their own expense, and were called the Prince of Wales' troop. Holland, who was even then suspected of treachery by Wentworth, seized the occasion to put a slight upon Newcastle. The latter had sent to him, as general of the horse, to ask that his troop might be given some precedence. The request was refused, for no obvious reason, and Newcastle, accepting the position with quiet dignity, merely showed his sense of the slight to his royal master by ordering that the Prince's colours should not be carried. Holland complained of this to the King, but Newcastle's action was upheld. The troops did not see active service, for the Pacification of Berwick put an end to this first "Bishop's War." Newcastle seized the first opportunity to challenge Holland, imputing his action to personal hostility, but that nobleman delayed the meeting so long that the King came to hear of it and used his authority to prevent it.

In May, 1641, Newcastle resigned his post of Governor to the Prince, and retired from Court. The cause of his retirement was probably his knowledge that Parliament meant to remove him. The revelations concerning the Army Plot had lately been made, and Newcastle was supposed to be implicated. It was said that his name had been suggested as Governor-General, for then the loyalty of the Army would be assured by the presence of the Prince of Wales. Believing, or professing to believe, these allegations, it was not at all likely that the Commons would acquiesce in Newcastle's continued guardianship of the young Prince. At any rate, the Earl conceived it to be for the welfare of his King that he should resign the appointment, and to the Marquis of Hertford was given the charge of the future heir to the throne.

Newcastle retired to the country, where he would fain have remained, occupied in quiet study and the care of his estates, but hurrying events soon called him forth again.

The King, owing to the increased hostility of the populace, had been forced to leave London for Hampton Court. Here on 11 January, 1642, he signed a warrant, appointing Newcastle Governor of Hull. It was in this town that the stores of armour and ammunition prepared for the northern expedition had been placed, consequently it was of importance to the King that it should be in loyal hands. Unfortunately for his purpose the Commons discovered his intention, and themselves appointed Sir John Hotham to the governorship of Hull. At first Newcastle had the advantage, he was in a fair way to secure the town when he was summoned to take his seat in the House of Lords. This summons he ignored, sending to the King for instructions; but Charles was so unfavourably situated at the moment that he thought it wiser to yield rather than perhaps to precipitate a crisis, and recalled Newcastle to London. Hull was therefore lost to the King; when he demanded admittance a little later the gates were closed to him. Newcastle, on his return, obtained permission of the Lords to retire to the country, where he remained until the King summoned him to his side at York, war being now inevitable.

His great influence in the North secured for the Earl his commission as Governor of the four northern counties, and especially of the town of Newcastle, which he was

instructed at once to secure. Its importance to the King
was great. The Navy, under the Earl of Warwick, had
declared for Parliament, and there was no other port
available by means of which he could obtain supplies
sent by the Queen from abroad, or obtain the assistance
of those Englishmen, hitherto in service abroad, but
now flocking home to stand by the side of their King in
his necessity.

For this great responsibility Newcastle had many
qualifications—his deep loyalty, his great wealth and
unbounded generosity, his influence in that part of the
country, his personal bravery and great reputation.
He had, however, other qualities which unfitted him for
the burden. As Sir Philip Warwick said, " his edge had
too much of the razor in it." He was not a soldier by
profession or inclination, his courage was liable to give
way beneath defeat or the fear of ridicule ; his whole
nature was contemplative rather than active. Zealous
for the King, he was unable entirely to lose sight of considerations of personal honour. His very culture was
a disadvantage, it led to too much introspection which
often paralyses action. Thus the choice, inevitable in
the circumstances, was none the less unfortunate in its
ultimate results.

At first, however, all went well. The Earl acted with
much prudence and skill—secured the port of Newcastle
and garrisoned it, also he restored order in the Bishopric
of Durham, the train bands there having mutinied. He
then occupied himself with raising forces for the King's
service in the four northern counties, and was speedily
successful in gathering together a body of some four or
five thousand men. He received the King's permission
to enlist Roman Catholics in his army ; and from that

circumstance, and possibly the countenance he received from the Queen, it gained from the rebels the name of the Papist army. Great use was made of this to persuade the people that the King was but an instrument in the hands of the Papists, who were plotting the downfall of the Protestant religion in England. The King's consent to this step was given in the following letter, dated 23 September, 1642 :

" NewCastel,

" This is to tell you that this Rebellion is growen to that height, that I must not look what opinion men ar who at this tyme ar willing and able to serve me. Therefore I doe not only permitt, but command you, to make use of all my loving subjects services without examining ther Contienses (more than there loyalty to me) as you shall fynde most to conduce to the uphoulding of my just Regall Power.
" So I rest
" Your most asseured faithfull friend,

" Charles R."

In the north the Earl of Newcastle commanding the four northern counties, and the Earl of Cumberland in residence at York and commanding the rest of the north, were faced by the Hothams at Hull and the Parliamentary forces led by the Fairfaxes, father and son. Newcastle gained some advantage over the latter ; but Cumberland was unfitted for his post, he had no knowledge of military affairs, and the result was that Sir Thomas, the younger Fairfax, made himself master of Leeds, Wakefield, and Doncaster, and threatened York itself. This would have been a disaster of such magnitude to the King's cause that he promptly commissioned Newcastle to the command of all forces levied north of the Trent, as well as in the counties of Leicester, Cambridge, Rutland, Huntingdon, Norfolk, Suffolk, and Essex, together with the extraordinary privileges of conferring knighthood, coining money, and publishing declarations. The Earl, reinforced by the advent of Goring, who brought officers and ammunition from Holland, marched south towards York. He was now at the head of some eight thousand men. At Pierce Bridge he was intercepted by a strong party of the enemy, whom, however, he successfully resisted. On reaching York the Earl of Cumberland gladly resigned his charge into Newcastle's more capable hands. Newcastle had now to make ready for the coming of the Queen from Holland; she was expected at any moment. As early as November, 1642, before Newcastle had entered York, the King wrote expressing his desire that at the earliest possible moment after Her Majesty's arrival the Earl should hasten south. Charles had made his plan. Edgehill had failed to open the way to London, therefore the enemy was to be surrounded. He himself, stationed at Oxford, would hold Essex in check, Hopton from the west would advance into Kent, Newcastle was to bring his northern army through the eastern counties into Essex. So London would inevitably fall. In pursuance of this plan Charles therefore issued his instructions to Newcastle to hasten his proceedings in the north that he might be ready to start immediately upon the Queen's arrival.

The Queen reached York in March, 1643, but, in spite of his early success, it was not until the early part of July that Newcastle succeeded in expelling the Fairfaxes from the West Riding. Immediately on the surrender of

York, Newcastle issued a declaration to the people of that county, stating his reasons for invading it, and defending himself against attacks due to the enrolment of Papists in his army. Then, on 6 December he marched on Tadcaster. An attack of Lord Fairfax was repulsed, and Newcastle therefore found himself in possession of Pontefract, and in the position of having cut the Parliamentary defence of Yorkshire in two. Fairfax had been forced to fall back on Selby, thus the clothing towns of the West Riding were isolated.

Two courses were now open to Newcastle. He might at once have pushed south to carry out his share of the King's strategical plan. He had an army of eight thousand, Hopton was already on the march, and the defeat of the Fairfaxes at Tadcaster had opened up the path. He did advance into Nottinghamshire, but the second course—the reduction of the West Riding—appeared to him of primary importance. The southward march was accordingly postponed. It is difficult to say what were the Earl's reasons. The local feeling so strongly displayed later on may have already appeared—his followers were possibly reluctant to leave their homes at the mercy of the Fairfaxes and Hothams—the glory and honour of separate command may have biassed Newcastle's judgment, or he may have deemed it prudent to await the Queen's arrival in order to safeguard her landing with supplies and her subsequent march to the King.

Whatever the reason, the attack on the towns of the West Riding was determined. The first attempt was a failure. Sir William Savile captured Leeds and Wakefield, but was forced to retreat from before Bradford, whereupon Sir Thomas Fairfax seized the opportunity, entered Bradford, and taking the offensive, recaptured

Leeds, thus forcing Newcastle to retire upon York, 23 January, 1643.

The strength of the Royalist General was, however, soon increased by the arrival from Holland of General King, an experienced soldier, who became Newcastle's military adviser. Moreover, in February the Queen herself landed at Bridlington, with arms and money; but her southward march, as well as that of Newcastle, was postponed till Leeds could be recaptured and the Earl of Derby, then hard pressed in Lancashire, succoured. One attack on Leeds was repulsed; but early in May Newcastle surprised Rotherham and Sheffield. Fairfax, in his turn, surprised Wakefield on 21 May; but Newcastle's preponderance in the north was too great to be easily shaken. Previous to the loss of Wakefield, the Queen, protected by a body of about five thousand cavalry and infantry, had been sent to Oxford, and the Earl then prepared for a final blow at the West Riding. On the 22nd he stormed Howley House, and then led his troops, now ten thousand strong, to attack Bradford. On the way he encountered a smaller force of the enemy, led by the younger Fairfax, and the Battle of Adwalton Moor resulted. It was a decisive victory for Newcastle, and one which had most important results. Bradford and Leeds at once fell into the victor's hands. He even hoped to secure Hull, for the Queen had so worked upon the fickle Hothams that they were ready to deliver the city into the hands of the Royalists. Owing to Hotham's timidity and indecision the plot was suspected by the townspeople, who arrested the conspirators and sent word to the Fairfaxes, who hastened to Hull and thus preserved it for the Parliament.

Newcastle has been blamed by most modern historians

for the excessive time which he spent over the conquest of the West Riding ; and Warwick, the King's herald, writing at the time, gave his views concerning the reasons. He agrees with Clarendon that the Earl was not a born General ; a good soldier, without doubt, but once out of action, too fond of his ease, too easily seduced by poetry and music to trouble to command, which duty he left to his officers. They complained that for days they could not obtain an audience to lay their plans before the General ! Further, Warwick maintains that his disposition of troops was faulty. He accuses him of creating too many commands, so that regiments and companies were never up to their full strength ; that, moreover, these skeleton companies were scattered too widely over the country, so that they were at the mercy of the more highly concentrated troops of the enemy, who gained false prestige by the overthrow of a nominal regiment which, perhaps, only contained the numbers of half a troop. Then, too, these small bodies, being widely spread, impoverished the country to a greater extent than a few large parties, posted in definite parts, would have done. These criticisms probably explain the length of Newcastle's campaign in the West Riding. His path to the south had, however, been opened by Adwalton, and he accordingly marched into Lincolnshire. Here, in spite of Cromwell's efforts, he captured Gainsborough and garrisoned Lincoln. Newark, too, was held for the Royalists. The danger of this advance from the north was clearly apprehended, not only by Cromwell, but by Parliament also, and active measures were taken to hinder Newcastle's progress through the Associated Counties towards London.

Probably at no given moment during the war did the

Royalist cause stand so near ultimate success. The Associated Counties were only defended by a small army under Cromwell; Newcastle's task therefore would seem a comparatively light one. In the south Dorsetshire was overrun by the Royalists; the King was in force at Oxford. Parliament was thus forced to act on the defensive. Waller was sent to oppose the advance of the victorious western army; Essex was set to watch the movements of the King, while Manchester was to reinforce Cromwell in the Associated Counties. Moreover, not only did Parliament labour under the disadvantage of being forced to adopt defensive tactics, but the three armies thus detailed were largely skeleton, their numbers yet to be levied.

The question then remains—Why were the Royalists, with all these advantages, not successful? Why was that triple attack on London never made? The answer lies in the fact that neither Newcastle in the north nor Prince Maurice and Hopton in the west, was able to bring his victorious army far from the counties where each had been levied. We find Newcastle turning his back on that task which would appear so light, in order to undertake the siege of Hull, where he frittered away his strength and the hopes of his cause. Though personal considerations probably had their share in Newcastle's decision, and though he was perhaps incapable of appreciating the importance of the moment, nevertheless it must be owned that the local difficulty was the determining factor. The Yorkshire squires and yeomen utterly refused to march south. Newcastle's influence was great, but entirely insufficient to induce them to leave their homes at the mercy of forays from Hull. It is, of course, possible that had Newcastle himself been in earnest he could have

so impressed his followers with his own determined zeal
as to cause them to put aside purely personal and local
interests. It is, on the other hand, certain that the action
urged by his followers jumped with his private inclination. Against that we must put the remembrance that
Hopton, of whose disinterestedness there can be no
possible doubt, was equally unable to infect his Cornish
followers with enthusiasm for national, as opposed to
local, considerations.

Newcastle therefore turned back into Yorkshire and
forced the enemy from before Beverley, where they had
a strong contingent. Early in September he laid siege to
Hull, and from this moment his good fortune deserted
him. The siege lasted from 2 September to 11 October,
and from the first there seemed little hope of its capture.
Newcastle was encamped at some distance from the
town, the weather was wet, and, to add to the discomfort
of the besiegers, Fairfax broke down the banks of the
Humber, which flooded the Royalist works for two miles
about the town. Warwick visited Newcastle on an errand
from the King, and found the troop standing ankle-deep
in mud. " You have heard us called the Popish army,"
joked Newcastle, " but you see we trust not in our good
works." He did, however, advance his troops along one
bank of the river until within cannon-shot of the town,
and many fierce assaults were made, only to be as fiercely
repelled. The town was defended with great courage and
resolution, the Governor putting each householder to
watch his own house to be ready to quench the flames
caused by cannon-balls, while the women volunteered to
carry earth to make strong the defences. On 5 October
Manchester sent a reinforcement of five hundred men, and
the younger Fairfax went into Lincolnshire with the

horses, which were useless, indeed a hindrance, to the
besieged. Finally, on 11 October the defenders resolved
on a sortie, which was altogether successful—the Royalists
being driven from some of their forts, and a huge cannon,
one of those called " the Queen's gods," or " Gog and
Magog," captured and turned against themselves. All
spirit for the contest had been taken from the Royalist
ranks long since by the discomforts of the siege, and these
events, together with the news of the defeat of his garrison
in Lincolnshire by the combined forces of Cromwell,
Manchester and the younger Fairfax at Winceby, left
Newcastle no choice but to raise the siege and retire to
York.

Thus the siege of Hull had failed, the undertaking for
which he had overthrown the King's plans, and with it
fell the Royalist hopes in the north. To fail to take a
town leaves no army in the position it held before the
siege was begun ; confidence has been shaken, prestige
overthrown. To add to this disaster came the news of
the advance of the Scotch into England to the help of
the Parliamentarians. Thus just when Newcastle needed
every ounce of prestige, all the confidence and loyalty he
could gather, he had, by the fatal siege of Hull, lost the
one and shaken the other.

The Marquis of Hamilton was the first to warn Newcastle of the approaching invasion of the Scotch, and he
recommended that Carlisle and Berwick should be
garrisoned. Newcastle, now a Marquis, a dignity to
which he had been advanced as a reward for the victory
of Adwalton, replied that such a proceeding would be
contrary to the terms of the Pacification of Berwick and
would prejudice his master's cause, seeming to justify the
Scots in their action. It is questionable whether such

legal niceties are to be observed in warfare, certainly it is only another example of the damage done to the Royalist cause by the over-scrupulosity of the King and some of his followers. Thus, though forewarned Newcastle refused to forearm, and spent the next few months in placing Derbyshire in a posture of defence and in Nottinghamshire at his own house, until an appeal came to him from the loyal people of Yorkshire to assist them against the advancing Scotch. In January, 1644, therefore, the Marquis returned to Yorkshire and raised fresh troops, whom he placed under the command of Colonel John Bellasis. Thence he marched to his own town of Newcastle, in order, if it were possible, to put a period to the Scotch advance.

He reached Newcastle in February, 1644. At the outset of this new campaign the Marquis must have had an anxious heart. He had left behind him a very insufficient force to cope with the vastly increased power of the Fairfaxes in Yorkshire. The East Riding was the elder Fairfax's, the West Riding was firm for Sir Thomas, though he was at the moment in Cheshire, while the North Riding was fast falling into their hands. For the moment, however, the more pressing danger was the Scots, who arrived before Newcastle immediately after the Marquis had entered the town. A garrison was placed in the port and Newcastle took the field, his design being to manœuvre so as to engage the Scotch in battle at a favourable moment, in the meanwhile doing his best to prevent their obtaining supplies. Unfortunately for the success of these plans Newcastle was no strategist, and the methods of his adviser, King, now Lord Eythin, were those of the Low Countries. Thus by no manœuvres were the Royalists able to outwit the wary Scotch, who were invariably found posted in a position impossible to attack with any sure hope of victory. Newcastle was at last compelled to retire to Durham, where he endeavoured to straiten the quarters of the Scotch and cut off their provisions. He also again resorted to fruitless manœuvres to induce the enemy to engage. Thus was occupied the month of March. It is probable that had Lord Eythin's military genius been of a more dashing nature, the Scotch might have been attacked and defeated on more than one occasion. They were certainly weak in horse, for Parliament ordered Sir Thomas Fairfax to make his way with all speed to the north to succour the Scotch, who were in great straits. No such attempt was made, however, and when Newcastle heard that Colonel Bellasis, the Governor of York, had been defeated by the Fairfaxes at Selby and forced to retreat into York, he turned to aid in the defence of that town. Thus freed from all danger the Scotch followed, joined the Fairfaxes, and laid siege to York.

During these last weeks Newcastle's self-confidence must have received a rude shock. From letters written by the King it may be gathered that as early as January, and again in February, 1644, the Marquis had sent urgent appeals to Charles for help, and for the help of no other than Rupert. From one letter it would appear that he desired his quittance from the King's service. Obviously Newcastle was not of the temper which rises to the greatest heights of self-sacrifice and devotion in times of difficulty and defeat. His sanguine temperament needed the stimulus of success; defeat, the sense of being over-matched, depressed his spirit to the point of inaction, almost of surrender. A letter in the King's own hand, dated Oxford, 5 April, 1644, clearly shows that New-

2

castle was weary of the conditions of loyal service, the strife of evil tongues, the sure accompaniment of any failure. Charles writes thus :

" NEWCASTLE,

    " By your last despatch I perceive that the Scots are not the only, or, it may be said, the least enemies you contest withal at this time ; wherefore I must tell you, in a word, for I have not time to make long discourses, you must as much contemn the impertinent or malicious tongues or pens of those that are, or profess to be, your friends, as well as you despise the sword of an equal enemy. The truth is, if either you or my Lord Ethin leave my service I am sure at least all the north (I speak not all I think) is lost. Remember all courage is not in fighting ; constancy in a good cause being the chief, and the despising of slanderous tongues and pens being not the least ingredient. I'll say no more, but let nothing dishearten you from doing that which is most for your own honour, and the good of (the thought of leaving your charge being against both)
    " Your most assured, real, constant friend,

                                      " CHARLES R."

Again a few days later Charles wrote, apparently in answer to an appeal for aid .

" NEWCASTELL,

    " You need not doubt of the care I have for the north, and in particular of your assistance against the Scots' invasion ; but you must consider that we, like you, cannot doe alwais what we would ; besydes our taske is not litle that we strugle with, in which, if we

faile, all you can doe will be to little purpose, wherefor
you may be asseured of all assistance from hence that
may be, without laing our selfes open to eminent danger,
the particulars of which I refer you to my Lord Digby."

Prince Rupert had started for the north, but his progress was necessarily slow as he had to recruit his army
in Wales on the way. His plans were to relieve Newark
and, if possible, Lathom House, where the brave Countess
of Derby had long held out against the foe. This would
have the advantage of enabling him to recruit from the
Lancashire adherents of the Earl of Derby, then with
the army thus strengthened he would march straight to
the relief of York, where, since 18 April, Newcastle had
been beleaguered.

His progress and the fate of the north depended
largely on the state of affairs in the west. There Waller
was contending with the army of Hopton and Prince
Maurice. Should the Royalists be victorious, Essex and
Manchester would be drawn from the Associated Counties
to the support of Waller. On the other hand, the victory
of the Roundheads would mean the reinforcement of the
Scotch and Fairfax by Manchester's troops. The Battle
of Cheriton (29 March) decided the issue. The King's
troops were defeated, and Manchester having gained the
whole of Lincoln, hastened with Cromwell to the siege of
York.

The King's own position was now precarious, and he
recalled Rupert, who advised him to establish a strong
ring of fortresses round Oxford, which would keep the
foe at a distance. The advice, in a modified form, was
followed, and Rupert hastened north again. Newark
had already been relieved ; he now succoured Lathom

House and captured Stockport and Bolton. June 5 saw him at Wigan, and on the 11th Liverpool surrendered. The position of Parliament was now wellnigh as desperate as the King's had been. After the Battle of Cropredy Bridge the King's prospects in the south were much improved; if his forces were successful in the north he could hardly fail to get the upper hand. All eyes were now on Rupert and York.

On 13 June Newcastle offered to treat for the surrender of the city, but his terms were rejected. He then wrote to Rupert that York could only hold out for another six days; but when on 30 June Rupert reached Knaresborough it was still beleaguered. On the arrival of the Prince the Parliamentarian and Scotch forces raised the siege. The work that Rupert came to do was, apparently, accomplished. York was relieved. The enemy withdrew to a portion of Marston Moor, about seven miles from York. Newcastle at once concluded that the Royalist army, now, with the addition of Rupert's forces, some twenty-three or twenty-four thousand strong, would engage in manoeuvres and await a fitting opportunity to attack the enemy. Rupert had, however, determined otherwise. He had received from Charles a somewhat ambiguous letter which he interpreted as an order to fight the Scots under any circumstances. The Prince had never yet met the cavalry he could not scatter before him, and a war of manoeuvre was an uncertainty. Moreover, he had the King's orders to march to him as soon as possible after the relief of York.

On the night of 1 July, Rupert encamped on the north side of York and arranged to meet Newcastle on the following morning. The circumstances of the meeting were somewhat unpropitious. Rupert had made up his mind to fight, and had no notion that any other idea could be entertained. His curt, hasty greeting of the Marquis was resented, and the latter at once began to put forward his objections to the proposed course. These were not without weight. It was known that there was dissension among the Parliamentary Generals, it would therefore be better to wait the inevitable division of their army ; moreover, Royalist reinforcements were on the way. There was wisdom in such counsel ; unfortunately Newcastle was not the man whose advice was likely to be accepted by the Prince. Latterly, at any rate, though his loyalty was unquestioned, his skill as a soldier and General had not been pre-eminent. The two men were utterly unlike. Newcastle, a courtier before all else, suave in manner, and expecting the like treatment—the Prince, impetuous, rough, giving and expecting no personal consideration when matters of moment were to the fore. Though Newcastle had sent for Rupert and must have known that he must yield the supreme command to him, yet he would have liked more outward deference paid to his opinions, the rôle of subordination must be made easy. Rupert thought little and cared less for such considerations ; to him the fight was the thing. Nevertheless there is something pathetic about the figure of Newcastle at this moment, the point at which his public career was about to end. The courtier, the polished gentleman, the poet and musician, suited for a quiet rather than a stirring life, had been thrust by his loyalty and the exigency of events into a position for which he was really unsuited. At first he had made some success, his great name and his personal influence in the north had counted for much. Day after day as his influence waned and his power grew less, as he saw defeat grow daily more imminent, his task grew more distasteful. The crowning humiliation of his career seemed now to be thrust upon him—he must subordinate himself to this headstrong soldier of fortune, whom he regarded as his inferior in all but the accident of birth, and even in that matter in his eyes an English nobleman was as good as a German princeling. Still, he had called Rupert to his aid and hurt pride was subordinated to loyalty, so that when the Prince announced that he had positive orders from the King to fight, Newcastle withdrew his objections, and, to his friends, who urged that it was unworthy of his position to serve under Rupert, he replied, " Happen what will, I will not shun to fight, for I have no other ambition but to live and die a loyal subject to His Majesty."

The disaster of Marston Moor followed. Newcastle's own regiment of " Whitecoats," so called because they wore coats of undyed cloth which they vowed they would colour red with their enemies' blood, were cut to pieces. The Marquis had borne himself gallantly in the fight ; but when it was over, and he realized that the whole of his northern army was annihilated—that army so painfully gathered together and on which he had built such high hopes—then Newcastle's spirit gave way utterly. Overwhelmed, he gave up hope, rode to Scarborough, and from thence he took himself beyond seas. It was not in him to play the losing game. He is said to have explained his action only by saying, " I will not endure the laughter of the Court." Clarendon thus comments on his action : " All that can be said for the Marquis is, that he was so utterly tired with a condition of employment so contrary to his humour, nature, and education, that he did not at all consider the means or the way that would let him out of it, and free him for ever from having more to do with it. And it was a greater wonder that he sustained the vexation and fatigue of it so long, than that he broke from it with so little circumspection." The destruction " of all the force the Marquis had raised and with so many difficulties preserved . . . so transported him with passion and despair that he could not compose himself to think of beginning the work again, and involving himself in the same undelightful condition of life from which he might now be free."

Whatever Charles may have thought of Newcastle's present desertion, he was generous enough to overlook it in face of his past services. He knew and could sympathize with the Duke's disgust with public life and desire for a life of peace and retirement. He must often have desired it for himself, but a stern sense of duty to his country, his Church, and his successors upheld him and armed him for a fight to the death—he therefore had no desire to wound a faithful servant who had found his task beyond his strength. The letter written by the King to Newcastle in his exile is full of kindly consideration and gratitude for services rendered, with no hint of dissatisfaction with his conduct :

" CHARLES R.

" Right, trusty, and entirely beloved Cousin and Chancellor wee greete you well. The misfortune of our forces in the north wee know is resented as sadly by you as the present hazard of the loss of soe considerable a porcion of this our Kingdom deserves, which also affects us the more, because in that loss so great a proporcion falls upon yourself ; whose loyalty and eminent merit we have ever held, and shall still, in a very high degree

of our royal esteeme.   And albeit the distracted condition of our affairs and Kingdom will not afford us
meanes at this present to comfort you in your sufferings,
yet we shall ever reteyne soe gracious a memory of your
merit, as when it shall please God in mercy to restore us
to'peace, it shal be one of our principal endeavours to
consider how to recompense those that have with so
great affection and courage as yourself assisted us in the
time of our greatest necessity and troubles.   And in the
meanetime if there be anything wherein we may express
the reality of our good intentions to you or the value we
have of your person, we shall most readily doe it upon
any occasion that shal be ministred.   And soe we bid you
very heartily farewell.   Given at our Court at Oxford,
28th day of November, 1644.

" By His Majesty's command,

" EDWARD NICHOLAS

" To our right, trusty, and entirely beloved Cousin and
Chancellor, Wm. Marquis of Newcastle."

The Marquis of Newcastle may have released himself
from an " undelightful 'condition of life," but that the
life of exile to which he was now condemned could have
presented itself to him as " delightful " is scarcely think-
able, especially as he had some ninety pounds with which
to support himself, two sons, and a considerable following !   To a man of his tastes the shifts to which he was
put must have been most painful and humiliating, and he
bore himself throughout with considerable courage and
dignity.   The one moment of weakness was doubtless
redeemed.

After leaving England, Newcastle went to Hamburg
and from there to Paris, where he arrived in the spring

of 1645. His wife had been dead for some time, and now, at the Court of Henrietta Maria, he met Margaret Lucas, a penniless Maid of Honour to the Queen, as she herself, in her Life of the Marquis, tells us. In December of the same year they were married. During his residence in Paris the Marquis was forced to live entirely upon credit, and on one occasion his wife was reduced to the expedient of pawning gifts made by her to her waiting-woman, in order to procure a dinner for the household! The Queen, out of her own poverty, gave him a sum of two thousand pounds, and when, by her request, he followed the Prince of Wales into Holland, she engaged herself to satisfy Newcastle's creditors. They, however, would only be content when he pledged his own name to pay his debts!

Newcastle now settled at Rotterdam, the Prince being at The Hague, awaiting the issue of the second Civil War; but on news of its failure, and seeing no prospect of a return to England, the Marquis retired to Antwerp, where he lived in retirement until the time of the Restoration. The years of exile were employed by him in literary pursuits, and in the " manage " of horses. His sole anxiety seems to have been to obtain the wherewithal to live, and his wife made a journey to England, accompanied by her brother-in-law, Sir Charles Cavendish, to endeavour to secure some fragment of her husband's estates. She failed in her mission, for, although Parliament had decreed that the wives and children of " delinquents " should be succoured from their estates, the claim of the Marchioness was not allowed, in that her marriage had taken place since the " delinquency." Sir Charles Cavendish compounded for his property, and managed to buy in for his brother his two estates of Welbeck and

Bolsover, but not before the latter had suffered considerable damage.

The necessities of the Marquis were however supplied; partly through the good offices of friends in England, the Marquis of Hertford and the Duke of Devonshire, but largely through the compliance of the tradespeople of Antwerp, who trusted—justly—the word of Newcastle that if ever he recovered his estates or any portion of them, they should be fully recompensed. Thus he was enabled to live in some comfort and even luxury. On one occasion, when entertaining Charles II, the latter jested that Newcastle could obtain better meat than his King! The last few years of exile were rendered less uncomfortable through the money which Newcastle obtained from his brother's estate. He had died within two years of his return to England, and the Marquis benefited to the extent of some two thousand pounds a year.

Newcastle was one of those who advised Charles II to come to terms with the Scotch, believing it to be the only way in which he could recover his throne. Here he was at issue with Hyde and Hopton. The former refers to this in a letter to Nicholas, in which he says: " You have a very precious junto to determine concerning three kingdoms; you will find the Marquis of Newcastle a very lamentable man, and as fit to be a General as a Bishop; but I doubt though you choose officers, you are not in the way of raising armies." It had been arranged, as this passage hints, that Newcastle should accompany Charles to Scotland, but " the Scots would not suffer him to come, or be in any part of that kingdom."

The hopes of the exiles were shattered by the news of Worcester, but his wife tells us that Newcastle would never repine; he was certain that in God's good time the restoration of the lawful Prince would take place. He knew, says the wifely biographer, that " it was impossible for the kingdom to subsist long under so many changes of Government, and whensoever I expressed how little faith I had in it, he would gently reprove me, saying I believed least what I desired most, and could never be happy, if I endeavoured to exclude all hopes, and entertained nothing but doubts and fears."

Newcastle's faith was to be justified. Charles was invited to return to his kingdoms, and the Marquis was one of the first to repair to The Hague to offer his felicitations and services. Here disappointment awaited him. Charles had, apparently, always designed the office of Master of the Horse for his old tutor. Now he had to say that General Monk had desired that office. Newcastle's reply was prompt, with no sign of the disappointed courtier in it—the gentleman was worthy of any honour his Majesty could confer. Newcastle's arrival in England was delayed, owing to his ship being becalmed. His joy was, however, so great at seeing the smoke of London that he desired he might be jogged and awakened from his dream, " for surely," said he, " I have been sixteen years asleep and am not thoroughly awake yet." His faithful wife had been left at Antwerp, hostage for his debts. As speedily as might be, for it was no easy matter for the returned exile to raise money, those debts were discharged and the Marchioness rejoined her husband—in London at first, but there they made no long stay. Newcastle would accept no offices, but was determined to retire to his estates and do his best to reduce his tangled affairs to order. He told the King that many would, he knew, attribute his retirement to discontent, but begged him to believe that his action had no such foundation, that he wished only to serve the King; "whatsoever your Majesty is pleased to command me, were it to sacrifice my life, I shall most obediently perform it; for I have no other will, but your Majesty's pleasure."

The repair of his ruined fortunes was enough to occupy Newcastle's time of retirement. Welbeck and Bolsover were still his, but both houses were sadly out of repair, the latter was half pulled down, all the furniture had been taken away or destroyed, with the exception of some famous pictures and hangings saved from the wreck by Newcastle's daughter, Lady Cheiny. The greatest grief to the returned exile was, however, the state in which he found Clipston Park, in which he had greatly delighted. Its timber had been famous, it had been well stocked with deer and all kinds of game. Now he found it denuded of timber, the deer destroyed, no sheltered place being left for them or for game. Here the generosity and restraint of the English gentleman was exhibited—Newcastle made no complaint, merely remarking that he had hoped it would not have been so much defaced. By dint of energy and economy he was able to leave his estates in some order and prosperity. Welbeck and Bolsover were repaired and in part rebuilt, his lands were restocked and manured, Clipston Park fenced and planted, and the Castle of Nottingham, because it had been a favourite seat of his father's, purchased and in part rebuilt before his death. All this was not accomplished without infinite labour. Many of his estates and manors had been sold, some to regicides, and as Charles II had given their possessions to his brother the Duke of York, Newcastle, on appeal to the King, obtained these without much difficulty. Others were only regained by wearisome and expensive lawsuits, so that we may not wonder that Newcastle had little time to spend at Court. In her " Life " the Duchess computes her husband's losses to amount to £941,303, a sum only approached by a similar computation presented to the King by the Marquis of Worcester.

It does not appear that Charles II was altogether unmindful of his former tutor, and of his sufferings in his father's cause and his own. He would probably have given him some high office had Newcastle been urgent in demand, for while others clamoured and often obtained nothing, he was made Gentleman of the King's Bedchamber, Justice in Eyre north of the Trent, and a member of the Privy Council. The honour of the Knighthood of the Garter, conferred upon him in exile, was now formally bestowed. Also, when by his diligence Newcastle had put his affairs in such order as made the title not unbecoming, he approached his royal master with the request that he might be advanced to the dignity of a Duke. In granting this request Charles said of him: " The great proofs of his wisdom and piety are sufficiently known to us from our younger years, and we shall always retain a sense of those good principles he instilled into us ; the care of our youth which he happily undertook for our good, he as faithfully and well discharged." Newcastle was therefore granted the title of Duke of Newcastle and Earl of Ogle, an honour conferred in June, 1664.

Newcastle enjoyed his dignities for some years ; he died in December, 1676, his wife having predeceased him by nearly four years. He left only one son, Henry, to inherit his titles and estates, the two eldest having died before their father. The last years of this noble-

man's life may well have been the happiest. Secure in
his position and in his possessions, untroubled by ambition or the cares and jealousies of office, he was free
to spend his time in the management of his estates and
of his horses, in which he never ceased to take delight, in
literary labours and philosophical and other discussions
with his learned and admiring Duchess.

He had no regrets for his course of action in the past:
in fact, his wife tells us that in speaking of the miseries
of the Civil War he declared that "if the same wars
should happen again and he was sure both to lose his life
and all he had left him, yet he would most willingly sacrifice it for His Majesty's service." As he was thus prepared to spend and be spent in that service, so he looked
for no reward, for he said "that his love to his gracious
master King Charles the Second was above the love he
bore to his wife, children, and all his posterity, nay, to his
own life," and when his wife remarked after the Restoration that "his gracious master did not love him so well
as he loved him," he replied "that he cared not whether
His Majesty loved him again or not ; for he was resolved
to love him." This fervent passion of loyalty it is that en-
titles Newcastle to a high place among the King's Champions—in face of it and his undoubted suffering, and
patience under that suffering, we would fain forget the
weakness displayed after Marston Moor.

SIR MARMADUKE LANGDALE
AFTER THE PORTRAIT BY HUMPHREYS

SIR MARMADUKE LANGDALE

SIR MARMADUKE LANGDALE, according to Lloyd " a very lean and much mortified man," belonged to a northern family of great antiquity. The surname was derived from the town of Langdale in the Hundred of Pickering in Yorkshire, of which the Langdales were lords before the reign of King John. This descendant of a younger branch of the family owned the estate of Holme in Spaldingmore, Yorkshire, and had been knighted by King Charles I in 1627. He was held in high estimation as " a serious and wise man of most scholarlike accomplishments and good husbandry," and was probably never much attracted to the lighter side of life. The family at the time of the Reformation had remained faithful to the Papal Supremacy, and to be a Roman Catholic in those days of would-be Puritan domination was a serious business. He, indeed, earned especial execration from the Parliamentarians as being one of those Papists who, they averred, formed the bulk of the army under Newcastle.

Sir Marmaduke's religion alone would almost settle the question as to which side he would take in the civil troubles of the reign. At the outset of the war he took a prominent part in the north on the Royalist side. Sir John Hotham from Hull was rapidly gaining possession of the country round about ; accordingly several of the northern gentry, including the Earl of Cumberland

Sir Thomas Glenham, and Sir Marmaduke, raised a party for the King, strong enough to force Hotham to retreat to Hull. Very soon, however, these Yorkshire gentlemen realized the danger their county was in from the more strenuous Fairfax, who seemed on the eve of capturing the town of York. A petition was therefore sent to the Earl of Newcastle, then Governor of Newcastle, begging him to come to their aid with the army he had lately raised. The bearers of the petition were Sir Marmaduke Langdale and Mr. Aldburgh, and the Earl assented to their proposition on condition that a committee of the nobles and gentry of Yorkshire should be appointed to march with the army and give the Earl the benefit of their counsel and assistance. Of this committee Sir Marmaduke was a member, and by his own efforts raised three companies of foot and a troop of seventy horse from the East Riding. On the Queen's arrival in the north he armed them from her ships, and formed part of her escort to York, February, 1643.

During this year Langdale was much employed in negotiation. He was apparently sent by the Earl to discuss terms with the Hothams, when they held out hopes of the surrender of Hull to the Royalists—hopes which were never realized owing to the vigilance of some of the inhabitants of the town, though the father and son suffered death for their intentions. Later, in December of the same year, it fell to Langdale's lot to open letters sent by Colonel Hutchinson, Parliamentary Commander of Nottingham, to Colonel Dacre, indignantly refusing to consider certain proposals made to him by that gentleman with the consent of the Earl of Newcastle. The tone of Langdale's reply was such as to call forth the approval of the Puritan leader. It is one of the few instances of self-revelation which the records concerning Sir Marmaduke afford us. It speaks eloquently of the simple loyalty of the man to his superior, whose actions he will allow no man to criticize or misinterpret, even when he himself would have acted otherwise. It also contains his profession of faith ·

"For John Hutchinson, Esq., Geo. Hutchinson, and Th. Poulton, these—

"GENTLEMEN,

"In the absence of Colonel Dacre I have received your letters and am sorry you so much mistake his affection for you, in endeavouring to draw you from that rebellious course of life you seem to glory in. If you please to read all the histories of this nation, from the Conquest to this time, and you shall find all rebels' pretences of taking up arms against the sacred person of the King varnished over with the title of love to the laws of the land, liberty of the subject, and loyalty to His Majesty; yea, in those times when they deposed their natural Prince and set up others; wherein, although the event sometimes succeeded for a while,' yet the authors had cause commonly to repent before their deaths, and certainly there was never yet law of this land, nor religion publicly professed here, did ever allow subjects to take up arms against their natural sovereign. For his excellency, the Marquis of Newcastle, you are much mistaken in his desire to corrupt any man. I rather believe it was his affection to you, having known two of your fathers, and his desire to preserve your estates that are now in a lost condition by your follies. For my own part, as I am not known to you, so I should never have tendered you that good offer, but will go on in that way, that I

3

doubt not shall gain the King his right forth of the usurper's hand, wherever I find it, wherein you shall find a gentleman called

'
"MARMADUKE LANGDALE

" *West Hallam, 18 Dec., 1643.*"

During this same year, 1643, Newcastle made three attempts to loosen the hold of the Fairfaxes on the West Riding, where the Parliamentary interest was very strong. It was by their power in this district that communication was kept up with Hull. At the third attempt he succeeded, defeating Fairfax at Adwalton Moor and driving him into Hull. Now Newcastle was apparently free to obey the King's command, and march south through the Associated Counties towards London. He proceeded to carry out this design, but after taking Gainsborough and garrisoning Lincoln, he returned to Yorkshire and laid siege to Hull. Various reasons have been assigned for the General's disobedience to his King's commands, the most potent probably was the dislike of the northern army to the southward march, which would leave their homes exposed to hostile raids from the unconquered Hull.

, Whatever the cause the siege of Hull was begun, and Langdale took part in it. His horse repulsed an attack made by the garrison on the besiegers with considerable loss. His preparedness thus prevented a surprise, and, for that time at least, the raising of the siege. The siege lasted from 2 September to 12 October, when Cromwell's victory at Winceby forced Newcastle to give up his futile attempt.

Sir Marmaduke Langdale remained with the army of the Marquis of Newcastle until its final dissolution. He was with that General when he endeavoured, early in 1644, to prevent the incursion of the Scotch army into England and their junction with the Roundheads. The Royalist plan was to hold Newcastle, and to deprive the enemy of provisions on the march by destroying the crops in the district round. The plan failed, for Leslie would not be forced or manœuvred into action. The one success of the northern army against the Scotch was won by Langdale at Corbridge, in Northumberland, who, although he failed to surprise the enemy, forced them to retreat. He followed the chase for three miles, killing about two hundred and taking many prisoners. It also had the result of forcing the Scotch army to withdraw further from Newcastle. Finally, however, Newcastle was forced to retreat to York, to save it from capture by Fairfax. Here he was besieged by the Scotch and the Fairfaxes, who had been able to effect a junction. The King, in response to urgent appeals, now sent Rupert to the help of Newcastle and the northern army. On the way he relieved Newark and Lathom House, and at the end of June reached York. At his approach the siege was promptly raised, but the fatal fight of Marston Moor—2 July—caused the surrender of the town to the victors. All that was left of the great army of the north was the body of horse under Sir Marmaduke Langdale— who did not follow the example of his chief and seek safety across the seas. With these troops, about two thousand in number, Langdale marched into Westmoreland, his intention being to join Prince Rupert. His march south was not an easy one, for the enemy set upon and harassed his troops whenever an opportunity offered. Then Lord Byron, in command in Cheshire, hoped to take advantage of the presence of Langdale's

horse to beat the enemy out of those parts, in order that
Chester might be securely held. He therefore brought
on an unnecessary encounter, and his forces not being
strong enough for the work, it was only by Langdale's
skill that a retreat was substituted for a defeat. Byron
desired that Langdale and his horse should remain at
Wrexham, in order to second his efforts in Cheshire; but
this was impossible. Provisions and forage were un-
attainable, for the people of Lancashire were only intent
on diverting the war from their own quarters. On
29 August Langdale was attacked at Malpas, his troops
defeated and he himself wounded. He persisted in his
determination to advance south, and at last brought his
two thousand horse into quarters in Monmouthshire.
Rupert, in October, dispatched Langdale and Gerard,
who had accompanied him south, to the King at Oxford,
and they assisted in the relief of Banbury Castle.

Early in 1645, to their great joy, the northern horse
found themselves on the homeward road. An urgent
appeal from Pontefract had reached the Prince, and
he sent Langdale to the relief of the beleaguered
garrison. On the way he encountered Colonel Rossiter's
Lincolnshire forces at Melton Mowbray and routed them.
Later, Fairfax attempted to intercept his march but was
also repulsed, and his forces chased from Kelford to
Doncaster. Thus Langdale won his way to Pontefract.
If the enemy indeed nicknamed him " the ghost," it may
well have been, as Lloyd declares, because " they were so
haunted by him."

At Pontefract the besieging army was commanded by
Colonel Lambert, and was superior in numbers to the
Royalists. The northern horse was driven back, not once
nor twice, by a galling fire from the Parliamentary foot

drawn up behind the shelter of a hedge, but they gallantly returned to the attack, until the garrison, sallying out, fell on the enemy in the rear. They were finally beaten off the field with the loss of many killed, wounded, and prisoners, together with guns, ammunition, and provisions. These last served to supply the fortress in preparation for a renewed siege, which was indeed undertaken a month later.

Having gained these successes Langdale turned south to rejoin the Prince, though he evidently hankered for further work in the north, for in a letter to Rupert reporting on his work, he wrote :

" We find the country infinitely willing to come in if we might have stayed ; but we all are, and ever will be, at your Highness's command, whereof one is your Highness's most faithful and humble servant,

"M. L.

" *Bingham, 6 March, 1645.*"

This vague longing of the northern horse was later to become an irresistible impulse, which Langdale could not restrain in his men. For the moment Langdale joined Prince Maurice and Sir Jacob Astley at Bridgnorth. They were in need of reinforcements after the loss of Shrewsbury, which had broken the line of communication with Chester.

Very soon, however, the northern horse were commanded to rejoin the King at Oxford, and when in May, 1645, Charles left his base with the intention of marching to the north, their hearts must have rejoiced. At the Council of War at Stow-on-the-Wold another plan was, however, mooted. Fairfax was reported to be marching to the relief of Taunton, and there were many of the King's advisers who hoped to repeat the feat of Lost-withiel. Prince Rupert threw his influence on the side of Langdale and his officers, with the result that a com-promise—fatal to the King's cause with the fatality of compromises generally—was arranged. The King and Prince Rupert were to advance northwards, Goring to go to the west to check Fairfax.

The King's advance gave the Roundheads some anxious moments; it was thought necessary to recall Fairfax from the west to lay siege to Oxford, the King having taken and sacked Leicester. Apparently too, he was threatening the Eastern Association, or -so Cromwell thought. There was some cause for Roundhead fears; the New Model Army was yet in the making, that of the King was strong and united, with veteran soldiers filling its ranks. Langdale and his horse had played no insignifi-cant part in the taking of Leicester. With his troop of fourteen hundred horse he was sent by the King to take up a position between Coventry and Leicester, to prevent provisions from the country being taken to the garrison of the latter town. They successfully drove back a body of the enemy's horse to the works beneath the town, and when the King came up and the town was attacked, Sir Marmaduke had charge of the reserve in the assault.

The forward movement of the Royalist army was checked by the news from Oxford. The town was not able to stand a protracted siege, and in the opinion of Charles and most of his advisers it would not be wise to advance and leave his base of operations in imminent danger of capture. It was therefore resolved to turn south and force Fairfax to raise the siege. The spirits of the men of the north fell to zero, and in their disappointment their loyalty showed signs of being strained almost to breaking-point. The fate of their distant homes seemed to them far more important at that moment than the success or failure of the cause for which they fought. At first they utterly refused to obey orders. It required the utmost efforts of Sir Marmaduke and even of the King himself to induce them to follow their master in the direction of Oxford. The news of the King's approach was enough to raise the siege of Oxford. The general opinion then was that the King should return at once to Leicester, recruit his weakened army, and either await Fairfax there or continue his northward march. Many of the officers thought, however, that the raising of the siege of Oxford was a sign of weakness, and were anxious to seek out Fairfax and try conclusions with him. Time was wasted in argument, and when at last it was settled to fall back on Leicester, it was only to hear at Harborough that Fairfax was within six miles !

The Battle of Naseby was the result. This neglect to acquaint himself with the enemy's movements must certainly be attributed to Rupert. He undoubtedly had too great a contempt for the " New Model." Nevertheless the Royalist defeat was primarily due to the fact that the King's army was outnumbered by almost two to one. Added to this was the presence of Cromwell, who had joined Fairfax ; Rupert's usual hotheadedness in pursuit, and the heaviness which lay on the spirits of the northern horse, weakening their vital force. In this fatal battle Rupert was not pitted against Cromwell. To Sir Marmaduke Langdale's horse fell the task of meeting the Ironsides, and at that moment they were the least fitted for the position. Their spirits had not recovered from the rebellious outbreak of a few days before. It cannot be maintained that they shirked their duty; they advanced with great resolution though the geographical situation was against them—they had to make an uphill charge—but they lacked the loyal enthusiasm necessary to enable them to withstand the determined onslaught of the Puritan enemy. Their edge was dulled; they turned and fled in such a manner that no efforts of their leader could induce them to rally, even if to rally had been possible. Thus the rout of the left wing of the Royalist cavalry, and the absence from the field of the right wing under Rupert, who, victorious in his charge, was engaged in pursuit, left the foot under brave old Astley absolutely unsupported. Langdale and the Prince, when at length he returned, made an attempt to get together enough horse for a second charge, but they were easily repulsed. The day was already lost and won.

After Naseby the King had no force of infantry to put into the field, until levies could be slowly and painfully gathered together by Prince Rupert and the staunch old Sir Jacob Astley. With his horse, therefore, Charles took refuge in Wales, almost his last resource.

Sir Marmaduke Langdale's force formed now his strongest weapon and, perhaps stirred to remorse and shame by the result of Naseby, they seem now to have made most valiant efforts in their King's behalf, following him uncomplaining into Wales. Langdale himself was appointed Governor of North Wales, with directions to make preparations for the reception of troops expected from Ireland. It was now believed that peace was concluded in that sad land. Very soon, however, the King's plans were changed. He had contemplated crossing the Severn and joining Goring in the west, but various difficulties had presented themselves. Coincidently had appeared a petition from the gentry of the north that the King would march into their country with his cavalry, and that levies of infantry would then be swiftly raised. Thus at the head of a new northern army he could force his way into Scotland to Montrose, who was still pursuing his victorious career in that country. News of the victory of Alford strengthened the conviction that this plan at least was feasible, and the northern march began, once more.

The King reached no further than Chester. At Chirk intelligence reached him from Byron of the dire need of the port. Charles, at once realizing the importance of keeping open communication with Ireland, laid careful plans for its security. Sir Marmaduke Langdale was sent over Holt Bridge to Rowton Heath, while the King, with a strong party, entered Chester. A Colonel Michael Jones was in command of the besieging force ; he had been repulsed on 22 September, and it was hoped that by this arrangement he would be caught between two fires. Unfortunately, the Parliamentary General Poyntz was in pursuit of the King, and of his movements the Royalists seem to have been entirely ignorant. At Whitchurch he received a message from Jones, telling of the King's arrival and of the disposition of his troops, and in return sent a letter to tell Jones of his coming. This letter Langdale intercepted and so faced about to meet Poyntz's attack, but he apparently failed to let the King or the Chester garrison know of the enemy's approach. This omission had serious results. It is likely that Sir Marmaduke was anxious that his northmen should retrieve their reputation, so fatally damaged at Naseby, and so determined to bear the brunt of the attack alone.

Whatever the cause, the result was disastrous. The horse certainly behaved gallantly, but Jones was able to reinforce Poyntz with musketeers, who, lining the hedges, so well seconded the efforts of the Parliamentary horse, that Langdale's troops, finding themselves between two fires, at last turned and fled. Informed too late of the state of affairs, Charles sent out a party from the garrison to endeavour to retrieve the fortunes of the day. Such belated efforts were naturally useless. If the soldiers within the city could have acted in concert with Langdale's troops, victory might have gone to the Royalists.

Thus the blame for the loss of the Battle of Rowton Heath must rest on Langdale's shoulders. The King's affairs were in too desperate a condition to allow a commander lightly to take such risks. To him the honour of the north counted for more, at the moment, than the cause of his master. The result of the battle was that Charles' march northward to Montrose was, of necessity, abandoned for the time.

Charles retreated to Denbigh in North Wales, where the scattered horse rallied round him to the number of about 2400, and then he marched to Newark to take up his quarters there   News reached him that the star of Montrose was still in the ascendant, and he at once determined to make yet another attempt to join him. At Welbeck a Council of War met, and the majority of the King's advisers endeavoured to dissuade him from the hazardous enterprise, for that Montrose continued successful was but unconfirmed rumour. Digby and Langdale alone supported the King's wishes in the matter, the latter believing that once across the Humber a northern army could still be raised which would make the King's advance secure. Very soon, however, the true position of affairs in Scotland was revealed. News came of the defeat of Montrose at Philiphaugh, and then of the failure of his attempt to raise a fresh army in the Highlands. To pursue the cherished plan would have been madness ; but Charles was reluctant to break his promise to Montrose, and to abandon his last hope. He therefore determined to send Langdale and his horse, who were to cut their way through to Scotland. Thus at last the Yorkshiremen had their way.

Langdale must have realized the desperate nature of the enterprise ; but he, too, was relieved at the prospect of being once again north of the Humber and cheerfully consented, begging only that Digby might be given the chief command. The adventure was one after that rash, impetuous man's heart ; moreover, he had strong reasons for desiring absence from the Court at that time. Nevertheless the gallant Secretary of State was to prove that he was no mean strategist. Poyntz was discovered to be blocking the Royalist road to the north, but was himself unaware that an enemy was near. Thus Digby and Langdale were able to fall upon a strong body of his foot, which was well in advance of the horse, and which, thus unprotected, was speedily routed by Langdale's men. This was on 1 October, 1645. Digby then marched into Sherburn. His plan was to post Langdale with part of the horse at the south end of the town to fall upon the enemy as they crossed the brook ; he himself with the remainder of the horse was to form a reserve and sally out to complete the enemy's discomfiture. The strategy probably emanated from Langdale, who certainly proved himself time and again fertile in expedients. It was at any rate sound, and would have been successful but for an unlucky accident.

On the approach of the enemy Langdale drew out his
men and besought them, in a stirring address, by the
memory of their gallant deeds in the relief of Pontefract,
to wipe out the stain of Naseby—" for mine own part,
I will not have you upon any design, but where I will lead
you myself." He kept his word. The defeat of Naseby
still smarted, and the horsemen too were determined to
wipe out the memory, at least from their own hearts.
Copley's men broke and fled before their vigorous onslaught. Unfortunately for the Royalists a party fled
north through the town, instead of south, the natural
route. Thus the reserves within the town thought the
fugitives to be their defeated comrades and, without
pausing to make sure, joined in their supposed flight !
The pursued soon became pursuers, and what had been
a victory was turned into a rout. The Parliamentarians
were not slow to take advantage of Fortune's trick ; the
pursuit of the panicstricken Royalists did not cease till
they had taken refuge within the walls of Skipton
Castle.

Still, Digby and Langdale did not despair. They
gathered together as many of their scattered troops as
possible and pushed northward—the vision of Montrose
ever before their eyes. They were fortunate in being able
to obtain guides who knew the intricate country they
were in, its lonely mountain passes, its treacherous sands.
Thus they were able, time after time, to outwit the Scotch
troops sent out by Leslie, who lay with his army on the
borders to prevent their entering Scotland. The end
though protracted was nevertheless inevitable. Digby
did indeed reach Dumfries ; but to avoid an engagement
was forced to retreat, and finally, at Carlisle Sands, was
caught by a small party under Sir John Browne and

utterly routed. His men, though superior in numbers, were sore discouraged. They had been wandering for days with no objective, and there seemed no hope of ever reaching Montrose. No one could even learn where that gallant hero was ; between them and him was a large Scotch army under an able and determined leader ; behind them were the northern levies of the Parliament. It was small wonder that all.spirit had left them, and they were thus easily put to flight. Two hundred kept together and fled towards Bolton, but the rest scattered in all directions. Digby and Langdale escaped in a small boat to the Isle of Man and thence to Ireland.

Fresh plans at once floated in the brain of the versatile Secretary of State. He was convinced that Irish troops could be organized and sent to England if only the Prince of Wales could be induced to come to Ireland and place himself at their head. Full of this hare-brained scheme he crossed to Paris to win Henrietta Maria to his side. He was accompanied by Langdale, but the level-headed northerner had no faith in Digby's plans. A Roman Catholic in faith, he would have no scruples as to the introduction of a Papist army into England, but the confusion of affairs in Ireland had not escaped his notice ; he warned some of the English then in France that Digby's Irish army was largely a figment of his imagination.

Later, Langdale returned to England ; but during the time of the King's imprisonment with the Scotch army, his transference to Parliament, and his seizure by the army, there was no employment for such men as Langdale, who was a soldier and no diplomatist. He scorned to make any composition with the Parliament, even had

such a proceeding been possible ; and on the break-
down of the negotiations between the King and the army
he realized that London was not a safe refuge for him.
Then followed the determination of the Scotch to break
with the English Parliament, to ally with the Royalists
and free Charles from the power of Cromwell and the
army.   The Scotch Commissioners sent to London to
negotiate with Charles and his followers at once realized
the importance of obtaining possession of the North of
England.   They therefore made known their plans to
Sir Marmaduke, and he was invited into Scotland until
matters were in train, London being no longer a safe
place of residence for him.

Langdale, with others, therefore set out for Scotland.
On the way they spent some time in the north, preparing
their friends for future events.   Some months were spent
in Scotland in disguise, but at the opening of the Parliament at Edinburgh, Langdale and Sir Philip Musgrave
appeared openly and were well received.   This Parliament
was to arrange the course of action.   Hamilton and his
party believed that they were strong enough to draw
Argyle and his faction to the side of the King.   Very soon
difficulties arose.   The English Parliament sent to demand
that " notorious malignants "—especially Sir Marmaduke
Langdale and Sir Philip Musgrave—should be banished
from that country or handed over to the Commissioners
from England.   Hamilton was afraid to use the power he
had, and persuaded the English Royalists to leave
Edinburgh or remain in hiding there until affairs were
more settled.

This was not the only indignity to which the Scotch
exposed these English gentlemen, on whom they depended
entirely for their entrance into England and for com-

munication with their English allies in the north. Matters having been arranged between Argyle and Hamilton and their respective parties, Argyle now demanded that the English officers should take the Covenant before being received into their army either as officers or soldiers. Hamilton and his friends clearly saw the folly of this proceeding. They knew that to force the Covenant on all and sundry would be to alienate every English Royalist, and was clean contrary to what the King had agreed upon with them. They were, however, afraid to speak their minds. Not so Langdale and Sir Philip Musgrave. They expostulated forcibly at this breach of faith, not only refused to take the Covenant themselves; but declared their intention of marching into England and warning their compatriots of what they had to expect from the Scotch army.

The Scotch leaders well knew how impossible their undertaking would be without the co-operation of these gentlemen, and it was left to Hamilton to find a way out of the difficulty. This he did by agreeing that Langdale and Musgrave should lead an advance expedition into England—the former to surprise Berwick, the latter Carlisle, of which city he had formerly been governor for the King. No commission was to be given them as they had refused to take the Covenant, but they were required to enter into an engagement to yield the towns to the Scotch when called upon. This they agreed to do. Accordingly, on 28 and 29 April, 1648, the two towns of Berwick and Carlisle were surrendered to the Royalists and the second Civil War had begun. In this Langdale was destined to play an important part. He and his northmen were to bear the brunt of the fray, and though victory was denied them, by their gallant conduct they were once and for all to wipe out the sad and bitter memories of Naseby.

The capture of Berwick is another instance of Langdale's ingenuity and foresight. It was exceedingly well planned and as successfully carried out. He had arranged with the loyal gentry of the neighbourhood that certain of them should join him on the Scotch side of the town the night before he intended to surprise it. Others were to be on the English side, and these last were in the morning to enter the town, not in a body to excite suspicion, but in small parties, some to post themselves on the bridge, others near the market-place. Langdale himself sent some foot to enter the town amongst the market-people. Thus, when he himself appeared on the bridge with one hundred horse, there was a large number in the town prepared to co-operate. The bridge was then lowered, the mayor seized, and, as there was no garrison save townsmen, all with no resistance. So easy was the task that in a few hours Sir Marmaduke was able, without fear, to reopen the town for the purposes of the market.

Langdale had made careful plans for the subjugation of the north. He had well gauged its inherent loyalty to the Royalist cause. Even before he had reached England the gentry of Yorkshire in the neighbourhood of Pontefract—where Langdale's earlier exploits were remembered with enthusiasm—had, not awaiting his orders, seized upon that stronghold. Moreover, they had gathered together such a formidable army from the neighbouring country that communication between London and York was rendered very difficult for the enemy. After the capture of Berwick Langdale received orders from Scotland to repair to Carlisle and make his army as strong as possible. Sanguine as he was, his highest hopes were fulfilled. In a very few days he had a well-equipped body of three thousand foot and seven hundred horse raised from the two counties of Cumberland and Westmoreland; also from Yorkshire and Durham came another force of five hundred horse. He then evolved a daring plan. At the head of this army he would march into Lancashire and subdue it, incidentally falling upon Lambert's troops, inferior to his own in numbers. He would thus be able to effect a junction with Lord Byron, then in Cheshire. Success is to the bold; the plan might well have been successful, and if so the north would be secure—the co-operation of the Scottish army might then be expected to do the rest.

The Scotch were, however, obsessed with the idea that the King's restoration must be achieved by their sole efforts, in order to ensure the permanence of the Covenanting religion in England. Therefore orders were sent to Sir Marmaduke that he must not fight upon any consideration; he was reproved for enlisting Papists in his army, and for not enforcing the taking of the Covenant upon all his men. The Englishman must have felt the insult to his religion keenly, but he put personal considerations aside in his desire for his country's welfare. Perforce he abandoned his forward movement and resigned himself to wait for the dilatory march of the Scotch. He was condemned to watch the Roundhead preparations becoming daily more complete, the hope of ultimate victory more remote. Nevertheless, he held on doggedly, merely sending Sir Philip Musgrave to protest against the demand of the Covenant for all—so certain to arouse English hostility to the Scotch alliance. Mean-

4

while, Lambert was able to get together a strong body of horse and foot with which he marched on Langdale, who, owing to his peremptory orders, and having by bitter experience learnt self-restraint, was forced to evade the issue, although success seemed within his grasp. He retired to Carlisle, thus allowing his path to the south to be blocked.

Finally, news that the Royalists were besieged in Colchester forced the Scotch to move, though even now they were not ready, the army that marched under Hamilton being deficient in horses and artillery. Hamilton entered England in the middle of July, 1648, came to Carlisle, joined with Langdale and took Appleby. On 2 August he had reached Kendal, whereupon Lambert was forced to retreat from Barnard Castle to Richmond in order to guard Yorkshire. For two courses were open to Hamilton—to march south into Lancashire, or to cross into Yorkshire, fall on Lambert, join the Yorkist Cavaliers and relieve Pontefract. Lambert obviously thought that this latter would be the course adopted, hence he took up his position between Knaresborough and Leeds in order to wait for Cromwell and check advance on Pontefract.

Instead of promptly falling on Lambert, Hamilton lingered at Kendal for a week. Impatient of such cowardly inaction when great issues were at stake, Langdale pushed on to Settle, hoping to obtain the surrender of Skipton Castle, and so spur the Scotch to advance on Pontefract. If he succeeded so far, the next step would be an eastward march to Colchester. Hamilton had no mind for such hardy enterprise. He could not even assert himself sufficiently to force Callander and Baillie, his subordinates, to co-operate with Monro. That general had arrived with well-seasoned troops from Ireland, and was forced to remain behind with his troops to await reinforcements from Scotland.

On 9 August Hamilton pushed forward to Hornby. Here, on the 13th, the anxious Langdale visited him to warn him of the gathering of Roundhead forces in Yorkshire and to urge immediate action of some sort. Clarendon says that Langdale already knew of or guessed at Cromwell's advance, and threatened junction with Lambert, while Scotch authorities maintain that he neglected to gain information of the enemy's proceedings. Clarendon was a friend of Langdale, and probably derived his information from him. Moreover, there is no doubt that Langdale was for action, and immediate action, the only wise course, whether he knew of Cromwell's coming or not. The question to be decided was what should be the line of march. Hamilton preferred the southward march through Lancashire to join Byron on the borders of Cheshire, and in this he had his way. Langdale would have chosen to march into Yorkshire in pursuance of his original idea, but action of any sort was better than none, and a diversion in North Wales and the Midlands might serve to relieve pressure on Colchester. Therefore he cheerfully set out for Settle to bring his forces to join Hamilton at Preston. By 16 August he most certainly heard rumours of Cromwell's presence with Lambert, but whether he acted on the information is again disputed. Clarendon declares that he sent urgent messages to the Duke informing him that Cromwell was within two or three days' march, and begging him to keep his army together. On the other hand, Scotch authorities affirm that he declared there were only small bodies of the enemy in the neighbourhood with whom he could easily deal. Langdale had acted rashly on earlier occasions, and it can be argued that he desired to meet Cromwell alone, to avenge, for himself and his followers, the disaster of Naseby. It is, however, hardly credible that he had failed to learn any lesson from past mistakes ; his conduct in later enterprises may be put in the balance against such an assumption. Moreover, the circumstances were entirely different. The fate of his master, of the whole country, hung upon one single issue—should the Scotch invasion fail, ruin must fall upon both. Again, he had urged instant co-operation against Lambert alone before Cromwell should have time to join him ; it is unthinkable that he should deliberately misinform Hamilton in order that he alone might meet their combined forces !

Cromwell, on his side, was determined to overtake and fight Hamilton before he could join with Byron. Such a junction would inevitably lead to an uprising of the Midlands, which might have its effect on London itself. In that case the work of the First Civil War would be to re-do, with the Scotch army against him this time.

Assuming that Langdale warned Hamilton, the disposition of the Scotch army on the 16th was the worst possible. The cavalry under Callander and Middleton had been sent forward to Wigan, sixteen miles south of the infantry which remained with Hamilton and Baillie at Preston ! This divorce of the two branches of the army was the real cause of the disaster that followed. Langdale, with three thousand foot and six hundred horse was posted to the north-west of the town, in a direct line with Cromwell's approach from Stoneyhurst. On the 17th Hamilton ordered Baillie to cross the Ribble and proceed south, but as he was carrying out this order Langdale was attacked by Cromwell. Still ignorant of the strength of the forces opposed to Sir Marmaduke, but anxious to be in a position to support him should he be in difficulties, Hamilton ordered Baillie to return. Before he could recross the bridge Callander, who had heard of Cromwell's approach and had ridden with Hamilton, overruled his commander, his arguments being that the position on the other side of the Ribble was more tenable, and that the junction of cavalry and infantry might then be more quickly accomplished. Both were sound reasons, but to carry them out meant leaving Langdale in the lurch to fight alone against the enemy. Reluctantly Hamilton gave way, with the result that the help of one thousand foot, which Langdale afterwards declared would have turned the scale, was withheld.

Valiantly Langdale and his English troops held their ground. Though pitted against double their number of the finest soldiers in the world, they so took advantage of the hedges in the fields that attack after attack of the New Model was repulsed. It was only after four hours' hard fighting, when it was quite clear that the help Langdale had sent for was not forthcoming, that the retreat into the town began. Here again there was no support, Hamilton having crossed the Ribble, and the defeated troops were driven out of the streets. Langdale and a few followers made their way with difficulty to Baillie, two hundred of his horse fled north to join Monro and Sir Philip Musgrave, his infantry were hopelessly scattered. Cromwell admitted that they had fought like heroes; it was the only real stand made against the Roundheads during the three days' fight.

Callander, whose advice had led to this disaster, failed to do his part in preventing the greater disaster of the rout of the whole Scotch army. The cavalry had not arrived when Cromwell fell upon Baillie's unprotected infantry and drove him from his position. It arrived only in time to cover his retreat. For three days the wearied, disheartened army fled south in torrents of rain, pursued by the victorious Cromwell. At Winwick a desperate fight ensued, only to end in failure. So hopeless was the plight of the Scotch that Hamilton sent orders to Baillie to make no attempt to hold the bridge at Warrington, and that brave veteran had then no alternative but surrender. After leaving Malpas the horse wheeled to the east, hoping to circumvent their pursuers and reach Scotland in safety. At Uttoxeter it was seen that even that hope had failed, and Langdale and some others there parted company from Hamilton and his officers, Sir Marmaduke being one of the seven whom the army had excepted from all pardon and could hope for no mercy if taken.

Hamilton and his principal officers surrendered at Uttoxeter. Langdale, with one or two companions, eluded pursuit for some time, but they were finally taken in a house not six miles from Nottingham. A contemporary account of the capture relates: " Sir Marmaduke Langdale being in an alehouse and suspected by some saints of the town, they have to examine him and the gentlemen with him who they were; they answered they were of the army; being asked under whom, they said Lord Cromwell; with which answers they went away satisfied. But meeting with three or four of their servants without, and questioning them likewise, they answered those gentlemen, within

were their masters, and that they were under Lambert,
so that this difference in the account wrought a jealousy."
Information was sent to Nottingham to Captain Poulton,
who, with Colonel Hutchinson, seized Sir Marmaduke
and his companions and conveyed them to Nottingham
Castle, where Langdale remained for some months.

Sir Marmaduke was so hated by the rebels, largely on
account of his religion, that there was no hope of mercy
for him—indeed, his captors determined to hang him
before the eyes of the garrison of Pontefract Castle,
still closely besieged by the Roundheads. That garrison,
however, and, in fact, all the Royalists of the north, had
too much love for him whom they affectionately termed
" our general " to allow such a deed to be carried out,
if by any means they could prevent it. A rally in force
from the Castle was beyond their power, but ready brains
and daring hearts were not lacking.

A certain General Rainsborough had lately been sent
from London with reinforcements to put an end to the
protracted siege. At present he was at Doncaster, some
twelve miles distant. It was resolved to seize him in
his lodgings and carry him to Pontefract, there to hold
him hostage. for the safety of Sir Marmaduke, and,
if possible, to exchange him. The plan miscarried, for
on being seized, Rainsborough cried out in spite of
warnings, and in self-defence he, with his lieutenant,
was killed.

This failure rendered fresh measures doubly necessary,
for the enemy would be more than ever disinclined to
mercy. Lady Savile, by judicious bribery, made the
way easy for Langdale's escape ; then, till the hue and
cry was over, he lay for weeks hid in a haystack. Afterwards, disguised as a clergyman, he made his way to

London to Dean Barwick, a trusted agent of Charles I, who afterwards became the chief medium of communication between the exiled Charles II and his secret adherents in England. Langdale was sheltered by this clergyman till an opportunity of escape from the country presented itself, it being given out that he was a clergyman driven from his benefice by Irish rebels.

During the sad years of exile that followed Langdale strove to advance his master's interests in every possible way. During the years 1653–5 he was at Brussels, and from letters to Secretary Nicholas was bent on advocating a policy of friendship with the Pope and Spain, as a counterpoise to Cromwell's friendship with France and Protestant States. In his zeal for such an alliance he sometimes incurred the blame of Nicholas and Hyde, who were too English and conservative to approve of such designs. They were the counsel of one who would leave no stone unturned to restore his royal master and unseat Cromwell, the usurper. Moreover, a Roman Catholic himself, he would scarcely be likely to appreciate the objections brought against his scheme. Occasionally he wrote of plots of the Levellers, with whose agents he negotiated, only to find that their designs would not in any way further his master's cause, their sole concern being the overthrow of Cromwell and the setting up of a Commonwealth on their own lines.

During this time Sir Marmaduke, in common with other exiles, must have suffered much from poverty, for he writes to Nicholas that he can send him but scanty news—merely what he picks up at the ordinary, for he is too poor to go into the society of people of quality. Probably he found service in some of the armies then fighting in Europe, but in the years 1657–8 he was again

in the forefront of an organization for a fresh Cavalier
rising.   Plans were on foot to murder Cromwell; of
this part of the proceeding Langdale was almost certainly
ignorant; letters which tell of his share in the arrange-
ments contain no hint of such knowledge.   There was
to be a rising of the Royalists, more especially in the
counties of Yorkshire and Sussex, and it was with this
that Langdale was concerned, as he was to have charge
of the north.   The undertaking was never carried out;
in some way plans miscarried, or the moment was not
considered propitious.   Thus Charles II's return to
England was delayed for two more years, and on his
Restoration he was accompanied by Langdale, who
spent the short remainder of his life on his Yorkshire
estates.   He once appeared in Parliament as Baron
Langdale, a title conferred on him by Charles II during
the period of exile; but his public career was over.
Though he had lost sixteen thousand pounds in the
King's service and spent the best years of his life in his
cause, he received no further reward—again, probably,
religion was the obstacle to advancement.

In August, 1661, Langdale died; in a happy hour,
maybe, for one of his strict character.   His labours may
not have signally advanced his master's cause; at
least, he worked whole-heartedly, with no thought of
self, and with the most complete loyalty to his superiors.
His failures were few and were due either to mistaken zeal
or loyalty to the men of his country, whom he had brought
from their homes.   The most strenuous work of the
Second Civil War was accomplished by his single efforts,
and, had he been sufficiently supported, that unlucky
enterprise might well have had a different result.   He
never, in his private life or public work, cast discredit

on the cause he supported. On the contrary, he " carried
that gravity in his converse, that integrity and generosity
in his dealings, that strictness in his devotion, that
experience, moderation, and wariness in his counsel,
and that weight in his discourse, as very much endeared
strangers to his royal master's cause and to his own
person, in all the countries he travelled."

WILLIAM SEYMOUR, MARQUIS OF HERTFORD
FROM AN ENGRAVING BY H. ROBINSON AFTER THE PAINTING BY VAN DYCK

TWO CHAMPIONS OF THE WEST

THE MARQUIS OF HERTFORD

WILLIAM SEYMOUR, Marquis of Hertford, was great-grandson of that Earl of Hertford who was created Duke of Somerset on the accession of Edward VI, but was afterwards executed and his children dispossessed of title and possessions by an Act of Attainder. In the reign of Elizabeth his son, the grandfather of William Seymour, was made a Baron with the title of Lord Beauchamp. He was also created Earl of Hertford; but, having married the Lady Catherine Grey who, according to Henry VIII's will, was in the direct line of succession after Elizabeth, he fell into disgrace. In fact, the culprits were imprisoned, and the legality of the marriage denied. There were three sons of this marriage, and the eldest, Edward, Lord Beauchamp, obtained letters patent from Parliament in the reign of James I, granting that he and his heirs male should be Barons of Parliament on the death of his father. Other letters patent were also granted, conferring on him the title of Earl of Hertford. This Lord Beauchamp died before his father, as did also his eldest son, Edward, thus the second son, Sir William Seymour, succeeded his grandfather in his honours.

Romantic marriages seem to have run in the family, for the youth of Hertford is rendered especially interesting by the story of his courtship and marriage of the Lady Arabella Stuart, with its sad sequel for that unhappy lady.

It is sometimes asserted that even in boyhood Seymour had formed an attachment for the Lady Arabella. This is, however, most improbable. In the reign of Elizabeth Arabella had certainly fallen into disgrace, owing to rumours of an understanding between her and one of the Seymours. This was probably the second son of Lord Beauchamp and Catherine Grey, William Seymour's uncle. It was natural that both Elizabeth and James should look with disapproval on any suggestion of a marriage alliance between the Seymours and Arabella. Whatever claims to the throne the latter might have would be doubled by such an alliance. Therefore, when James heard that a treaty of marriage had been arranged between the young William Seymour and the Lady Arabella he summoned them both before his Council, and the gentleman excused his conduct in a letter containing the following : " Being but a younger brother, and sensible of mine own good, unknown to the world, of mean estate, not born to challenge anything by my birthright, and therefore my fortunes to be raised by mine own endeavour, and she a lady of great honour and virtue, and as I thought of great means, I did plainly and honestly endeavour lawfully to gain her in marriage."

Whether young Seymour was moved solely by these mercenary considerations, can only be a matter for conjecture—certainly the lady was considerably her suitor's senior, though disparity of years is notably no barrier to love, and, in spite of the Royal displeasure which he knew he must incur, and which would be an effectual bar to " the raising of his fortunes," the marriage was secretly performed. Moreover, when in later life Hertford again married, one of his daughters was named Arabella, which would seem to point to other motives than those purely worldly ones to which he owned in his Apology to the Council.

The marriage was soon discovered, and in July, 1610, the pair were imprisoned or, as a contemporary letter-writer has it, " The great match which was lately stolen betwixt the Lady Arabella and young Beauchamp, pro-vides them both of safe lodgings ; the Lady close prisoner at Sir Thomas Parry's house at Lambeth and her husband in the Tower."

They found means to communicate and soon laid plans of escape. The Lady Arabella left the house after disguising herself, " by drawing a pair of great French-fashioned hose over her petticoats, putting on a man's doublet, a man-like peruke with long locks over her hair, a black hat, black cloak, russet boots with red tops, and a rapier by her side." Thus attired she rode to Blackwall, where a ship awaited her ; but Mr. Seymour, who had made his escape from the Tower at the same time, had not yet appeared.

The fears of the Lady Arabella's attendants caused her to set sail at once ; but as the ship lingered in the hope that Seymour would arrive, it was overtaken by a pinnace, and Lady Arabella Stuart again taken and imprisoned. Thus when Seymour arrived he found the ship with his wife gone. Knowing nothing of her capture he set out in another, and succeeded in reaching Flanders. He did not return to England until after the death of his wife in September, 1615. This occurred in captivity, for in spite of many petitions James would never con-sent to allow her freedom. It has been often asserted that she lost her reason, but this does not seem to be borne out by the evidence. In a letter the Venetian Ambassador, who seems to have been much interested in her story, mentions her death, saying that she died " contumacious," a term scarcely likely to be applied to one bereft of her reason.

Seymour returned to England in January, 1616, and in November of the same year he was admitted a Knight of the Bath at the creation of Charles Prince of Wales. In the next year he married Lady Francis Devereux, the sister of the Earl of Essex. In April, 1621, at the age of thirty-three, he succeeded his grandfather as Earl of Hertford, his father and elder brother being already dead.

The new Earl of Hertford attended the Parliament of 1626 ; but until 1640 he lived in retirement, for which he was much more suited and which was more congenial to him than public life. He was therefore fifty years of age when he responded to the call of duty, and began to take an active part in public affairs, for which the years of studious ease had been poor preparation. In spite of his disinclination to exertion, the Earl of Hertford exercised considerable influence on those who surrounded him—on the outbreak of the troubles there were very many who waited to see what course he would adopt before deciding upon their own. The serious state of affairs in that year, 1640, convinced him that his position entailed a duty to the public, consequently in the Short Parliament Hertford was in constant attendance at the House of Lords. He was one of those Peers who met at York and advised the King to call the Long Parliament. He was appointed one of the commissioners to treat with the Scotch at Ripon, and this because it was thought that he would be acceptable to those of that nation.

Hertford also signed the petition for a Parliament presented to the King by twelve peers, and altogether, previous to the trial of Strafford, his deeds and words were more likely to find favour with the popular than with the Court party. On the question of Strafford, however, he could not conscientiously follow the lead of the dominant party in the Commons. He was no friend of Strafford ; but he began now to see that Parliament was going too far beyond the bounds of its own province, in making " new law " to cover the guilt of a person who, under the " old law," would have escaped the desired penalty. Up to this point he had acted with the popular party ; he had sat on Committees to reform the Court of Star Chamber, abolish Ship Money, etc., but, in common with Hyde and Falkland, he now began to draw back. He was probably in favour of sparing Strafford's life if the King would make him incapable of holding office. Finding the Commons determined on exacting the extreme penalty, he absented himself from the House when the voting on the Bill of Attainder was taken.

Previous to this, while still acting with the popular leaders, he, together with six other peers of more or less similar views, had been added to the Privy Council by the King, probably as a concession to that party. In that capacity he acted with conspicuous and careful loyalty towards both King and Parliament. Some of these newly exalted members seem to have used their position to advance the most extreme measures of the Commons, " withholding or giving advice subversive to monarchy." Hertford was no party to this " slim " policy. No want of good faith can be urged against him. As an example of these methods many members of the Privy Council would have postponed the King's return from Scotland, when delay had already been and would be still more disastrous to his interests. Hertford was at one with his most faithful friends in urging Charles to an immediate return.

In May, 1641, the Earl of Newcastle resigned the office of Governor to the Prince of Wales, considering that by continuing to hold it he was doing the King no service, he being in such ill-odour with the popular party, and suggested the Earl of Hertford as his successor. The suggestion was a happy one, for Hertford was not only acceptable to the King, but the appointment would increase the prestige of the Court, since, if accepted, it would prove to the populace that there were persons of undoubted popularity and loyalty to established institutions, who could still conscientiously serve their sovereign. It was such considerations that led the Earl to accept a post, not congenial in itself, too arduous for one of his ease-loving nature, and for which he felt himself unfitted both by nature and age. In the following month the Earl was raised to the Marquisate, but neither this nor his acceptance of the office forfeited the confidence of the popular party. Probably, from subsequent events, they hoped to use him for their own ends.

In August, 1641, the King set out on his unfortunate journey to Scotland: he deputed Hertford one of the commissioners for passing bills in his absence, and before leaving England arranged that the Prince of Wales should have a separate establishment, Richmond being chosen as his place of residence. The King's absence afforded the malcontents in Parliament an excellent opportunity for interference in his domestic affairs. They at once framed an order to the Marquis of Hertford

that he should take every care of the person of the young
Prince, and the evidence seems to favour the opinion
that they had very early formed a plan to obtain possession of his person. Certainly they claimed supreme control over his actions, for on one occasion when the Prince
spent a few days with his mother at Oatlands, they protested at the absence of his governor. So far Hertford
was willing to submit to the interference of Parliament ;
at any rate, he gave an explanation of his absence, saying
that he spent the day at Oatlands, but that " there was
no room for him to lie there." Both he and the Queen
promised that in future he should not be separated from
his charge.

In November, owing to the urgent entreaties of his
friends on the Privy Council, including Hertford, the
King returned from Scotland and was accorded a magnificent reception by the City of London. Shortly afterwards
it was decided that the Queen should set out for Holland,
taking her daughter Mary, who was to be married to the
Prince of Orange. In order that he might take leave of
his mother, the King sent for his son to Hampton Court.
Parliament protested ; the King returned a dignified
answer, but sent the Prince back to Hertford's care,
while he himself escorted the Queen to Dover. He informed the Marquis that he should again require his
son's presence on his return. Therefore, when he arrived
at Greenwich on his way back, Charles sent a message
commanding Hertford to bring the boy to him. The
Marquis was ill at the time, but Parliament having given
him strict orders that the Prince must either be accompanied by him or not go at all, he made shift to obey
the King's order in person. At Greenwich he resigned
the care of the Prince to the King, without previously

5

informing Parliament of his intention.   Here the real
motives of the popular leaders were revealed.   They
demanded that the King should " continue the Prince in
these parts, in S. James's, or any other of his houses near
London."   Obviously they had planned that the Prince
should become a hostage in their hands, when, they
opined, the King would be able to refuse them nothing.
The King's answer illustrates his innate dignity, which
never deserted him.   " For my son I shall take that care
of him which shall justify me to God as a father, and to
my dominions as a King."

It is scarcely surprising that from that time the Marquis of Hertford severed himself entirely from those men
who could so far forget the respect they owed to the King
as to presume to dictate to him the residence he should
choose for his son, letting him see quite clearly that they
meant to use the Prince as a pawn in their game that
they might bring the King to his knees by working on
his paternal feelings.   It is probable that, the Prince once
in their possession, they would have threatened to depose
Charles in his favour, should he continue to resist their
demands.

Hertford was not present during the debate on the
militia, but it was on that question that he definitely
split with the Parliamentary leaders.   He held the position
of Lieutenant for the County of Somerset.   On 5 March,
1642, the Commons proceeded to appoint new lieutenants
in pursuance of the Ordinance passed by both Houses,
but to which the King had refused his assent, for if
Parliament appointed the lieutenants they thereby controlled the forces of the militia, a power till that day
indisputably a royal prerogative.   The Lieutenancy of
Somerset was offered to Hertford, who replied that he

was not at the debate of the militia, and therefore was
utterly ignorant of what had passed in it, " neither doth
he yet know that the King hath given his consent to it,
without which he hopes your Lordships will not impose
it upon him."

The last act of Lord Hertford in Parliament was to join
with the minority of peers then present in protesting
against the first Article of the nineteen Propositions presented to the King at York—that all the great officers
and Privy Councillors should be removed and others,
recommended by Parliament, be put in their places. A
few days after this ineffectual protest Hertford was with
the King at York, fulfilling his duties as governor to the
Prince. His presence in the House of Lords was at once
commanded, together with urgent directions that he
should not allow the Prince to leave the kingdom. Hertford's answer was addressed to his brother-in-law, the
Earl of Essex :

"-My noble Lord,

" It being expected from me that I should give an
answer to the House of Peers whether I should undertake
that the Prince should not be conveyed out of this kingdom, I humbly desire your Lordship to make this answer
for me. That I will undertake that the Prince shall go
no further than His Majesty goeth, for so it hath pleased
His Majesty to assure me and that he shall not stir from
him. For any other undertaking I do utterly disclaim as
being a thing out of my power, and consequently a great
rashness and presumption in me to undertake. Thus
much I humbly pray your Lordship to present, with my
humble and earnest desire that the order may be taken
off, which may be so prejudicial to me, especially since I

have thus far declared myself. God remove all jealousies
from us, and put a true understanding between the King
and his Parliament, which shall ever be the earnest and
hearty prayers of

" Your Lordship's most faithful brother and humble
servant

" HERTFORD "

After receiving this straightforward answer, Parliament made no further attempt to interfere with the
Marquis in his governorship of the Prince. They could
have no possible ground of complaint with his conduct
in the matter, which was that of an honest, straightforward man, who believed that no Parliament had
authority to interfere with a father's guardianship of his
child.

In June, 1642, the Peers present at York, forty-five in
number, pledged themselves " not to obey any orders or
commands, not warranted by the known laws of the land ;
to defend His Majesty's person, crown, and dignity,
together with his just and legal prerogative, against all
persons and power whatsoever ; and not to obey any
ordinance concerning the militia that had not the royal
assent." Two days later they signed a declaration that
they were assured the King had no intention of making
war upon the Parliament. Both these documents bear
the signature of Hertford. He had now definitely
decided to throw in his lot with the King. He did more
than sign declarations to show his loyalty ; at his own
expense he raised a body of sixty horse, with maintenance
for three months. The King soon found that the time
for declarations was past and over, that active measures
were necessary, for the Parliament, acting on the Militia

Ordinance, was making its power felt in every direction. Therefore Charles sent the leading nobles and gentry into their respective counties to execute the commission of array. Among their number was Hertford, who was also given a commission as the King's Lieutenant-General of the West. He seems to have been very confident of success, a confidence probably bred of his considerable influence in that part of the country, " where his interest and reputation was greater than any man's." A letter written to the Queen at about the time of his receiving the commission, is written in an unwontedly buoyant and light-hearted vein. " By His Majesty's commands I am with all speed to repair unto the west, to put his commissions of array in execution, which I make no doubt to perform without any great difficulty. If God prospers us, as I trust He will, in so good a cause, we shall then shortly (I hope) be blessed and cheered up with Your Majesty's long-wished-for presence. And hey then, down go they, and to our greater encouragement. Sampson is come over to us."

This letter was written from Beverley, from which town Hertford advanced with so light a heart on his mission to the west. It was high time that the King's cause was championed in that part of England, for Parliament had practical control of all the south of England, with the exception of Portsmouth, the position of which was but precarious, seeing that it was held by the fickle, unreliable Goring. Danger from him was not, however, apprehended by the Royal party, who were much encouraged that Portsmouth had declared for His Majesty, and was held by " such a good officer."

Hertford first made for Bath, but met with little encouragement from that city, and so passed on to Wells, as the centre of the county, where he was joined by a brave band of local gentry, including his brother, Lord Seymour, Lord Paulet, Sir John Stawel, Captain John Digby, Sir Ralph Hopton, Sir Francis Doddington, and others. Here he found that the work before him was of a much more difficult nature than he had foreseen. The Marquis was of a gentle, peaceable disposition, not a leader of men by nature ; moreover, he was of that party among the King's advisers who urged that every action on his side should be legally justified, in order to win the support of the neutral and that the enemy might be given no occasion to blaspheme. Consequently his efforts to increase his forces and strengthen the King's cause in the west were mainly persuasive, and he was no match for the agents of Parliament, who did not hesitate to translate the Latin of the commission of array into whatsoever English best served their purposes ; as, for example, that two-thirds of the estates of the yeomen and free-holders were to be taken from them, that every peasant was to be made to pay a tax equal to one day's labour per week to the King, with other similar flights of imagination. The result was, that while the Marquis had only three troops of foot and a company of horse to defend himself and relieve Portsmouth, the Parliamentary forces were rapidly growing in strength. Moreover, owing to his passion for legality, which, throughout the early stages of the war, was a drag on the Royalists, Hertford was afraid to use any small advantage that occasion offered. When, for instance, at Shepton Mallet Sir Ralph Hopton turned the tables on those who accused him and his companions of disturbing the peace, by proving that he had a commission from the King to preserve the peace of that country and to quell any unlawful tumult, and so turned the justices to his support, the natural course to have taken would have been to drive the rebel leaders and their followers completely out of the county. This, however, he was not able to do, his hands being tied by strict orders from the Marquis that no hostile act should be undertaken. Thus it was that when the army of the Earl of Bedford, seven thousand foot and eight troops of horse, appeared, the Marquis of Hertford had already been forced, by the rebels of that and the neighbouring county of Gloucester, to retire from Wells to Sherborne. Bedford wished to capture Sherborne and, if possible, secure the persons of Hertford and the other commissioners who had, since the affair at Shepton Mallet, been declared delinquents and incapable of sitting in Parliament, Hertford himself being impeached. Hertford's desire was the relief of Portsmouth, but this it was absolutely impossible for him, with his " great little army," to accomplish. Nevertheless, for a considerable time he made it equally impossible for the representative of Parliament to attain his end. He sent a personal challenge to the Earl of Bedford, with the fantastic, if chivalrous, idea that a personal combat would avoid the meeting of the two armies. Bedford refused the challenge and, on his second attempt to capture Sherborne, Hertford surrendered, probably seeing how utterly useless it was to hold out longer. Portsmouth had been yielded by Goring, some regiments of horse he had expected from Sir James Byron had marched instead to the King, all the more important towns in Somerset, including Taunton and Wellington, had declared for Parliament. Hertford and his troops marched to Minehead, hoping to garrison the castle there, and so make a new centre for the upholding of the King's fortunes in the West Country. Mr. Luttrell, the owner, refused to allow the castle to be garrisoned, and Hertford, having no superabundance of self-confidence, and being easily discouraged, could see no hope for the royal cause in those parts. He therefore determined to return to the King. Some of his followers, led by the gallant Hopton, were of stronger calibre ; they determined to remain and make still more efforts to uphold the King's standard in the west. Their bolder, more strenuous efforts met with the success they deserved, but it must be remembered, before we blame Hertford over-severely, that he was no longer young, being fifty-four when he joined the King at York, that for many years his sinews had been relaxed, his nervous energy lain dormant, study and ease had claimed him for their own. Moreover, it was no love of war or of action, but the simple call of duty that had led him to accept the King's commission. His was the artistic temperament which foresees all, and more than all, the possibilities of defeat—the soldier, the man of action, must see only the goal to be attained. That Hertford remained at his post, that he did not retire at once into private life on this first great disappointment must be held to his credit. For he must have been bitterly disappointed, he knew himself beloved and esteemed by all in his neighbourhood, he believed in the righteousness of the cause he had espoused. It was excusable that he should imagine the western counties ready to follow him at a word. The reality wounded his vanity, and for a while he lost heart. It was no small thing then that he held by his master, and determined not to forsake him but to serve him, if not here as leader, in some other place, perhaps, in some other capacity.

In September, therefore, the Marquis crossed the Bristol Channel from Minehead to South Wales, where he busied himself in raising troops until he could rejoin the King. By the end of the year he was with the King at Oxford. On his way from Wales with troops, in December, he had attacked Cirencester, but unsuccessfully. It was on his advice that in February Prince Rupert made another attempt on the town and captured it. The advice was excellent, as the result proved, for it kept open the country to the Royalists between Oxford and Worcester and so into South Wales, to be in the future Rupert's chief recruiting ground. As a Parliamentary writer acknowledged, " the news of the disaster at Cirencester operated far and wide. Upon the report of it the castles of Sudley and Berkeley were abandoned. Tewkesbury yielded and was garrisoned by the King. The south was still kept open towards Bristol, but on the northern and eastern frontier, Gloucestershire was entirely excluded from intercourse with London."

At about this time the King wrote to the Queen mentioning that Hertford desired some office near His Majesty's person, either as Treasurer or " of my Bedchamber." This points to a desire to relinquish his office of Lieutenant-General in the west. If this were the case, Hertford quickly surrendered his own desires to the public welfare, for in two months' time he had resumed active exercise of that office.

In the month of March, 1643, hostilities ceased for a time, and negotiations for a treaty were begun. As in nearly every similar case, Hertford was one of the commissioners, and would seem to have been especially acceptable to the other side, owing to his ' known

moderation and desire for peace. The negotiations
ended in failure, neither side being anxious to come
to terms, each believing that its party was assured
of speedy victory. The King's affairs were certainly
in a promising condition. All Gloucestershire save the
county town itself was obedient to him, and the way
into Wales was thus kept open. Hopton had won the
brilliant victory of Stratton and was advancing into
Devonshire. Waller, in May, had been forced to leave
Hereford, and had failed to take Worcester—now he
was on his way to hinder Hopton's advance. This was
not an easy task, for in addition to Hopton and his brave
Cornish forces, Hertford and Prince Maurice had left
Oxford for the west with a considerable army. There
had been some heart-burnings before the army had
started from Oxford, and the arrangement finally made
was not one which promised to make for peace. The
Palatine Princes had felt it derogatory to their rank
and dignity that Maurice should be subordinate to
Lord Hertford, and the King showed some disposition
to yield to their importunities. Hyde, however, pointed
out that a divided command would be ruinous and
impossible. Thus Hertford retained for the time his
rank as Lieutenant-General in the west, though from
their widely differing dispositions it was certain that
the Marquis and Prince Maurice would not for long
work together in harmony. Then, too, the Marquis
had thoughtlessly filled all the posts in the army before
he joined hands with Hopton, whom he would, in the
natural course of events, supersede when the two bodies
united. Thus the Cornish officers found no chance of
preferment left open to them ; the junction, indeed,
decreased their individual importance, though it was to

them that the favourable position of the King's forces
was due. Their loyalty was, however, proof against all
temptations to discontent ; they quelled the murmurings
of the soldiers and inferior officers and prepared to do the
work assigned to them in the coming campaign.

The two armies met at Chard, and immediately on
their advance Taunton, Bridgwater, and Dunster Castle
fell into their hands. News came that Waller was at
Bath, within two days' march. As he had the advantage
of position, it was decided to advance and, if possible,
draw him out to engage. The Royalists marched to
Bradford-on-Avon, and so to Marshfield, the army so
placed as to threaten Bath and cut off Waller's way of
retreat to London, while at the same time he would be
tempted to fight to prevent the junction of the western
army with that of the King at Oxford. So far their
plans were skilfully laid. Waller did draw out his troops
on to Lansdown, but the Royalists, conscious of their
strength and over-confident of victory, attacked at a
disadvantage, when they should have held their ground.
The result was that at first Hertford's horse was driven
back by Hazelrigg's "Lobsters," and the Royalists
only gained the hill at great loss. Sir Bevil Grenville
and many other officers were killed, and Sir Ralph Hopton
was so badly wounded the morning after the fight by
the bursting of a barrel of powder as to be incapacitated
from active leadership for some time. Hertford was
forced to retreat to Devizes, closely followed by Waller,
who advertised the battle as a victory for the Parliamentary forces. At Devizes the Royalists entrenched
themselves—they could not fight unless reinforced,
neither could the whole army retreat over open ground
to Oxford. It was therefore decided that Hertford and

Prince Maurice, with the cavalry, should retreat to Oxford by way of Salisbury, and return with the help so badly needed. Hertford has been severely censured for this "desertion." Certainly Hopton and his gallant men were in sore straits in Devizes, but the step was taken with the advice and consent of the officers, who probably knew their own difficulties, and it was justified by results. Hertford himself did not at once return to his post, but Prince Maurice and Wilmot set off with twelve hundred horse and successfully attacked and routed Waller's army where it was posted on Roundway Down. The action was so decisive that Waller was forced to flee to Bristol, and the King's troops possessed themselves of Bath. They were naturally elated that they had put to such ignominious flight the great Waller, in whom Parliament had placed its trust, and their delight and confidence in the future were vented in such rhymes as the following, in which Sir John Denham ridiculed Waller's flight together with his appellation of the " Conqueror."

> " And now without lying, you may paint him flying,
>   At Bristol they say you may find him ;
> Great William the Con, so fast did he run,
>   That he left half his name behind him."

Another popular Royalist rhyme testifies to the feeling of joyous confidence :

> " Bristol taking,
>   Exeter shaking,
>   Gloucester quaking."

After Roundway Down it had been immediately decided that Bristol should now be besieged, and the victorious western army was to combine with Rupert's forces from Oxford to this end. Hertford and Prince Maurice were to lead their forces to attack the city on the Somerset side, Prince Rupert, with the Oxford army, was to lie on the Gloucester side. There was difference of opinion as to the method of the siege. Prince Rupert wished to assault; Hertford and his officers disapproved of this method. Both parties were equally right from their own point of view. From the Gloucester side assault was the ideal mode of attack, while it would be almost impossible from the Somerset side. Nevertheless, an assault was determined, with the result to be expected. The Cornish storming party was driven back with great loss, Prince Rupert's attack was successful, so successful indeed that a parley was called, and the town ultimately surrendered. Thus, from no fault of the Cornish army or its officers, their share in the capture of Bristol was but negative. Possibly the fact that his troops, by his strategy, had won the city caused Prince Rupert to adopt an attitude of absolute superiority towards Hertford. He failed to consult him before signing the articles of surrender, though, as Lieutenant-General of the west, Bristol came within the Marquis's jurisdiction, Hertford's sensitive, highly-strung temperament was at once in arms. Without consulting the Prince, he, in his turn, asserted his authority by appointing Hopton governor of the captured city. Rupert had designed that office for another, but on hearing of Hertford's action, wrote off at once to the King begging the office for himself. Knowing nothing of the circumstances, Charles readily granted the boon, in itself a small reward for so great a service as the capture of the second city in the kingdom. The King's answer was no sooner dispatched than there arrived a message from Lord Hertford also telling of the taking of Bristol and mentioning that, subject to His Majesty's approval, he had nominated Sir Ralph Hopton to the governorship. The King's dilemma was great, for he had no mind to repulse either his nephew or the Marquis, while the fact that the dispute concerned Hopton, who had served him so well and was withal so much beloved, made the question no easy one to solve. Charles therefore set out for Bristol, and prevailed upon the Marquis to surrender his nomination on the understanding that the Prince should only have the titular governorship, the real power remaining with Hopton as Lieutenant-Governor. So the matter was settled. It was, however, clear to the mind of the King that it was undesirable to continue Hertford in his position as Lieutenant-Governor of the west ; his great name and his personal popularity were desirable assets, but he had no practical experience of leadership, and was easily affronted. To expect hearty co-operation between him and the Prince for the future was out of the question. Therefore Charles decided to accede to the request made by Hertford some time previously, and give him some office about his person. This decision he very tactfully made known to the Marquis, assuring him that he needed a person of such tried loyalty and wide experience near him to give him the benefit of his counsel and advice.

That the King was wise in this decision from the practical point of view is proved by the incident concerning the governorship of Weymouth. This town fell into the hands of the Royalists very shortly after the fall of Bristol, and again there was a dispute—this time between Prince Maurice and Hertford—as to the appointment of a governor. The King at first absolutely refused to confirm Hertford's choice, and he, his sensitive nature still sore from the late affront, complained " that he was fallen from any degree of credit with the King, and was made incapable of doing him farther service ; that his fidelity should never be lessened towards him, but since he was become so totally useless to the King and his friends, he hoped His Majesty would give him leave to retire to his own house, where he doubted not he should be suffered to live privately and quietly to pray for the King." Though, owing to the intercession of Hyde, the choice of Hertford was afterwards confirmed by the King, it was obvious that a man of this temperament was unfit for the rough life of a camp—though it was a nice question whether his withdrawal might not do harm to the King's service by giving some show of reason to the complaints of those who urged that the advice and wishes of the nobles were disregarded in favour of the foreign princes. Nevertheless, as soldiers the princes were decidedly superior to Hertford, and if choice between the two had to be made, it was perhaps wise as well as natural that it should fall on them.

Wounded pride did not long hold Hertford in its sway. He retired to Oxford, though not for some time did he obtain the position of Groom of the Stole promised him by the King at Bristol—at one time the Queen seems to have desired to see it conferred on the renegade Holland. From this time his name is only occasionally met with in the records of the time ; he played no prominent part in the King's affairs, but remained at his side, his faithful servant, ready to serve in whatever capacity best pleased his sovereign. When appointed Groom of the Stole, he finally resigned his office of Governor to the Prince of Wales. In October, 1643, he was appointed Chancellor of the University of Oxford in the

place of the Earl of Pembroke—a sufficient compliment.
Most of the documents emanating from Oxford contain
his name; he was one of those who addressed a letter
to the Lords of the Privy Council in Scotland touching
the expedition into England, and pointing out how few
peers were left at Westminster. He was a member
of the Parliament summoned to Oxford, 1643-4. Hertford took a prominent part in any negotiations for peace,
and his share in the discussions concerning the Treaty
of Uxbridge is especially interesting, for it discloses his
attitude towards the theological controversies of the
time, and his impatience of discussion which could
lead to no definite end. He was one of the sixteen
commissioners for the King, and when a lengthy argument
ensued between Dr. Steward and Dr. Henderson on
Church government, the one maintaining that Episcopacy,
the other that Presbyterianism was *jure divino*, the
Marquis broke in: "My lords, here is much said concerning Church government in the general; the reverend
doctors on the King's part affirm that episcopacy is
jure divino, and reverend ministers of the other part
do affirm that presbytery is *jure divino*; for my part,
I think that neither the one nor the other, nor any
government whatsoever, is *jure divino*, and I desire we
may leave this argument and proceed to debate upon the
particular proposals." Here spoke the practical man
of affairs, unconcerned with theological differences,
but much concerned to bring about peace by definite
proposals of " give and take." If peace was not to be
obtained, such controversy was idle.

During the remaining years of the war Hertford
remained with the King, ready to give counsel if that
was desired, but, with the remnant of the King's original

body of advisers, falling more and more into the position of a friend, as the issues of the conflict depended ever more and more upon the sword.

After the departure of the King to the Scotch army, and the surrender of Oxford, Hertford petitioned Parliament to be allowed to reside at Windsor, probably with the idea of being close at hand should the King return to London. When, however, Charles was handed over to Parliament by the Scots, Hertford, with the rest of his faithful followers, was not even allowed to visit him. At Hampton Court that embargo was apparently removed, for with the Duke of Richmond and many others Hertford was allowed to see the King, though not to reside there with him. While in the Isle of Wight, negotiations for the Treaty of Newport were begun, and Charles was then permitted the comfort of the presence and advice of Richmond, Hertford, Lindsey, and Southampton, though when the actual terms were discussed they were not allowed in the room. Thus, as far as advice was concerned, their presence was a mere farce.

When the Parliamentary commissioners left the Isle of Wight, Hertford, Southampton, Sir Philip Warwick, and the Bishop of Salisbury obtained leave to attend to their own affairs for a fortnight, thinking they would not be needed for that short space of time. They little thought that they had held their last personal communication with their sovereign. The same night the King was seized by Cornet Joyce and taken to Hurst Castle, and from that time to his execution they never saw him again. It has been stated that Hertford, with the Duke of Richmond and the Earls of Southampton and Lindsey, begged permission to suffer the extreme penalty in the King's stead, as they were his advisers

6

and therefore responsible for his actions. Beautiful and pathetic as the story is, and very nearly contemporary, it lacks corroboration. In itself, it is not improbable, the devotion of his followers to the King's person is well known. Moreover, the doctrine of the responsibility of ministers had been promulgated on several previous occasions.

It was to these four that permission was granted to bury the body of their loved master, though they were not allowed to accompany it from London to Windsor, nor were they allowed to use the Burial Service of the Church of England. Thus deprived of the last rites of the Church for which he gave his life, the body of the King was placed in a vault where Henry VIII and Jane Seymour were buried.

From that day to the Restoration Hertford lived in retirement—he was allowed to compound his estates, for he supplied Charles II with money to the extent of five thousand pounds a year. He is reported to have been held in such high honour by Cromwell that he once asked him for advice as to his conduct, to whom Hertford replied : " I will declare to Your Highness my thoughts, by which you may continue to be great and establish your name and family for ever. Our young master that is abroad—that is, my master and the master of us all—restore him to his crowns, and by doing this you may have what you please." The Protector answered that he " had gone so far that the young gentleman could not forgive."

On the Restoration Hertford was one of those who met Charles II at Canterbury, and was there invested with the Order of the Garter. He was named a member of the Privy Council, and Parliament, on Charles's proposal,

restored to him the title of Duke of Somerset. When the
Act was passed Charles addressed the House in person,
saying: "I cannot but take notice of one particular
Bill I have passed, which may seem of an extraordinary
nature—that concerning the Duke of Somerset—but
you all know it is for an extraordinary person, who
hath merited as much of the King, my father, and
myself as a subject can do, and I am none of those who
think that subjects, by performing their duties in an
extraordinary manner, do not oblige their princes to
reward them in an extraordinary manner. There can
be no danger from such a precedent, and I hope no man
will envy him, because I have done what a good master
should do to such a servant."

The new Duke did not enjoy his honours for many
months. He was seventy-three years old at the time
of the Restoration, and died in October of the same year,
leaving a grandson, a boy of nine years old, to succeed
him. He had five sons, but one only survived him.
Hertford may be accounted happy in that he lived to see
the son of his beloved master restored to his rightful
heritage, happier still, perhaps, that he did not live long
enough to see the glories of that Restoration tarnished
and dimmed.

SIR RALPH HOPTON

SIR RALPH HOPTON, the hero of the west, was born in 1598 "heir to one of the most powerful and ancient families in Somerset." His father was Robert Hopton, of Wytham, in Somerset, where the family had been settled for more than four centuries; his mother was Jane, daughter and heir of Robert Kemeys, of the Wandry, Monmouthshire. He received his early education at a good country school, and very early showed a great aptitude for study, especially languages. In his "Memoirs" Lloyd gives us an amazing picture of youthful precocity. "His education was such that he learned to pray as soon as he could speak, and to read as soon as he could pray; before three years old he read any character or letter whatsoever in our printed books, and within a while any tolerable writing hand, getting by heart at four and a half years five or six hundred Latin or Greek words, together with their genders and declensions"!

He left school for Oxford, and became a gentleman commoner of Lincoln College, where his tutor was Robert Sanderson, afterwards Bishop of Lincoln. His teaching was evidently remembered with gratitude, for Hopton is said to have blessed God for the habit instilled into him by Mr. Sanderson "of considering matters proposed to him leisurely and soberly, of recollecting the proper circumstances of a business pertinently, of searching into the bottom of things quickly."

SIR RALPH HOPTON

FROM THE PAINTING ATTRIBUTED TO VAN DYCK IN THE NATIONAL PORTRAIT GALLERY

In spite of his studious disposition, it was the life of action that appealed to him : he determined to do great things for future ages to meditate upon, leaving others to consider the great things done in the past. He left the University to serve as a volunteer in the Low Countries, and afterwards had a regular command in the Palatinate. He took an active part in the early scenes of the Thirty Years' War, and fought in the battle of Prague. It was seated on horseback behind Hopton that the young Queen of Bohemia escaped from the city, the scene of her greatest triumphs. In the service of the " Queen of Hearts " Hopton spent five years of his youth.

By the year 1624 he had returned to England, for his name occurs in a list of some of the regiments of foot designed to take part in Count Mansfield's expedition for the relief of the Palatinate. The next year he was in England again, apparently with the object of raising men to recruit the body of troops then in Germany. In this he was not successful, for he wrote to Sir Dudley Carleton, who had already urged him to throw up his employment with Mansfield and join the fleet, begging him to procure his discharge, for he had not raised the six hundred men he had hoped for, and was afraid "to command men without the means to support them." During his years of service abroad Hopton had gained great military skill and a reputation for undaunted courage. On his discharge he did not join the fleet ; he was probably desirous of a time of peace after his activities abroad, and looked forward to the life of a country gentleman. Doubtless the studious side of his nature now demanded satisfaction.

He had married Elizabeth, the daughter of Sir Arthur

Capel, and widow of Sir Justinian Lewin, a lady of considerable beauty and wit, who was evidently a most suitable wife for the simple soldier. In the year 1625, at the Coronation of King Charles I, Sir Ralph Hopton was made a Knight of the Bath.

He enjoyed fifteen years of peace ; what part he had taken in the controversies of that period is unknown, but when the Long Parliament met he was elected to it as a burgess for the city of Wells, and at that time his sympathies were certainly on the side of the popular party. So strong was his adherence to it, in fact, that he was appointed one of the Committee which drew up the Remonstrance of November, 1641, and was chosen to read it to the King when presented. From that time, however, he began to draw back, perhaps recognizing that a course which such patriots as Hyde and Falkland refused to countenance could not be consistent with loyalty to the King, perhaps for the first time perceiving the ends aimed at by the leaders of the popular party— the subversion of the established government in Church and State. He took objection to some expressions in a Declaration in which Parliament set forward some of their fears, especially that they " had information from Rome, Venice, etc., that the King had a design in hand for the altering of religion," as being too distant from that reverence which ought to be used to the King, and saying that when they assumed that the King would change his religion, that " they seemed to ground an opinion of the King's apostasy upon a less evidence than would serve to hang a fellow for stealing a horse." For this plain speaking he was committed to the Tower for several days, though apparently Parliament took his advice and made the clause complained of less grossly

insulting than had been at first intended. He made
other efforts to curb the extravagances of Parliament.
Thus in January he excused the action of the King in
coming to the House with armed followers to effect the
arrest of the five members—he was probably roused to
defence on this occasion by the bitter invective of a
certain Harbottle Grimstone. In pursuance of this
course he opposed the adoption of the Declaration, expressing the sense of the House that its privileges had
been violated, pointing out that at the time Parliament
itself had servants in the lobby, armed in an unusual
manner with carbines and pistols. Again he opposed
the appointment of a Grand Committee of the House
to sit at the Guildhall—this on legal grounds—and the
motion was modified to meet the objection, by the appointment of a Select Committee with leave for all other
members to attend who chose to do so.

Finding all his efforts to stem the now resistless current
utterly futile, Hopton finally retired from Parliament,
after having, according to Lloyd, impulsively challenged
several of the leaders of the Parliament in Westminster
Hall. Once more he abandoned the sphere of thought
for the sphere of action. In his own county he set himself
to make preparations for the war, which he now perceived
to be inevitable, by providing arms and ammunition
at his own expense, directing the strengthening and
fortifying of all tenable places in Somerset, Devon, and
Wiltshire. By his eloquence and personal interest he,
with the help of Sir Bevil Grenville, Sir John Stawell,
and Sir Nicholas Stanning, had raised a choice army
by the time that Lord Hertford appeared, in the summer
of 1642, as Commander-in-Chief in the west. At Wells
Hopton joined his chief at the head of two troops of

horse, raised and armed at his own charge and trained by him to be ready to fight at once.

If he had hoped to find Hertford at the head of a strong force, ready to take the offensive, he was sorely disappointed. His army consisted of a troop of horse raised by Mr. John Digby and Sir Francis Hawley and about one hundred foot gathered together by Colonel Harry Lunsford. To these were now added Hopton's own body of horse and a small troop of dragoons. With these, in the midst of the hostility of the common people, Hertford was unable even to hold Sherborne, and, utterly discouraged, he determined to cross into Wales from Minehead and so return to the King. The country was, however, so thoroughly disaffected that he could not embark even the whole of that small army, so with a part he crossed into Glamorgan with the idea of organizing the defence of South Wales.

Sir Ralph, finding himself thus deserted, and thoroughly disapproving of his chief's course of action, resolved to take the charge of affairs into his own hands. He realized that the defence action had been a failure, and determined to take the offensive and win a neutral county for the King. He therefore entered Cornwall and occupied Pendennis Castle, his object being to make a centre of loyalty in the west before the agents of Parliament could forestall him. He recognized that careful tactics would be necessary. To secure the adherence of the Cornish he must avoid any appearance of taking the offensive—for the people of that county had a reputation of reverence for the name of Parliament, with a great love for the established government in Church and State, and no reverence at all for the Court. Of the gentry, the most part were for the King, but a few, and these the most active, were for the Parliament. Hopton, recognizing the delicacy of the situation, contented himself with the occupation of Pendennis Castle for the moment, and quietly awaited his opportunity, which the Parliamentarian gentry soon proceeded to give him. They had formed themselves into a Parliamentary Committee at Launceston, in which town they collected forces to prevent Sir Ralph's escape; they then indicted him and other leading Royalists at the Bodmin Quarter Sessions as "divers unknown men lately come armed into that country against the peace." When they arrived at the town they found the tables turned. Hopton met them bearing his commission from Hertford as Lieutenant-General of the King's Horse in the West, and called upon all men to submit to the King's authority as vested in him by virtue of that commission. Hopton and his followers were accordingly acquitted, and the jury declared the gentlemen from Launceston guilty of promoting a riotous assembly, and the sheriff was called upon to rally the forces of the county against them. This was done, a body of three thousand foot raised, and the enemy driven from Launceston and Saltash. Hopton then proposed, as Cornwall was now entirely loyal, to pursue the advantage and drive the enemy from Devonshire.

This proved a different matter, for the train-bands, who had willingly served under Hopton in their own county, to free it from Parliamentary interference in matters religious, refused to cross the Tamar. Forces raised by the sheriff were for the defence of the county, and were not bound to leave it. Thus early in the struggle appeared the difficulty, which was to be one great cause of Royalist defeat—the strength of purely local as opposed to national feeling. Again Hopton showed his good sense ; he saw the futility of argument or force, surrendered gracefully to the exigency of the situation, and prepared to attain his end by other means. The train-bands were dismissed till their services should be again required, and Hopton turned to Sir Bevil Grenville and other gentry, including Sir Nicholas Slanning, John Arundel, and John Trevanion, suggesting that each should use his influence to obtain, by voluntary enlistment, a body of foot for permanent service. With the small body of fifteen hundred men thus raised, Hopton advanced into Devon, and before the end of November he had occupied Tavistock and even threatened Plymouth, then held for Parliament by Ruthen, a Scotchman.

Thus by December the position of Parliament was serious enough to cause certain members to propose calling in the aid of the Scotch. Everywhere the Royalists seemed to have the advantage. In the north Fairfax had been forced to retreat from Tadcaster ; the Queen was indefatigable in sending supplies to the northern army. Stamford had been forced to evacuate Hereford, a fresh army of Welshmen was being raised by Lord Herbert, while the King's position at Oxford, within his girdle of fortresses, was practically impregnable. Then had appeared the cloud in the west, which, at first no bigger than a man's hand, had now assumed alarming proportions. Hopton was clearly a man to be reckoned with. The Houses agreed that at any cost his advance must be stayed. It was thought advisable to form a combination of the forces of Devon, Somerset, and Dorset to oppose him. The appointment of the Earl of Stamford as commander of this western army seems to point to an undue respect for wealth and position, with a too small appreciation of Hopton's military skill and power of handling men.

Sir Ralph Hopton is one of the few commanders on either side who came through the ordeal of civil war with an absolutely untarnished reputation. No contemporary pamphleteer, no matter how vindictive, ever ventured to bring an accusation against that loyal, upright soldier—no envious colleague, not even the unscrupulous Goring, dared asperse that pure character, whether in his conduct as soldier or man. The success of Hopton in the west was due more to his personal character and to his influence over his followers than to his military skill, though that was not inconsiderable He was sincerely religious, so much so that he was accounted a Puritan before the war, more especially owing to his great reverence for the sanctity of Sunday. More than once, in contemporary accounts of Hopton's engagements, occurs such a phrase as " after solemn prayers at the head of every division they charged and carried all before them." He seems to have had skill in the choice of men to serve under him, being careful to note other men's worth and reward it—though he was ever modest in his estimate of his own. He acquired a great reputation for the discipline of his troops, allowing no profanity, no plundering, and rigidly training his men that they might be ready to fight with intelligence when called upon. At the same time he was careful to pay them regularly as long as funds permitted, providing the means from his own pocket when the King's resources were strained. He knew how impossible it is to keep under discipline a starving, discontented soldiery. Though none knew better than Hopton how to preserve the

dignity of commander—yet none knew better how to
win the hearts of men—no service was demanded of
them in which the leader did not reserve the most difficult
part for himself, "his language was not ' Go ye,' but
' Go we.' " His honesty was recognized by all, and the
fact that he, who had up to a certain point supported
the Parliament, should now have cast in his lot with the
King must have exercised considerable influence on
thoughtful men.

The extraordinary affection of the men of the west
for their leader is thus partially explained by a study
of his character, but to win such devotion a general
must not only be a good man, but a good soldier. And
Sir Ralph Hopton was a good soldier—he had been trained
in the Low Countries, he had observed the methods of
that genius among soldiers, Gustavus Adolphus. Like
him, he knew how to choose his own time for fighting
and how to avoid having an engagement forced upon
him. He was careful of his men, running no unnecessary
risks, for he knew that an army once destroyed is not
easily resuscitated, and that veteran troops are of all
troops the best. Yet he never neglected an advantage,
being as watchful of his enemy's movements as he was
careful of his own Thus through the conduct of the
western campaign shines clear and steady the bright
star of Hopton's loyalty. He was not only a soldier, but
a politician as well, in the best sense of the word. He
was acquainted with all the points at issue, and when once
convinced that the King had been asked more than he
could or ought to grant, he threw in his lot with his royal
master, and, his path chosen, he did not look behind
him. Never wavering, though the task set him might be
hopeless and the conditions impossible, he stands out

in vivid contrast in his steadfastness to the vain and unstable Newcastle; in his unwearying persistency against heavy odds to the hesitating Falkland, who allowed despair to numb his active energies; in his modesty and humility to the proud, high-spirited Rupert, who could not bear reproof.

In January, 1643, Stamford appeared in Devonshire. The western campaign was to begin in earnest. Hopton retreated across the Tamar; the Cornish train-bands rallied round him, so that his force, though still smaller than that of the enemy, was a very formidable one. Ruthen, the governor of Plymouth, should have waited for Stamford, his superior in command, but confident of success, he pushed on into Cornwall in pursuit, making the common mistake of despising his enemy. He marched towards Liskeard, and the King's forces, under Hopton and Grenville, advanced to meet him, Hopton being desirous of fighting before Stamford could come up with his subordinate.

The armies met on Bradock Down, where the Parliamentary troops, being raw, were soon overpowered. Ruthen fled to Saltash, which he had regained from the Royalists, for he was reluctant to lose influence in Cornwall, while Stamford fell back on Tavistock, in order to prevent the invasion of Devonshire. The Royalists carried Saltash and Okehampton by assault, then divided—one wing to lay siege to Plymouth, the other to pursue the enemy, until that pursuit was checked by the victory of the Parliamentarians under Sir John Northcote in a skirmish at Chagford, in which fell the young Sidney Godolphin, the friend of Falkland. The Royalists were now forced to retire to Tavistock owing to lack of ammunition and money; also they were unable to communicate with the King or learn his wishes. A truce was finally agreed upon which lasted until April, when Chudleigh tried, though in vain, to drive Hopton from Launceston. Two days later, however, he succeeded in dislodging him from the heights of Sourton Down.

Hopton had achieved his first end. Single-handed he had secured Cornwall for the King; he now desired permission and assistance to advance into Somerset, that the success might be followed up and the west won for the King. The early months of 1643 had been occupied by the King in peace negotiations, but when these fell through a new plan of campaign for the year was formed. Two proposals were laid before the King and his council. The first that the western army, the importance of which was fully realized by the King's military advisers, should join the main army and an immediate advance be made upon London, that is, to try again the plan that had failed in 1642. The second was an entirely new plan, suggested by the Royalist success in north and west. That the King should " act from circumference on centre "—Newcastle advancing from the north on London, while the western forces should also remain a separate army, subdue the petty garrisons still recalcitrant, capture Portsmouth, subdue Sussex and so on to Surrey and Kent, where forces would be raised to join with them. This was the plan adopted, and in pursuance of it the Marquis of Hertford was again dispatched to the west as head of the army there with Prince Maurice as his Lieutenant-General. They did not arrive until early in June, and in the interval Hopton had still further demonstrated the value of his Cornishmen.

On hearing the news of Chudleigh's success at Sourton

Down, Stamford decided to make a forward movement into Cornwall. His troops were double the number of the Royalists', who also were short of provisions for two days each man had subsisted on the scant allowance of a biscuit a day. Stamford sent twelve hundred horse under Chudleigh to Bodmin to prevent the reinforcement of the Royalists by the train-bands, and took up his position on a high hill near Stratton. In this he had a twofold object : he wished to secure himself from attack till his cavalry had returned, also in the event of victory, which he regarded as certain, he would thus have cut off the enemy's retreat.

Stamford's position was an exceedingly strong one, as Hopton realized. Yet it was impossible for the latter to act on the defensive, owing to lack of provisions; equally impossible to retreat. Accordingly, on the morning of 16 May the Royalist general divided his army into four, with directions to storm the hill from all quarters. This was done, but at first every effort seemed in vain against both superiority of position and numbers. Word was brought to Hopton that their stock of ammunition was nearly exhausted. A decisive effort was therefore absolutely imperative. The leader ordered a last desperate assault with pike and sword. Resolutely the Cornish army stormed the slope on all sides, and, perhaps stricken with a sense of the futility of resistance in face of that stern determination, the enemy's hands seemed weakened. On two sides the defence gave way, and the capture of Chudleigh, the second in command, was the signal for a general flight of his horse. The leaders of the fourfold attack shook hands on the height, with thanksgiving in their hearts, and then proceeded to turn their own artillery against such of the foe as yet remained. They turned and fled, while rumour had it that they only followed the example set by their incompetent commander. Whatever may be the truth concerning that, the fact remains that the hill has ever since been known as Stamford Hill.

The victory of Stratton was fruitful in results. Chudleigh joined the King ; the whole of Devonshire, with the exception of Bideford and Barnstaple in the north, Plymouth, Dartmouth, and Exeter in the south, was soon in Hopton's hands. To remedy Stamford's incapacity, Sir William Waller was sent to take command in the west, though he had been obliged to abandon Hereford and had failed to take Worcester.

Hopton was later rewarded for his signal services with the title of Baron Hopton of Stratton ; to the people of Cornwall the King addressed a gracious message of thanks which was placed in every parish church in the county, and in some may still be seen.

Hopton now gained his desire ; the western army was reinforced by Hertford and Prince Maurice with troops from Oxford. The influx of numbers was of great advantage to the Royalists, followed as it was by the prompt surrender of the Somerset towns of Bridgwater and Taunton, together with Dunster Castle. At the same time Hopton's anxieties were increased thereby. In the first place, Hertford had distributed the chief posts in the newly-constituted army to new adherents ; thus the loyal men of the west, who had borne the burden and heat of the day, found themselves relegated to inferior positions. There was little or no complaint, yet Hopton must certainly have felt the slight to his loyal followers deeply. Nominally now the command of the army was vested in Hertford, in all practical military affairs

Hopton was still the chief; yet there were other matters, and matters which touched his sensitive spirit deeply, in which he was powerless to interfere. The troopers of Prince Maurice were courageous and energetic beyond doubt, but they were also great plunderers. The Cornishmen had been faultless in this matter, and the reputation of his men was dear to Hopton's heart. Then, too, the plundered people were men of his own native-county, his friends and neighbours, who confidently looked to him to prevent this abuse, and looked in vain. Hertford probably felt the matter as deeply as Hopton, but Prince Maurice was not the man with whom appeals in such a matter would have any weight—he had been trained in a school of war where plunderings were everyday matters. There was also another consideration which probably deeply affected Hopton at this time. He was to be pitted in the field against Waller, his friend and companion in the wars in the Low Countries and Palatinate. It is not one of the least evils of civil war that such situations are created. Added to these anxieties was the consciousness that in Waller Hopton knew that he had to encounter his equal in military skill, the man who adopted his own tactics, and when not master of the field knew how to choose and shift his ground in order to win every possible advantage.

Waller had established himself with his army at Bath, and was not to be forced to take the offensive. A skirmish ensued at Chewton, the advantage of which rested with the Royalists; but Waller was not to be drawn from East Somerset, the population of which was favourable to the Parliament; moreover, an advance west would leave Bristol unprotected. While the two armies were thus waiting an opportunity, Hopton seems to

7

have made some sort of overture to Waller, perhaps hoping by an appeal to friendship to strengthen his arguments for loyalty to the King. Hopton's letter has never been discovered, but Waller's reply is fortunately preserved, and it does honour to both. Waller writes as to one who will understand and appreciate his feelings :

SIR WILLIAM WALLER TO SIR RALPH HOPTON.

" SIR,

" The experience I have had of your worth and the happiness I have enjoyed in your friendship are wounding considerations to me when I look upon this present distance between us. My affections to you are so un-changeable that hostility itself cannot violate my friend-ship to your person. But I must be true to the cause wherein I serve. The old limitation, *usque ad aras*, holds still, and where my conscience is interested all other obligations are swallowed up. I should most gladly wait upon you, according to your desire, but that I look upon you as engaged in that party beyond the possibility of a retreat, and consequently incapable of being wrought upon by any persuasions. And I know the conference would never be so close between us, but that it would take wind and receive a construction to my dishonour. That great God, Who is the searcher of my heart, knows with what a sad sense I go upon this service, and with what a perfect hatred I detest this war without an enemy. But I look upon it as sent from God, and that is enough to silence all passion in me. The God of Heaven in His good time send us the blessing of peace, and in the meantime fit us to receive it ! We are both upon the stage, and must act such parts as are assigned to us in this tragedy. Let us do it in the way of honour and without personal animosities. Whatever the issue be, I shall never wittingly . . ."

The Royalists hoped to get between Waller and London, and at the same time draw him from his position by threatening Bath from the valley of the Avon. To that end they advanced by way of Frome to Bradford-on-Avon, but Waller was not to be drawn from his good position on the other side of the valley under Claverton Down. The Royalists were therefore obliged to give up the idea of reaching Bath by that route, for Waller would give them no opening, and to cross the river in his face, or to march on towards Bath, leaving him in the rear, would be equally unwise. The King's army then marched to Marshfield with the idea of approaching Bath from the north, along the ridge of Lansdown. Waller was determined to prevent this, and when the Cavaliers pushed on from Cold Ashton to Tog Hill they found that Waller had command of every available approach. On 5 July, therefore, the order was given to retreat. This was too much even for Waller. Sir Arthur Hazelrigg's " Lobsters," a newly-formed regiment of London cavalry, was sent in pursuit, but after a sharp fight was driven back on Lansdown, the victors again taking up their position on Tog Hill. The Cornishmen were eager to attack, and advanced up through the woods towards the ridge. The horsemen, obliged to advance along the open road, were at first repulsed, but Sir Bevil Grenville advanced in support with pikemen and musketeers as well as horse. The Parliamentary cavalry charged five times, but vainly, in spite of their advantage in position. At last the whole Royalist army surged over the breastworks, and the day was won. It was, however, a dearly-bought victory; of two thousand horse only six hundred were left. Sir Bevil Grenville, only second to Hopton in the affections of the soldiers, was slain in the thick of the fight. Moreover, Waller had saved his cannon, and during the evening and early hours of the night the position of the Royalists was perilous; a vigorous assault might possibly have dislodged them from the dearly-won height. A careful watch was set to guard against surprise, and soon after eleven the welcome news was brought that Waller had retreated to Bath. Perhaps it was only this which prevented a Royalist retreat; the army was certainly too shattered to pursue, and it had not sufficient ammunition to undertake the siege of Bath. The " Lobsters " had proved themselves dangerous foes, the best horsemen the Parliament had as yet been able to place in the field.

The misfortunes of the Royalists were not yet over. During the retreat next morning a wagon-load of ammunition, almost all that remained, exploded, and, worse than the loss of the ammunition, was the fact that Hopton, " the soldiers' darling," was struck down and seriously injured by the explosion—so seriously, indeed, that his life was despaired of for a time. Saddened by this last blow, the weary troops fell back on Marshfield, then, on intelligence of the near approach of the enemy, hurried on to Devizes. Waller had heard of the loss of the gunpowder and of Hopton's accident, and so hastened to cut off the retreat of the army to Oxford, as also the possibility of reinforcement from that direction, by taking up his position on Roundway Down, a hill north of Devizes, which commands the Oxford road. Waller felt himself secure of victory; he captured a convoy of ammunition on its way from Oxford under the Earl of Crawford, but failed to prevent the escape of the Royalist horse under Hertford and Prince Maurice, which made its way to Oxford by way of Salisbury.

The siege of Devizes began on 11 July. The whole work of defence devolved on Hopton, chained as he was to a sick-bed, unable to see, but capable of hearing, and, as his preparations showed, in full possession of his faculties. His organization of the defence was masterly, and served, if anything more was wanting, to increase the enthusiastic love of the men for their leader. Barricades were thrown up at the entrances of the streets, match was provided by collecting ropes from the townsmen's beds and boiling them in resin, but even Hopton's ingenuity was not equal to the replenishing of empty powder-casks. The only hope lay in speedy succour from Oxford.

Waller had planned a general assault on the town for the 13th, but a few hours before the time fixed Prince Maurice, with a large body of horse, commanded by Wilmot, appeared on Roundway Down. Here Waller suffered a great defeat, his army being practically annihilated. Hopton, of course, took no personal part in this battle, though he let no opportunity slip, and it was the sight of the Cornishmen sallying from the town to take the disordered army in the rear, which had completed the rebels' discomfiture. Thus was shattered Waller's hope of " scattering if not destroying this mighty army of the west." It is even said that Waller had already announced the capture of the Cornish army, promising to send the list next day. The Roundhead commander fled first to Bristol, thence to London, leaving the few Parliamentary garrisons in the west to

Sir Ralph's mercy, who in a fortnight took five of them by assault and seven upon surrender.

· In this connection Lloyd, in his "Memoirs," quaintly remarks · " He was excellent at the contriving at the scaling of walls, as his soldiers were in executing, and yet more excellent in taking hearts, being so civil, even to the most obstinate, that they chose rather to be conquered by him than protected by others." A tribute, indeed !

The news of this victory, in conjunction with Newcastle's success at Adwalton Moor in the north, revived the plans of Parliament for securing the aid of the Scotch. It caused ill-feeling between Waller and Essex, for the former thought that Essex should have prevented the Royalist march from Oxford to Roundway Down, while Essex believed the defeat to be due to Waller's disobedience. On the Royalist side it fixed the time for the attack on Bristol. This had been determined upon since the spring, when a promising plan had failed—two merchants, Yeomans and Bourchier, who had plotted to admit Rupert, having been discovered and executed by order of Essex. On 18 July Prince Rupert marched out of Oxford, met the victors of Roundway Down, and with them sat down before Bristol on the 23rd. The Cornish army was posted on the Somerset side of the town, which was unfavourable for attack, so on the 26th, when a general assault was made, it was repulsed with heavy loss. Prince Rupert, on the Gloucestershire side, was more fortunate, and managed to break through the defences at a weak spot. He did not, however, imagine that his task was accomplished, though such proved to be the case. A trumpet arrived with an offer of surrender from the governor,

Nathaniel Fiennes, terms were arranged, and the Royalists were in possession of the city almost before they had deemed the work of assault begun. The capture of Bristol was of great importance to the Royalists; it was the second city in the kingdom, also it gave them access to the sea and made more easy communications with Wales. It was now that one of the fatal sources of weakness in Charles's army was openly revealed—the divisions among the leaders. Through the whole course of the war effective action was hampered by the perpetual quarrels between civilian and military advisers on the one hand, between professional soldiers and noblemen holding office because of their position and influence, rather than because of their military skill, on the other. Such a dispute now arose over the question of the governorship of the newly-captured city. Hertford, the great noble but dilettante soldier, owing his position as Lieutenant of the Western Counties solely to his loyalty and great influence in those parts, had not been consulted by Rupert concerning the articles of surrender. Sensible of the slight, Hertford, without informing the Prince, appointed Hopton governor of Bristol. Thereupon Rupert at once wrote to the King requesting that he might retain the governorship for himself. Charles, who knew nothing of Hertford's action, at once consented. The feeling aroused was very strong on both sides. The King was obliged to journey to Bristol to settle the dispute, and his decision, after hearing both sides of the question, was that Prince Rupert should have the title but Hopton the power. A message was sent to Hopton from the Prince to that effect, and that self-forgetting gentleman was placed in an extremely awkward position. Should he accept the appointment from the

Prince, the Marquis would think he was joining in the slight laid upon him, and he and others might attribute Hopton's action to revenge for Hertford's desertion of him in the early part of the war, and the placing of new officers over the heads of the old when the western army was reorganized. Should he refuse, on the other hand, confusion in the King's affairs might result, as it was most unlikely that the Prince and the Marquis would agree in the choice of a substitute. Moreover, for the sake of their mother, Hopton had great affection for the children of the Queen of Bohemia. He therefore decided, even at the risk of losing the friendship of Hertford, that his own feelings in the matter must be ignored, and " according to his rare temper throughout this war, to let him whom he professed to serve choose in what kind he would be served by him, and cheerfully received the commission from Prince Rupert." The King took Hertford with him to Oxford, and Hopton was left at Bristol to regain his strength and to reform the garrison and defences of the town.

While at Bristol the King had definitely decided on laying siege to Gloucester, but the Cornish troops were unwilling to accompany him there or to join with the King's forces at all, and were therefore sent against Dorchester under the command of Lord Carnarvon, a man whose character made him eminently suitable to be their leader. Prince Maurice was to follow later with foot and artillery. Thus Hopton was now entirely divorced from his faithful Cornishmen, and never again was he as happy, or they, the personality that had bound them to the King thus taken away, as successful in the King's service as they had hitherto been. The King had, at any rate for the time, abandoned his second plan of campaign—the threefold advance on London. The difficulties in the way had proved insuperable. Newcastle had refused to march south, and the western army was beginning to show signs of the same local feeling. The plan of an immediate advance upon London was abandoned for the siege of Gloucester, many thinking it dangerous to leave such an important garrison in hostile hands in their rear.

The failure of the Royalists before Gloucester and the battle of Newbury led the King later to revive the old plan. The capture of Bristol had been followed by the surrender of Exeter early in September. Hopton was now to be sent into Hampshire, the plan of campaign being to capture Winchester Castle, open up Sussex, and so establish communications with the loyal party in Kent, with the idea that in the spring a compact body might be ready to advance on London from the south. The intervening months Hopton had spent in recruiting the garrison of Bristol, strengthening its defences as far as might be, and in gathering together the nucleus of an army for his fresh enterprise. In November, then, he found himself at the head of a new army, consisting of a good body of horse and foot which he had raised about Bristol, a body of foot brought by Sir John Berkeley from Exeter, and an English regiment, about two thousand in number, from Ireland, set free by the Cessation. Another new army was in process of being raised in Cheshire, also partly composed of an English regiment from Ireland, to be under the command of Sir John Byron, which was first to free Lancashire from the rebels, and then either to reinforce Newcastle and enable him to overcome the Fairfaxes and push south, or itself fall upon the Eastern Association, and in this way to make

Newcastle's southward march possible. Thus again
there were to be three armies in the field whose task
would be first to overcome their enemies singly, then to
overwhelm London from different points.

Early in November Hopton marched to Winchester,
which he made his head-quarters in his new undertaking.
His task was no light one; Parliament had again sent
Waller to oppose him, the man whose methods were
Hopton's own, and who would be sure to anticipate his
every movement. Also Hopton had no longer his old
tried Cornish army, that was now engaged before
Plymouth. The Irish regiments were Protestant to a
man, more inclined to sympathize with Parliament
than with the King, and were frequently mutinous;
the other levies were raw and undisciplined. Further,
his own plans for the campaign had been rejected at
head-quarters—the dashing tactics of the younger
commanders being preferred to his more cautious proposals. The general opinion held of Hopton by these
youthful enthusiasts then dominant in the King's
Councils is probably reflected in Clarendon's words:
" The Lord Hopton was rather fit for the second than
for the supreme command in an army." Hopton had
wished to capture the fortresses held by Parliament in
Wilts and Dorset, and so to secure his rear before taking
the offensive, and the plan had much to recommend it.
Against this advice, however, Lord Ogle had been sent
to capture Winchester, obliging Hopton to advance
to his support. He, possessing a " generosity that was
not to be exhausted," cheerfully undertook the task of
which he disapproved, and threw all his energies into it.
·The capture of the town of Arundel (6 December) and
the surrender of its castle (9 December) were the im-

mediate results. The tone of a letter written by Hopton
to Prince Rupert, and dated 12 December, shows clearly
that so soon after such a notable success as the capture
of Arundel he was fearful of the future. The Prince
had sent to him for a regiment, and after explaining his
difficulties, Hopton adds : " The truth is, the duty of the
service here were insupportable, were it not in this
cause, where there is so great a necessity either of pre-
vailing through all difficulties, or suffering them to
prevail, which cannot be thought of in good English."
The earlier note of confidence and determination
is lacking here ; the war had taught Hopton too
much.

This capture of Arundel proved to be the furthest limit
of Royalist success. Parliament, London, and the
south were roused to strenuous action ; Waller's army was
strongly reinforced, and on his approach Hopton retired
to Winchester. He knew very well that his army was
insufficient to hold such an extended field in face of an
experienced general and able tactician such as Waller.
He was, indeed, unable to prevent Crawford being surprised and overcome at Alton. This reverse caused
Hopton to withdraw his troops from Petersfield, with
the result that his line of communication between
Winchester and Arundel was broken. Waller therefore
moved on Arundel and recaptured it on 6 January.
Hopton retired to Oxford, but in March was again at
Winchester, and, reinforced by the Earl of Forth with
two thousand men, prepared to face Waller. The news
of Rupert's success at Newark had raised the spirits of the
Royalists still higher. Hopton insisted that the Earl of
Forth should take the supreme command in the engagement that was expected. Waller was at West Meon on

25 March guarding the road from Winchester to Petersfield.

The Royalists, under their two able generals, secured
the advantage of position, occupying Alresford before
Waller could reach it. This gave them command of
the road to London, and Waller was cut off from his
base unless he could win a decisive victory.

Superior in strategy, the Royalists seemed also to
have superiority in tactics. On the 28th Forth and
Hopton occupied the crest of the hill between Alresford
and Cheriton, while on a slightly lower eminence was
posted a detachment under Sir George Lisle. Waller's
army was stationed in a field south of the river Itchin
surrounded by a hedge, with the artillery on a slope
behind. Waller's first impulse was to retreat, but in the
morning he decided to make a fight, and under cover
of a thick mist he threw a good force into Cheriton Wood.
By this movement he outflanked Lisle, who withdrew to
the main army. In the forlorn hope that he might induce
the Royalists to leave their strong position and attack,
Waller posted his horse in front of his foot, ready to
fall upon the enemy's cavalry, which, if they fell into the
trap, could only advance by way of a narrow lane.
Hopton succeeded in driving Waller's forces from Cheriton
Wood, and then would have pressed this advantage
home with a charge of both horse and foot on the rebels'
main body. Such an attack, made at once, might well
have proved successful, for Waller's troops seemed
shaken. Forth was, however, determined to abide by
the advantage of position and force Waller either to
attack or retreat, both equally dangerous movements.
Unfortunately for the Royalists, the advantages of
either course were lost by the insubordination of one

young officer, Sir Henry Bard, who determined to attack,
and advanced down the hill with a half of his regiment.
At first he was, naturally, unsupported, and when the
general advance was made it was too late to win any
advantage from the course Hopton had at first proposed.
Waller was able to fall upon each disordered regiment
as it emerged on the common, and the result was victory
for the Parliamentary army. The Royalists performed
prodigies of valour, but that was insufficient to avert
the consequences of insubordination. Forth managed
the retreat with admirable skill, and Hopton with a
party of horse succeeded in bringing off the guns. Waller
was therefore unable to push his victory home, though he
pursued the Royalist army to Winchester and Andover,
and succeeded in capturing Lady Hopton, who was,
however, treated with all courtesy and escorted to
Oxford " together with her plate and jewels."

Thus the King's project for the invasion of Kent
and Sussex from the west was entirely overthrown. Moreover, the armies of Essex and Manchester were now
free to take the offensive, whereas had the Royalists
crushed Waller they would have been forced to march
against Hopton, and it would have been the King's
forces that were thus set free to take the offensive.
This was the result of one unconsidered act of zeal—
only one, but a symptom of a fatal disease, lack of
discipline among the Royalist gentry—occurring, too,
when the necessity for discipline was being clearly perceived in the ranks of the rebel army, and being perceived
was slowly but surely being attained.

Saddened by this defeat, for that his fears have proved
amply justified is no consolation to a general who has
the success of his cause at heart, Hopton returned to

Bristol to strengthen his garrison and to gather recruits in South Wales, while waiting for the King's order to rejoin him. While here, in August, 1644, Lord Percy was removed from the office of General of the Ordnance, which was given to Hopton, with apparently the approval of all, for, as Clarendon remarks, " the one had no friend, the other was generally beloved." Not the same approval met the appointment of Goring in place of Wilmot, who, it was believed, was deprived of his post because he desired peace, though it was on accusation of treachery.

The King had now conceived the idea of forming a Royalist Association of the West as a counterpoise to the Parliamentary Eastern Association. It was to comprise the counties of Cornwall, Devon, Somerset, and Dorset. There were many difficulties in the way. Geographically, it was difficult to open up communication between this western peninsula and the Royalist districts further north. Local feeling would prevent the western army from advancing out of its own counties till they were safe from attack by the enemy's garrisons; it would therefore be necessary first to capture Taunton, Plymouth, and Lyme. To render it still more useless, this western army fell practically under the command of Goring. Hopton, to whose lot as Field-Marshal of the West it had fallen to organize it, was by special order recalled to Bristol, lest there should be disputed command between him and Goring. He obeyed at once and without complaint, but we may guess with what a pang he left his beloved west at the mercy of Goring. The latter had received no commission to command in the west; he had been appointed Lieutenant-General of Hampshire, Sussex, Surrey, and Kent, his intention, as expressed to the King, being to advance into Hants, and from thence into Sussex and Kent, to co-operate with the Royalists there and make a diversion. In Hampshire he was beaten off with loss from Christchurch, through his want of vigilance Weymouth was captured by the Parliamentary troops, and in February, 1645, he even allowed Waller to relieve Taunton, though from failure of support and lack of money the Parliamentary general was unable to follow up the advantage. Thus driven back to the west, in the west Goring elected to remain, and the coming of the Prince of Wales to keep his court at Bristol afforded the pretext for the recall of Hopton. Thus the command in the west, nominally still Hopton's, was for all practical purposes in the hands of the dissolute, selfish Goring

A council of six had been appointed to advise the Prince ; Hyde, Culpeper, Capel, and Hopton were the most important members of this body. As commander of the garrison, it fell to Hopton to provide for the reception of the Prince, and he seems to have supplied his establishment mainly from his own purse. For a year the Prince was resident in the west, and during those twelve months Hopton's position must have been well-nigh intolerable. He was forced to look on while those western counties, whose loyalty he had done so much to stir up and encourage, were gradually alienated through the license of Goring's troops and the negligence of their commander, beset by contradictory orders from Digby and Rupert, subject to the indignity of the perpetual intrigues of Goring and Greenville, who would fain have ousted him from all military command in the west—till at last, when all the harm that could be done in that part had been accomplished, he was called upon

to take command, when to command such an army was
dishonour, to remedy its condition absolutely impossible,
defeat being imminent and inevitable.   No greater test
of loyalty could possibly have been invented : Hopton's
loyalty stood the test.

The outlook in the west on the arrival of the Prince
was in no sense hopeful, though with efficient generalship
much might have been done to make it once more a
centre of loyalty to the King.   Dorset was in possession
of the rebels with the exception of Sherborne and Portland.
Somerset was to a great extent loyal, but Taunton still
held out for Parliament, and its influence was felt through
a large circuit.   Devonshire was at one end occupied
with the blocking of Plymouth, at the other it was open to
incursions from Lyme and not uninfluenced by Taunton.
Cornwall was wholly loyal, but its utmost resources
were taxed to block Plymouth and provide for its own
garrisons.   Throughout the west the King's garrisons
were stronger in fortifications, though these were nowhere
finished and in some places scarcely begun, than in men
and provisions.

Goring's forces lay on the borders of the three counties,
plundering everywhere and doing nothing against the
rebels.   It was believed by many that he had prevented
the capture of Taunton in order that he might have an
excuse to remain in the west.   He certainly tried every
means to obtain the absolute command, and even
approached Hyde on the subject.   It was felt by all
who had the King's cause really at heart, that the hope
of the west lay in Hopton.   In fact, Greenville's officers,
when their commander lay wounded before Wellington,
sent to implore him to take over the command, but he
had no mind to serve with Goring, unless by the King's

command, knowing that he would render all his efforts nugatory. He remained quietly at Bristol, patiently bearing the calumnies of Greenville and Goring. For a short time the west breathed freely. Goring was recalled to the King, who had been advised to march north with all the forces he could draw together, to cut his way through to Montrose in Scotland. Other counsels prevailed, however, and Goring was sent back to the west, and this time with full powers, while the King marched northwards. The Prince of Wales and his council were dismayed at this action, but after the disaster at Naseby the King sent other commands. The Prince had left Bristol, owing to the plague, and was then at Barnstaple. Here directions were brought from his father that Hopton should command in chief under the Prince. Meanwhile Goring had allowed Fairfax to relieve Taunton, and was defeated by him at Langport on 10 July. This necessitated the retreat of the Prince into Cornwall. In August the Prince marched from Launceston to Exeter, which was still held by the Royalists, with the idea of marching to the relief of Bristol. This was prevented by the news of Rupert's surrender. At Exeter Goring made another attempt to win the command in the west, but was advised by Hyde that any such attempt would be in vain, and was, moreover, unnecessary, seeing that neither the Prince nor Lord Hopton interfered with his dispositions in any way.

It was felt that Devonshire must soon be entered by the rebels, so it was determined to hold Tiverton to prevent any such invasion. Goring neglected every precaution, with the result that Tiverton fell and Exeter was threatened. Goring at last, having done all the mischief in his power, retired to France, but there was

8

still a considerable army in the west, consisting of Goring's horse under the command of Lord Wentworth, and a good body of troops under Sir Richard Greenville, besides the garrisons. It was therefore arranged that these forces should unite and march to the relief of Exeter. The Prince thereupon marched to Tavistock and thence to Totnes, but hearing that Wentworth's horse had been routed at Ashburton, he withdrew with the foot to Launceston, ordering the horse to remain on the Devonshire side of the river.

The situation was sufficiently dangerous. The enemy was in close proximity, an engagement in the near future was certain, but the Royalist army was utterly unprepared; the command was divided, the troops undisciplined. One forlorn hope remained: the army must be put under one command, and Greenville suggested that that commander should be Lord Hopton. To this supreme test was his loyalty put: he was to take command of an utterly disorganized, undisciplined body of troops " whom only their friends feared and their enemies laughed at," with no time to reorganize or discipline them, the enemy being close at hand and prepared to fight. With only a prospect of certain defeat before him, probably no other man would have attempted the task, but the simple loyalty of Hopton dictated his reply to the Prince that " it was a custom now when men were not willing to submit to what they were enjoined to say that it was against their honour; that their honour would not suffer them to do this or that; for his part he could not obey His Highness at this time without resolving to lose his honour, which he knew he must; but since His Highness thought it necessary to command him, he was ready to obey him with the loss of his honour."

The task once accepted, Hopton set himself with characteristic energy and thoroughness to the best accomplishing of it. At once new difficulties arose. Greenville, who had himself petitioned that Hopton should be given the sole command, now refused to serve under him, for which disobedience to the Prince's orders, he was imprisioned at Launceston.

Fairfax, by the defeat of Wentworth, had secured himself from immediate danger, and so turned on Dartmouth and captured it. He then returned to the siege of Exeter. The garrison sent urgent messages to the Prince's army for relief, and Hopton, hoping to fall on Fairfax before Exeter, resolved to march by way of Chumleigh in order, by keeping between the enemy and Barnstaple, to obtain help from the garrison of that town. Fairfax, however, left the siege of Exeter in the hands of Sir Hardress Waller and himself marched to meet Hopton. The armies met at Torrington, and here was fought Hopton's last engagement. All that a brave soldier could do was done. In his report to the Prince of Wales after the defeat, Hopton clearly pointed out the causes of his failure: the weakness of his foot, both in numbers and resolution; the insubordination of much of the horse, insomuch as the guard posted in advance to give notice of the approach of the enemy failed to do so, and it was only by accident that he heard that Fairfax was close upon the town; and lastly, his lack of artillery, for though he waited at Launceston to the latest possible moment in the hope of supplies arriving, he waited in vain. Thus, when he heard at Torrington of the near vicinity of the enemy, Hopton had to choose between two alternatives, each desperate: A retreat into Cornwall: this would be ruinous, because the county could not maintain so large a body of horse and foot, and the ground was so narrow that he would not be able to make any efficient defence. The alternative was to make a stand: the only hope for the western army now was a victory, and the position was fairly suitable. Hopton decided on the latter course, the more soldierly, and that which, though wellnigh hopeless, had at least the element of uncertainty. The town was therefore barricaded, but when the enemy forced the barricades the foot promptly gave way, and their example was followed by the horse—in fact, it would have been practically impossible for cavalry to defend itself in the narrow streets of the town against Fairfax's victorious foot Hopton, wounded and unhorsed, called in his own reserve of horse, on which he could rely, and they made a stout resistance; but as there was no foot to support them their efforts were of no avail, and as a last disaster the whole of the remaining stock of ammunition was blown up in the church.   The foot having all run away, retreat with the horse was the only possible course, and the next day, 17 February, saw the remnants of the western army on the borders of Cornwall.   It was suggested that the horse should break away to the King at Oxford, but they had been two days and nights in the field, and the enemy's horse was within two miles; they must have been overtaken and the attempt frustrated.   At Stratton, the scene of his earliest victory, Hopton rested till the 19th and gathered together the scattered remnants of his foot.   These day by day grew less in number, and the officers counselled retreat further west, or their tiny army would melt before their eyes.   Hopton hoped to make a stand at Bodmin, and put a guard three miles off at Cardinham Down to watch the enemy.   So careless

were these that the enemy's army was within three miles
of them before they had any knowledge of its movements,
and Hopton had only time to retreat from Bodmin and
Lostwithiel to Probus. Every further attempt to draw
together to offer resistance was frustrated by the disobedience of the troops, until at last the officers at the
Council declared that only surrender was now possible.
Hopton was still loath to give up his trust, and though
a trumpet came from Fairfax offering to treat, he
delayed till he had news that the Prince had left Pendennis for Scilly and was therefore safe. He then strengthened the garrisons of Pendennis and the Mount with his
remaining foot and ammunition. Finally, he gave the
horse permission to treat for themselves alone, and
honourable terms were obtained. For himself Hopton
refused to accept any terms save permission to leave the
country. Fairfax's own words give some idea of the
estimation in which Hopton was held by the enemy :
" For yourself, besides what is implied in common with
others, you may be assured, such mediation to the
Parliament on your behalf, both from myself and others,
as for one whom for personal worth and many virtues,
but especially for your care of and moderation towards
the country, we honour and esteem above any other
of your party, whose error (supposing you more swayed
with principles of honour and conscience) we most pity,
and whose happiness, so far as is consistent with the
public welfare, we should delight in more than in your
least suffering." In his dignified refusal to make any
terms for himself, Hopton " owns Fairfax's kindness to
him in particular and his Christian consideration of
sparing blood, but it cannot be expected by a man of
honour that his Lordship should renounce his Master's

house, to whom he is a sworn subject and servant, upon whose account he will suffer anything rather than taint his honour in that particular. However, he is desirous of the peace of the kingdom, and willing to spare blood by all honest and honourable ways. He had lately heard that the King was advanced in treating with the Parliament, and desires Fairfax to deal freely with him in that point, because it will spare him the labour of further treaty, he being willing to obey whatsoever His Majesty shall agree to. He acknowledges that God had humbled them for their personal sins by ill successes of late, but the prosperity of the other party was not a sure sign that God was altogether pleased with them."

These last words breathe the same spirit as that which animated Charles himself—humble submission to defeat as a punishment from God for personal sins, but in no way to be regarded as a token that the cause for which they fought was a wrong one and disapproved by Him.

On receiving Fairfax's assurance that the negotiations between King and Parliament had again come to nought, terms were arranged for the remainder of Hopton's troops, he himself being free to leave the country. Thus, on 10 March, 1646, was disbanded the last remnant of that brave army of the west which Hopton, with such bright hopes, had gathered together for the King's service in 1642 and 1643. Its spirit had long departed; loyalty and enthusiasm could not endure in face of Goring's licence and plunderings; the men had long since recognized that the cause for which they fought stood no chance in face of the New Model, and that peace for themselves and their distressed country could only be obtained by submission. Within a month Exeter had surrendered, and the west was regarded by Parliament as " pacified."

Private as well as public grief fell to the lot of Hopton at this time—in the death of his wife. It was in March that Hyde wrote from Jersey on hearing the news, and expressed a longing for his coming. Hopton, therefore, having done his uttermost for the King and failed, joined the Prince of Wales and the rest of the Council at Jersey. There he and they did what lay in their power to prevent the Queen obtaining her will, the removal of the Prince to France. Their efforts were useless, and when, in June, 1646, the young Charles set sail, the only protest Hyde, Capel, and Hopton could make was to refuse to accompany him. Intrigue, the very atmosphere of the French Court, was repugnant to these honest Royalists, and when, later in the year, the Queen and Jermyn, her trusted adviser, went so far as to propose that the Channel Isles should be ceded to France to purchase aid against Parliament, these same three would have appealed to Parliament, hateful as the step would have been, rather than countenance such treason to their country. They were spared the necessity, for, like many other of the plots and plans evolved by the fertile brains of Jermyn and the Queen, the proposal came to nothing. It was probably realized that French aid would never be forthcoming, be the bribe what it might.

Later in the year Hopton left Jersey to visit an uncle at Rouen, but when Hyde at last joined the Prince in France, and later in Holland, Hopton accompanied him; but his honesty and uprightness were quite out of place amongst the perpetual intrigues that now pervaded the

Royalist Councils. " There was only one man in the Council of whom nobody spoke ill, nor laid anything to his charge, and that was the Lord Hopton." Yet even he did not lack enemies who " had drawn the Prince himself to have a less esteem of him than his singular virtue and fidelity, and his unquestionable courage and industry (all which his enemies could not deny he excelled in) did deserve." In 1648 he was with the Prince on the Royalist fleet, but on the death of Charles I and the subsequent negotiations of the young King with Argylle and Hamilton, he retired from the Court. He disapproved entirely of the treaty with the Scotch ; his sympathies were with Montrose, and partly in disgust at the action of the Court, partly on account of poverty, Hopton retired to Utrecht. During his residence there he was in continual correspondence with Hyde and Secretary Nicholas, and at last, finding that he could be of no service to the King, that, in fact, he was only an additional burden, he began to think of saving some part of his estate by compounding with the Parliament. Apparently, from letters of Hyde, he also contemplated a second marriage, the lady in question being the daughter of Lady Morton. Hyde, in a letter to Lady Morton, wrote that he was exceedingly glad to hear of Lord Hopton's proposals : " He is the most virtuous, pious man living, and will certainly make the best husband." The Lady Elizabeth Hopton had brought her husband no children, and he probably desired to perpetuate his barony ; his uncle and heir, Sir Arthur Hopton, having died in 1650. The negotiations were being carried on in the year 1651, but the matter either fell through or was ended by Hopton's death at Bruges in 1652 of an ague. The news was conveyed by Secretary Nicholas

to Lord Hatton in the following words : " The gallant
and virtuous Lord Hopton died on Tuesday se'nnight
(8 October), at Bruges, of an ague, in whom all honest
and well-affected men had a loss, but none so, great as
the King." His title died with him ; his four sisters
succeeded to his estates as co-heirs. The body of the
gallant soldier was preserved unburied at Bruges till
the Restoration, when it was brought to England to rest
in that country for which he had fought and suffered.

Hopton was before and above all a patriot, and so
may be placed in the same category with Hyde and
Falkland ; but in character he differed from both. He
lacked the somewhat cold analytical power of Hyde,
the philosophical tendencies of Falkland, for his was the
simple directness of the soldier. Subtleties of thought
and diction escaped him, and this was probably why he
remained for so long on the side of the leaders of Parliament ; he believed their aims to be as they described
them, and did not look beyond. It is the weakness of
frank and simple natures that they believe others to
be as honest as themselves. When he was at last convinced that the cause of his country was bound up with
her King, he took no half measures, but threw in his lot
whole-heartedly with the Royalists. He decided to
serve his King as a soldier, and took no further part in
politics, leaving questions of peace terms to those whom
he considered better qualified to deal with them. With
characteristic modesty he refrained from expressing any
opinion on such matters ; perhaps his earlier experiences
in Parliament had convinced him that his talents lay in
a more practical direction. His course once chosen,
there was no looking back, no difficulties, no reverses
could dismay him ; personal considerations were for-

gotten, never even considered, in his steadfast loyalty to the cause he had adopted.

As a soldier Hopton excelled; he was a born leader of men, and to him, personally, a larger measure of the early success of the King was due than to any other leader. Clarendon's criticism that he was more fitted for the second than for the command-in-chief was perhaps justified; but he was never given the chance of proving what he could do as first in command, though he showed himself in no way ambitious for the position. A general who combined in himself the qualities of Rupert and Hopton, the superb dash of the one with the prudence, foresight, and experience of the other, would undoubtedly have won the Civil War for the King in the early campaigns. Hopton brought the same qualities of leadership into the later unsuccessful struggle in the west; but the condition of affairs was wholly changed, and he only surrendered when every hope of resistance, or even of retreat, was gone.

Exile is a hard test of character, but throughout the later years of his life, all spent abroad, his conduct was that of the few upright Englishmen, who ignored the intrigues that surrounded them on every side. It must have been a deep feeling of isolation and loneliness which caused Hyde to write to Nicholas, on hearing of Hopton's death: " I do concur with you in your full sense of the irreparable loss in our good Lord Hopton, who was as faultless a person, as full of courage, industry, integrity, and religion as I ever knew man, and believe me—sad consideration of that instance of God's displeasure to us in the taking away such men from us makes my heart ready to break, and to despair of seeing better times, and brings other melancholic thoughts into my head which I am willing and, I think, obliged to shake off." His grief being real, Hyde forgot his usual cold analysis, as deep feeling animates these words as pulses in the inimitable character sketch of Falkland, and they form an epitaph not unworthy of their object.

A CHAMPION FROM THE FENS
THE EARL OF LINDSEY

THE Earl of Lindsey may seem but little to merit inclusion among the champions of the Crown in the Civil War, since he lost his life so early—in the battle of Edgehill, the first engagement between the two parties. That life was, however, freely offered in the King's service. He was the Commander-in-Chief of the royal army ; moreover, for many years previous to the outbreak of war he had been a loyal servant to his King and country, and had held many important offices.

He was of noble extraction. His grandmother was Catherine, widow of Charles Brandon, Duke of Suffolk, who married as her second husband Richard Bertie. His father was Peregrine Bertie, Lord Willoughby, of Eresby, who commanded an expedition sent by the Queen to the aid of Henri Quatre against the Guises, and who had several times served in the Netherlands on behalf of the Dutch against the Spanish. There is a story of how this valiant nobleman, " when an insulting challenge surprised him a-bed of the gout, returned this answer : ' That although he was lame of his hands and feet, yet he would meet him with a piece of a rapier in his teeth.' " This Peregrine Bertie married Mary, daughter of John de Vere, Earl of Oxford. Their son,

ROBERT BERTIE, EARL OF LINDSEY

FROM AN ENGRAVING BY H. ROBINSON AFTER THE PAINTING BY VAN DYCK

Robert Bertie, was born in December, 1572, and had for godparents Queen Elizabeth herself and the Earls of Essex and Leicester. He inherited his father's martial instincts; from early childhood he delighted in those things appertaining to war, for when asked by Sir Walter Raleigh to choose a fairing, his choice fell unhesitatingly on toy swords and pistols; he would have none of books or pictures.

In accordance with the practice of the time, the education of the young Robert Bertie received great care, but, following his predilections, he gave most attention to those subjects bearing on the profession and practice of arms, history, mathematics, heraldry, and geography, though others were not neglected. His education was not one of mere book-learning; it had been begun at home in early infancy. He had grown up amongst those friends of his father who were absorbed in the spirit of the times: discoveries, battles and sieges, adventurous buccaneering voyages, the wonders of new and distant lands, were in all probability fully discussed in his hearing. Thus the school, the University, and the Court but continued what home-life had begun, and a four years' course of travel completed it—that is, if we regard education as being a preparation for the serious business of living.

During that time of travel the young student devoted his attention almost entirely to military affairs. He was with the Earl of Essex on his expedition to Cadiz, but whether he took any active part in it is uncertain. His next expedition was to the Low Countries, where he probably accompanied his kinsman, Sir Francis Vere, and here he certainly fought, it being recorded that he was three times unhorsed in the battle of Newport, where, of fifteen hundred Englishmen engaged, not one escaped scatheless. In the year 1597 he visited the Earl of Shrewsbury, then English Ambassador in Paris, where he took care to see something of whatever fighting was toward, since he was certainly present during some part of the siege of Amiens. Then followed journeys to the Spanish West Indies, to Moscow, to Denmark and Sweden, and to Essex in Ireland. In 1602, though his father was now dead and he was therefore the owner of great estates and advanced to the dignity of a peer, the new Lord Willoughby sailed, with Monson and Levison, on one of those piratical cruises against the Spaniards which were then so fashionable. It was they who captured the great galleon said to have contained treasure to the value of a million ducats. A visit to Italy and an embassy to Madrid brought these wanderings to an end, and the young Lord Willoughby was content to settle down to the life of an ordinary English nobleman. His mother's death led him to claim the earldom of Oxford, which, with several baronies and the hereditary position of Lord High Chamberlain of England, came to him in her right. There was considerable dispute, but finally he obtained the office, but not the dignities, though he was allowed to take his seat in the House of Lords above all the barons.

During the remaining years of James I's reign, Lord Willoughby, having married Elizabeth, daughter of Edward Lord Montague, of Boughton, lived a quiet country life. He settled on his estate in Lincolnshire, where he won golden opinions and, apparently, deserved them. One writer tells us that he attended to his estates with the greatest diligence, not disdaining to add to their value by skilful trading, " having learned at Florence

and Venice that merchandise is consistent with nobility."
He was generous, almost prodigal, in hospitality, but
this was rendered possible by the fact that he grew his
own corn and bred his own fish, fowl, beef, mutton, and
venison. He cared for the needs of the poor " as if his
house had been an hospital," and, more broadly, looked
to their future interests by preventing the enclosure of
common land as far as lay in his power.

Among his neighbours he acted as peacemaker, and
was much beloved by all. Evidence of the respect and
affection felt for him by the whole county was forthcoming on the outbreak of civil war, in the zeal with
which the population followed his lead, so that he was
very quickly able to rally to the King's banner a brave
regiment, and that when most of the other counties
were holding back to see in which direction lay greater
security.

While thus attending to private and local interests,
Lord Willoughby did not forget the duty he owed the
State. He attended Parliament with regularity and
spoke on various questions, his wide experience giving
his opinions great weight, especially on such topics
as plantations, trade, and the draining of the Fens.
Of the last question he later proved himself completely
master.

Such was the life of a nobleman in Stuart times.
No life of ease and luxury, but one in which the responsibility of great possessions was realized to the full,
and no shirking was practised. Such men deserve well
of the State they serve.

On the accession of Charles I, Lord Willoughby returned
to Court and resumed his share in the public official
life of the time. This seems rather to point to some

misunderstanding with James, and this may have been due to the disappointment concerning the Earldom of Oxford, for one of the first acts of Charles, who, we are told, held Willoughby in great esteem, was to create him Earl of Lindsey (November, 1626). From this time he rose rapidly. In 1630 he was elected a Knight of the Garter, while in 1628 he had been given command of the fleet. This was on the death of Buckingham, and the responsibility far outweighed the honour. From this the Earl did not shrink, but strove valiantly to retrieve his predecessor's failure—in the relief of Rochelle; but misfortune marred all Charles I's plans, and in this case a cross-wind forced Lindsey to bring off the fleet. Later, in 1635, he was made Lord High Admiral of England and given command of the fleet, which was fitted out by means of ship-money. Here again Lindsey strove to give dignity to what was a mere farce, but though men might mock at the fleet, none dreamed of mocking its commander, who, like others of loyal heart, served his master as he should choose to be served. So great was the confidence placed in his loyalty by Charles, that on the rising of the Scots he was made Governor of Berwick.

In the next year he sat as Lord High Constable of England at the trial of Strafford. During the troublous months that followed Lindsey took no prominent part in debates. He was probably no politician, and held no elaborate theories on government, his political creed consisting of the one clause, " Loyalty to Church and King." When the time came for action, therefore, it would be a foregone conclusion on which side the Earl of Lindsey would be found; his creed would then be upheld by the sword. A man of simple nature, his sphere was that of action rather than of words.

When the military question was being discussed in Parliament, the hostility of the populace to many of the peers, who were known to support the King's prerogative in that matter, vented itself in open threats, so that they no longer took their places in the House of Lords, but followed the King to York. Among them was the Earl of Lindsey, whose name is also to be found in the list of peers who signed the Protestation that Charles had no intention of war. Shortly afterwards he, in company with Lord Savile, was impeached by the Commons before the Lords, declared to be enemies of the kingdom, and disabled from sitting in the House again during the session. This was due to an action at York of which they were accused. The supporters of the Parliament in that city wished to present a petition to the King, but he refused to receive it. Parliament accused these two nobles of violence against the petitioners, and on this count they were proscribed without being able to make any defence. They were therefore impeached on mere rumour.

Seeing that war was inevitable, Lindsey had, several months before its actual outbreak, retired to his estates, and, with the help of his son, made such preparations as were possible, drilling and arming his tenants and dependants. Thus, when Charles raised his standard at Nottingham, he was able to summon to his master's banner a complete regiment of foot, officered by the principal knights and gentlemen of Lincolnshire. At York the King had made him Lord General of the Army —9 July, 1642. No better choice could have been made. Lindsey had won a great reputation in earlier days by his exploits in the Low Countries; he had served under and been approved by a leader of such great renown as Prince

Maurice of Orange. Moreover, his experience was wide ; he had been present at battles and sieges in many different parts of the world, his loyalty had been severely tried and had stood the test, and, greater perhaps than all, he was acceptable to all the chief men on the King's side. Civilians and military men alike were well content with the King's choice, the former confident in the tact and kindliness as well as loyalty of the man—an Englishman and one well-beloved—the latter approving his known military skill and experience.

From York the new General-in-Chief accompanied the King to Nottingham, and was present at the gloomy ceremony of the raising of the standard. At that moment the King's hopes of an army strong enough to enable him to take the field seemed very small, but the contingents raised by Lindsey and his son from Lincolnshire arriving put a different aspect on affairs. " The General, the Earl of Lindsey, had brought a good regiment of foot out of Lincolnshire of near a thousand men, very well officered. And the Lord Willoughby, his son, who had been a captain in Holland, and to whom His Majesty had given the command of his guards, had brought up from Lincolnshire another excellent regiment, near the same number, under officers of good experience." Moreover, these good examples were speedily followed ; discontent at the stern action of Parliament against those whom they termed " delinquents " was spreading rapidly ; also Prince Rupert had arrived, bringing life and spirit into the King's service. Soon, therefore, the King found himself strong enough to leave Nottingham, and he proceeded to march by way of Shrewsbury towards Chester to see to the security of that port, so important because of communication with Ireland. Then occurred the action near Worcester, in which Rupert, although surprised by a large body of the enemy, scattered them in such decisive fashion that he earned for himself in that short engagement such a reputation that for many a long day his very name struck terror into the hearts of the Roundheads.

It was probably the success of this engagement that caused the King to give Rupert command of the horse, and to yield to his demand to be exempt from receiving orders from any save the King himself. The fact that the Prince was made general of the horse caused no disturbance; it was generally known, Clarendon says, that that office had been reserved for him, but the clause in the Commission exempting him from receiving orders from any other than the King was a very different matter. It, in fact, divided the command of the army. The General-in-Chief could now only direct the movements of the foot, and had no control over the horse on whose support the foot must depend. In military science the separation of the two branches is the most fatal error; the combined movements of the whole army should proceed from one brain, for so only can tactics be capable of readjustment should necessity arise. To expect the Earl of Lindsey to submit to such a position was demanding more than the stoutest English loyalty could enable a man to bear.

The plan of campaign decided on by the King was to strike straight at London, the possession of which would probably have ended the war at a blow. With that end in view he effected a junction with Rupert at Shrewsbury. On the march towards London, Charles reached Edgeworth, hoping the next day—Sunday, 23 October—to proceed to Banbury, but during the night Rupert brought news of the close proximity of the enemy. A council of war decided that the army should take up its position on Edgehill. Lindsey, whose opinion on the conduct of the battle had been overruled in favour of Prince Rupert's plans, could bear no more. To be general in name of an army, yet to have no control over the cavalry, and to be forced to carry out tactics which he disapproved, was more than human nature could stand. He declined to assume the position of Commander-in-Chief, electing to serve, a simple colonel, at the head of his regiment. Thus in the battle the command of the foot was given to the Earl of Forth.

The events of the day proved the unwisdom of the divided command. Rupert's dashing charge scattered the Roundhead horse, then, subject to no man's commands, he dashed in pursuit, forgetful of the unprotected foot behind him. Wilmot, commanding the horse on the left wing, made the same error. The infantry were in consequence quickly overcome, and the Royal Foot Guards, the King's Red Regiment, were left alone to bear the burden of the fighting, with the inevitable result. When Rupert, at last wearied of the pursuit, returned to the field, it was to find the Red Regiment broken, Sir Edmund Verney, the standard-bearer, slain, the Earl of Lindsey wounded and a prisoner. The return of the cavalry served to prevent another attack by Essex, but the want of co-operation between cavalry and infantry had effectually prevented the victory on which the Cavaliers had counted. On the other hand, the road to London lay open before the King, for Essex had retreated. Banbury surrendered, and two days later, on 29 October, Charles entered Oxford in triumph.

The General meanwhile, during the night after the

battle, lay a prisoner in the Roundhead camp. His wounds were unattended for hours. This was due to no negligence on the part of Essex, but to the inability to procure surgeons. Lindsey's wound would not have proved mortal could the bleeding have been stopped. He had the consolation of the presence of his son, Lord Willoughby, who had fought his way to his father's side and surrendered to the enemy in order to be near him. He was also visited by Sir William Balfour and other officers of the Parliamentary army, but he spoke so vigorously to them of their disloyalty that they soon withdrew and dissuaded Essex from carrying out his intention of visiting his some-time friend. Lindsey, however, sent a strong message to the Roundhead general, " that he ought to cast himself at the King's feet to beg his pardon—which, if he did not speedily do, his memory would be odious to the nation." On the following morning, when surgeons at last arrived, he died in their hands from loss of blood. " He had very many friends and very few enemies, and died generally lamented."

Clarendon, in one of his inimitable character sketches, says of Lindsey : " He was a man of very noble extraction, and inherited a good fortune from his ancestors, which, though he did not manage with so great care as if he desired much to improve, yet he left it in a very fair condition to his family, which more intended to increase it. He was a man of great honour, and spent his youth and the vigour of his age in military actions and commands abroad, and albeit he indulged to himself great liberties of life, yet he still preserved a very good reputation with all men and a very great interest in his country, as appeared by the supplies he and his son brought to the

King's army, the several companies of his own regiment
of foot being commanded by the principal knights and
gentlemen of Lincolnshire, who engaged themselves in
the service principally out of their personal affection
to him. He was of a very generous nature, and punctual
in what he undertook and in exacting what was due to
him, which made him bear that restriction so heavily
which was put upon him by the commission granted to
Prince Rupert, and by the King preferring the Prince's
opinion in all things relating to the war before his.
Nor did he conceal his resentment, for the day before the
battle he said to some friends that he did not look upon
himself as general, and therefore he was resolved when
the day of battle was come that he would be in the head
of his regiment as a private colonel, where he could die."

Clarendon's stricture that the Earl did not try to
improve the family fortunes does not appear to be wholly
deserved. He was probably lax in expenditure, but
he did attempt to extend his estates, and at the same
time to develop the resources of the country. At that
period there was much concern at the waste of land
in the Fens of Lincolnshire, which, if proper measures
were taken, could be made serviceable for agriculture.
Many attempts were made in this and previous reigns
to reclaim these districts, but the landowners in the
district refused to pay the charges, and the work had
remained undone. At last, in 1636, the Commissioners
who had been appointed to inquire into the matter
made a contract with the Earl of Lindsey that he should
drain the fens lying between Kyme, Eau, and Glen,
and in return he should receive twenty-four thousand
acres of the reclaimed land. In three years he had
accomplished the work, which is said to have cost some

forty-five thousand pounds. The land granted him he then enclosed, farmsteads and houses were built, and the whole brought into cultivation. Later on disputes arose, the men of the fens claimed the land which the Earl and others had reclaimed, and when their possession was confirmed, wreaked vengeance by destroying drains, buildings, and crops, and, a writer of 1662 says, " still hold possession to the great decay and ruin of these costly works and exceeding discommodity of all that part of the country."

The attempt to improve the family fortunes was thus rendered futile, but from it we may gather some idea of the public spirit of the man and of his capacity in other than military affairs. Lindsey deserves to be remembered by his country, even though, as Clarendon hints, in his private life he may not have been devoid of faults. He may have been influenced in this respect by his long wanderings in foreign lands, which were unusually protracted, and which seem to have had an extraordinary fascination for him in his younger days. On the other hand, Clarendon's strictures would seem to be discounted by the undeniable facts that in his own neighbourhood he was honoured and looked up to as leader, and that Charles I repeatedly singled him out for distinction, and at that period no form of free-living was countenanced or condoned by those in high places.

Certainly in his public capacity Lindsey was a man to be revered. Active in local as well as in larger political affairs, in many practical matters he was an expert whose advice was welcomed, in every public capacity he showed energy and loyalty. That at the age of seventy he was willing to undergo all the hardships of an arduous campaign and all the responsibilities of high office shows

loyalty and courage of the highest kind, while that he
finally refused to undertake a divided command is no
proof of an undue regard for his own dignity. As commander-in-chief it was his business to secure victory
to the King's arms, when he realized that failure was
practically certain to ensue, it was his duty to protest
and to give weight to that protest by resignation. Loyalty
to his master controlled his actions all through ; though
his resignation failed of its effect, his best services were
still to be given to his cause, as he proved by taking
his stand at the head of his regiment and by his vigorous
protest against rebellion when a prisoner in the hands of
Essex.

His single-minded loyalty and devotion were continued in his son, who supported Charles to the end,
and who, with Hertford and Richmond, performed the
last sad offices for his murdered King.

SIR JACOB ASTLEY
FROM THE ETCHING BY THOS. WORLIDGE

A CHAMPION FROM THE MIDLANDS
SIR JACOB ASTLEY

SIR JACOB ASTLEY, "the very type of an
English Royalist," was a member of an old
Warwickshire family. He was the second son
of Isaac Astley, of Hill Morton, in the county of Warwick,
and of Melton Constable in Norfolk, and of Mary, daughter
of Sir Edward Walgrave, of Boreham, in Essex. The
family was one of undoubted antiquity. In the reign of
Henry II, a certain Philip de Estley was certified, in the
assessing of an aid for the marrying of the King's daughter,
as holding three knights' fees of the Earl of Warwick, all
in the county of Warwick, which had been held by the
family since the time of Henry I. These fees were, moreover, held by the service of "laying hands" on the Earl's
stirrup when mounting or dismounting. In later times
a descendant of this Philip was slain at Evesham, fighting
on the side of the barons. Again, in the reign of Edward
III there is a record that an Astley founded the Collegiate
Church at Astley, in Warwickshire. On the whole,
however, the family was not one whose members were
very prominent in public affairs.

Sir Jacob was born in 1579, and when only nineteen
he joined the expedition sent out by Elizabeth, under the
command of Sir Francis Vere, to the assistance of the
revolted Netherlands against Spain, and for thirty years
he fought on the Continent. He took part in the battle

of Newport in 1599, and in the siege of Ostend, and so distinguished himself that Prince Maurice of Orange gave him a commission, and in the course of the war he was advanced to high command. In 1621 he was one of that little band of Englishmen who volunteered their services to the Elector Palatine, son-in-law of James I, in his attempt to secure the throne of Bohemia. Ten years later, the Bohemian question being merged in the complications of the great war of religion in Germany known as the Thirty Years' War, Gustavus Adolphus formed a league to intervene in support of the Protestants. James Duke of Hamilton obtained permission from Charles I to raise a body of six hundred men to serve under that great leader, and Astley was given a commission by the Duke. That Astley was on very intimate terms with the Palatinate family is shown by a letter written to him on this occasion by the " Queen of Hearts " herself :—

"Honest little Jacob,

      " This is to assure you that I was very glad to know by your letter, that you had so good fortune in getting your suit of the King, my brother. I hope shortly to see you here, for the Prince (Maurice of Nassau) means to be very suddenly in the field, and means all shall be cashiered that are not at the rendezvous. Therefore, like a little ape, slip over quickly ! Your Colonel swears cruelly that the Prince will not give him leave now to go to my uncle. His daughter is here, I do not find her changed. I end with this, that I desire you to believe me ever,

                    " Your most assured friend,
                              " Elizabeth

    " The Hague, this 4th of May, 1630."

Another ten years of foreign service, and the year 1641 saw Astley, a man of some reputation as a soldier and leader of men, recalled to serve the King against the Scots. Here he seems to have won the approbation of the King by the way in which he kept the army, mutinous for want of pay, under control. In fact, his influence over the men was so great that he was able to offer them for the King's service, if he thought fit, to curb the city and free Parliament from the influence of the people of London during the stormy months of 1641. This was no inconsiderable performance, considering that Sir Jacob himself describes the men under him at that time as " the arch-knaves of the Kingdom." When peace, for the time, was made with the Scots, Astley was given command of Plymouth as a reward for his past services, and as a post of ease for his declining years, for he was no longer a young man.

The name of Sir Jacob Astley is prominent in that tangle known as the " Army Plot." The Royalists declared this to be a simple petition to Parliament by officers of the Army on the matter of their pay, their opponents believed, or feigned to believe—it is difficult to ascertain the truth, that the document covered a design to force the King's will on Parliament by means of the army. The document, whatever its real purport may have been, bore the King's initials, C.R., thus signifying his approval of its contents. Clarendon's explanation of this is that Captain Legge asked the King's permission to present the petition, but that Astley would not sign it until he had proof of the King's consent, and that Charles therefore affixed his initials for the satisfaction of Sir Jacob. That the proposed petition covered any further design rests solely on the testimony of that villain of villains—Goring—who betrayed the " Plot " to Pym. In any case, no imputation can rest on the character of Astley, who acted in the matter as an honest man, refusing to meddle in political affairs, which were not his business, unless assured that it was by the King's wish. His attitude also points to considerable acumen ; he probably realized the delicacy of the situation at the moment, and that any ill-considered action might seriously prejudice the King's interests.

Astley's period of quiet was of no long duration ; when the King unfurled his standard at Nottingham, he was found in his place beneath it. A man of his experience and reputation would be needed for other work than the defence of a fortress. At Nottingham he was made Serjeant-Major General of the King's army ; but of so phantom a character was that army at the time, that Astley told Charles that he might easily be taken out of his bed if the rebels were but bold enough to make the attempt ! The office was only that to which his experience and tried courage entitled him. As Sir Philip Warwick, a contemporary, wrote of him, he was " purely a soldier, and of the most loyal heart."

An incident which occurred before the battle of Edgehill illustrates another side of Sir Jacob's character, the simple piety which he, in common with most of the best men on his side, possessed, but which, with true English reticence, was only displayed on rare occasions. With no parade of religion, but in simple natural fashion, Astley knelt at the head of his division of infantry and prayed : " O Lord, Thou knowest how busy I must be this day ; if I forget Thee, do not Thou forget me ! " Then rose and gave the word of command : " March on, boys ! "

It was in such men as Astley and Hopton that the King's strength really lay—men whose religion was as deep and true, and whose belief in the justice of their cause was as firm as that of the best men on the other side, whose loyalty could not be destroyed, whose patriotism was beyond suspicion of taint or reproach. To such men the confidence of the middle and lower classes was readily given, so it was they who were able in those early days of the war to fill the King's army with disciplined, courageous troops, and to lead them on to victory. They were even able in the last evil days to lead forlorn hopes to the aid of the King when more brilliant but less stable men had given up the struggle in despair.

The office held by Astley implied his presence in the King's main army, and in the battle of Edgehill his infantry did good service. The foot fought valiantly, though deserted by the horse, and gave way no inch before the enemy till they were absolutely overpowered. The Earl of Lindsey was himself shot in the thigh, and Astley too was wounded, though not dangerously.

After the battle of Edgehill the King marched on towards London, but after the capture of Brentford was obliged to retreat, and the winter was spent in defensive operations round Oxford. The plan of campaign for the next year—the threefold attack on London —proved a failure, and it was decided to lay siege to Gloucester. Had this been successful the west would have been solid for the King with the exception of Plymouth, which had been held by the Roundheads since its cowardly surrender by Goring. Then, indeed, the royal armies might have marched on London with every prospect of success.

In the siege of Gloucester Sir Jacob Astley played an

important part. One of the two approaches to the town was committed to his care—the other to that of the general, Brentford. This arrangement was due to the fact that Astley had had great experience in the Low Countries in the conduct of sieges, and was highly esteemed for his judgment and skill in that branch of military service. During the siege a sally was made from the city with the object of nailing the Royalist cannon. The party left the north gate intending " to fall upon their trenches at the east gate, but the guide mistook the way and brought them round to Sir Jacob Astley's quarters at Barton, where about forty musketeers encountered five colours of the enemy and were forced to retreat." Sir Jacob was shot in the arm, but a false report was spread that he was dead, whereupon the Royalists retorted : " Was he slain with a musket or a cannon bullet ? Sir Jacob himself desires to know." The Royalists were forced to raise the siege, owing to the magnificent march made by Essex from London to its relief, one of the greatest feats of the Civil War.

Though the siege of Gloucester had failed the King hoped to bar Essex's return to London, and there was a race for Newbury. Here a battle was fought, indecisive in effect, but the King failed in his object, for Essex marched on to Reading, which had been seized and garrisoned by him some time before. Here he rested his army and then retired to Windsor, so that the King sent Sir Jacob Astley to re-occupy the town, which he did on 3 October, 1643, and was for the time installed there as Governor. In December of the same year he was sent by the King to the aid of Hopton. Taking with him one thousand men from Reading garrison, he aided in the capture of Arundel Castle.

The defeat of the western army at Cheriton, which set Waller free to co-operate with Essex against the King, together with the desperate state of affairs in the north caused by the incoming of the Scotch, for the moment paralysed the energies of Charles and his advisers. In haste he recalled Rupert, then on his way to the aid of Newcastle against the Scotch, and a new plan of campaign for the year 1644 was sketched. Rupert advised that the King should strengthen his garrisons of Oxford, Wallingford, Abingdon, Reading, and Banbury, leave a good body of horse about Oxford, and send the rest to Prince Maurice in the west, thus acting from the centre on the circumference. So many fortified places would prevent Essex and Waller from penetrating to Oxford, while they would be unable to march either north or west with such a strong position behind them. Thus Maurice in the west and Newcastle in the north would find their respective tasks so much the easier.

This plan, accepted at the time, was considerably modified after the departure of the Prince. It was finally decided to abandon the outlying fortresses of Reading and Abingdon, destroying their fortifications that they might not be garrisoned by the enemy, and to draw these garrisons to strengthen Oxford and the King's main army, with which he was to take the field. The body of military advisers who were, presumably, responsible for the King's action in disregarding his nephew's advice were at that time Brentford, Wilmot, Hopton, and Astley. It is not certain that their plan was inferior to that of Rupert. It had the advantage of setting the King free to strike a blow at Essex or Waller.

Reading and Abingdon were abandoned, but for a

time the King's army remained at Oxford to repulse any attempt which Essex or Waller might make upon that city. Two such attempts were made—one by Waller, who attempted to cross the Isis at Newbridge but was repulsed, and one by Essex, who tried to cross the Cherwell at Gosworth bridge, where he was opposed by Astley, who with great skill beat him off. Later both Waller and Essex succeeded in crossing the Isis and Cherwell, whereupon the King, fearful of being shut in between the two Parliamentary armies, decided to leave the town with his horse and part of the foot under Astley, the rest being left for the defence of the city. The danger was so great that one person, said to be of undoubted loyalty, advised Charles to surrender to Essex, who replied that " Possibly he might be found in the hands of the Earl of Essex, but he would be dead first."

When the enemy discovered the King's escape the two leaders decided to separate, Waller to pursue the King, Essex to march into the west. For three weeks the King wandered about the country, his chief aim being to avoid Waller. By skilful manœuvring he was able at last to circumvent that general and return to the neighbourhood of Oxford, where the army was strengthened by the foot he had left behind, so that he was able now to pursue Waller, who before had pursued him. The two armies met at Cropredy, and though the battle was indecisive, the advantage lay with the King, for Waller's army melted away from him, and it was thought that if the King had pursued his advantage it might have been annihilated. He, however, was anxious to pursue Essex, who had relieved Lyme and was marching towards Exeter. Bad news met both Charles and the Parlia-

mentary general. Marston Moor might well have caused
the courage of the Royalists to flag, as the news of Waller's
repulse most certainly did that of Essex, who abandoned
the idea of laying siege to Exeter and marched into
Cornwall. Here occurred the famous surrounding of
the Parliamentary army by that of the King, ending in
the surrender of the whole of Essex's foot at Lostwithiel.
Much of the Royalist success was due to Sir Jacob Astley,
who took advantage of the negligence of Essex to possess
himself of certain positions which prevented supplies
being brought in to the Roundheads by sea.

The King and Prince Maurice were stationed at
Boconnock, Sir Richard Greenville at Bodmin. This
blocked Essex on the land side. There remained the sea.
Essex had possessed himself of Fowey on the western
side of the harbour, but had no single point on the eastern
shore in his possession. This fatal omission was seized
upon by Astley, who promptly occupied View Hall,
a house on the top of the steep hill on the eastern side of
Bodinnock Ferry. From that point the Royalists took
possession of Polruan Fort opposite Fowey, and at the
very mouth of the harbour, so that it was practically
impossible for vessels to enter with supplies. Essex
therefore had to subsist on the provisions already in
hand, and his horse to be content with what forage
there was still in the fields around. When that was
exhausted surrender was inevitable, and the King's army
gradually contracted the circle till Essex was forced to
recognize the hopelessness of the situation. He himself
escaped by sea, his horse having been allowed, by Goring's
negligence, to escape ; the foot were left to the mercy of
the King.

Great dissensions in the Roundhead ranks followed

10

these events, but a temporary union was formed of Manchester, Essex, and Waller, in order to cut off the King as he returned from the west. Manchester was, however, intolerably slow, and the King, hearing of the siege of Donnington Castle, marched to its relief. On his approach the siege was raised, and, before he could reach Oxford, the King was attacked by the united forces of Essex, Manchester, and Waller. Rupert, who had gone to Bristol to bring up reinforcements, had not yet returned; thus it fell to Sir Jacob Astley to command the greater part of the army. In that indecisive battle, the second of Newbury, the foot under Astley acquitted themselves well, that part of the field being held by him against Manchester. The King's horse had, however, been unable to prevent Waller from occupying their part of the field and capturing much of the artillery. Thus Charles thought the day entirely lost, and decided on retreat. That the enemy were in evil case and not disposed to renew the fight is fairly evident from the fact that they made no attempt at pursuit, though the night was light and they must have known of the retreat.

The next mention of Astley is as Governor of Oxford, a post he held at the time that proposals for peace were made to the King in February, 1645. In January of that year he wrote to Rupert a piteous letter, showing his anxiety in the King's cause, his efforts to secure supplies and attend to the comforts of his men, as well as his aversion to plunder. It also illustrates the great and ever-increasing difficulty of the King's generals—lack of money. "After manie scolisietations by letters and messendgeres sent for better paiement of this garrison, and to be provided with men, armes, and amonition for ye good orderinge and defence of this place, I have reseeived no comfort at all. So yt in littell time our extreamities must thrust the souldieres either to disband, or mutiny, or plunder, and then ye fault thereof will be laied to my charge. God send ye Kinge mor monnie to go throw with his great worck in hande, and me free from blame and imputation." Rupert's answer to this letter is written in an entirely different strain from that of most of his replies to the complaints of governors and generals. Astley had been governor to him and Prince Maurice in their youth, and they probably owed much to his simple honest teaching, and—what speaks more plainly still for Astley's worth—Prince Rupert, at least, seems to have been conscious of the debt. Certainly his letters to Astley are all respectful, if not deferential in tone; they have none of that peremptoriness which won him so much unpopularity. Now, while regretting he has no money at all to send, he wrote: " For such precise orders as you seem to desire, I must deal freely with you. You are not to expect them, we being not such fit judges as you upon the place. I should be very loth by misjudging here, to direct that which you should find inconvenient there."

Astley can only have remained at Oxford a very short time. He was with Prince Rupert in Shropshire and at the relief of Beeston Castle, and aided in the collection of that army which enabled the King to leave Oxford and march north, and with which he fought the battle of Naseby.

The King's plan of campaign for the year 1645 was less decided and masterly than in the two preceding years. He had two enemies to beat—Fairfax and the Scots; but he could not make up his mind to crush each in detail, while it was impossible for him to concentrate his forces in Oxford, because that town was unable to withstand a long siege. He therefore tried to hold Oxford, and at the same time march against one or other of his enemies. For some time he hesitated between marching north to the aid of Montrose against Leslie, or west against Fairfax. Finally he divided his army, leaving Goring in the west; he himself marched north and captured Leicester, but hearing of the siege of Oxford he returned to its defence. Fairfax promptly raised the siege, and once more Charles turned his face northwards. There was, however, a difference of opinion among his advisers as to the course to be pursued. Some were for delay and an encounter with Fairfax. Astley was of Rupert's opinion that delay would be fatal, and that the King's only chance of success lay in at once marching north or into the Associated Counties.

Before the question was settled Fairfax and Cromwell were upon them; there was no longer a choice. Rupert had failed to keep himself posted concerning the New Model Army, with the result that that army was upon him before he was prepared.

The King was at Lubenham; the Roundheads were so near that he could not even make for Belvoir. It was therefore resolved to await the enemy's approach at Harborough. Astley was placed in command of the foot, Rupert and Maurice commanded the right wing of horse, Sir Marmaduke Langdale with the northern horse was on the left wing. Astley's plan was to occupy a long hill two miles south of the little town of Harborough and compel the Roundheads to attack. This was wise, for the Royalists were outnumbered by nearly two to one, and by leaving the attack the Roundheads would have the disadvantage of mounting the hill in face of the enemy.

Rupert's impatience lost the benefits of Astley's wisdom; the Roundheads did not appear, and he went in search of them. Seeing them, as he thought, in retreat, he advanced opposite the army, only to find that the movement he had taken for retreat had merely been a change of position, which would give the Roundheads those very advantages which Astley had sought for the Royalists. Rupert sent orders for the whole army to advance to an eminence to the right of the enemy, known as Dust Hill. The Royalists had now no choice but to attack, and at a serious disadvantage.

In the battle itself it was again Rupert's rashness that gave victory to the Parliament. Overcoming Ireton's cavalry, he pursued it with his usual unconsidered zeal, regardless of the fortunes of the rest of the field. Langdale's cavalry had been very quickly put to flight by Cromwell's " Ironsides," and the foot were therefore practically unsupported. They made a valiant fight, and had the Parliamentary leaders been as thoughtless as Rupert, would probably have stood their ground; but Cromwell retained most of his cavalry to support the actions of the foot, with the result that the Royalist infantry was overwhelmed. When Rupert returned from the pursuit, it was to find the day lost and the King's foot absolutely annihilated. From that time he had only his cavalry to depend upon, and was never again able to face the Parliamentary army in the field.

The King retreated to Wales, hoping to raise a new army in what had been a favourite and fertile Royalist recruiting ground. Leslie, for the time released from Scottish duty, was besieging Hereford, and the King attempted to rouse the Welsh men to march with his cavalry to its defence. Then arose a great and unexpected difficulty. The Welsh were at that time governed by General Gerard, who, by his exactions and plunder and other excesses, had aroused an universal spirit of discontent among the Welshmen. "Instead of providing men to march with the King they provided a long list of grievances." Charles was forced to listen to the accusations of the Welsh and counter-accusations of Gerard; neither party seemed to be thinking of its duty to the King, each of its own injuries. To appease the Welsh the King removed Gerard from his command, and made Astley Lieutenant-General of all His Majesty's forces in the west and the Marches. Before Naseby he had been appointed to levy contributions in the counties of Worcester and Gloucester, in which he succeeded so well that, as a Roundhead writer of the time remarked: "Sir Jacob Astley sends warrants for contributions to the gates of Gloucester." Thus he was known on the borders of Wales, and as he had a reputation for justice and restraint, the Welsh gentry accepted him with alacrity as their governor. It was, however, too late to undo the mischief. The loyalty of the Welsh—Celtic in its swift discouragement if self-interest is too much encroached upon—had been too severely shaken to be easily restored. Wales was never again to be the recruiting ground it had been in the past.

In September, 1645, the King relieved Hereford, but, although Lord Astley (as he now was, having been made a Baron in November, 1644) by superhuman efforts had held the Welsh back from openly supporting Parliament, they would no more fight for the King or his cause. From that time to March, 1646, Astley would seem to have been struggling to raise forces for his master.

In that month Charles found himself in Oxford with a small force and, Banbury being in a state of siege, hopelessly cut off from the army in the west—now, indeed, on the point of surrender at Torrington—with no northern army left since Langdale's defeat at Sherburn and flight into Ireland, and with no hope of help from Ireland, since Chester had fallen in February. There was only the remote possibility that the Queen might be able to send auxiliaries from France. Charles therefore called upon Astley to join him near Oxford, hoping that with the three thousand troops that general had painfully collected from Ireland and Wales, his own cavalry, and the possible French troops, he might be enabled once more to take the field and make a final effort against the rebels. This last desperate hope was crushed by the defeat of Astley at Stow-on-the-Wold, in Gloucestershire. The brave old veteran had marched from Worcester with his three thousand troops, expecting to be met by the King's horse, but apparently letters had miscarried, for the King knew nothing of his march till he heard of his defeat; while Brereton, now released by the fall of Chester, and Colonel Morgan from Gloucester, were aware of his approach, and fell upon him when his troops were weary with their long march. The foot behaved gallantly and twice repulsed the Roundhead attack, but the horse fled at the first charge and carried the news of the battle to Oxford. Finally the Royalist troops were utterly routed, large numbers were slain and the rest surrendered, so that Lord Astley had no choice but to do likewise. The victors brought a drum, and, seated on this, the grey-haired old man showed his sense of the finality of the King's defeat by his sadly humorous words to the enemy's officers : " You have now done your work and may go play, unless you will fall out among yourselves."

It was true, the King had played his last stake. Very soon he surrendered himself to the Scots, the beginning of the end. Walker, the King's herald, maintained that the King should not have sent for Astley to come to Oxford with foot and horse, a march taking time and almost impossible to keep secret. In his estimation it would have been better if the King, with his horse, had gone to Astley. The end was, however, inevitable, the mistake, if mistake it was, merely accelerated it.

Lord Astley was taken prisoner to Warwick Castle, where he remained till June, when, Oxford being surrendered to Fairfax, his release was made one of the terms upon which that city capitulated. One would be glad to think that this stipulation was made at the instance of Rupert, who was in the city at the time of its surrender, though there is no evidence to that effect.

Charles had always held Astley in high esteem, and in a letter which he wrote to him on hearing of his defeat and capture, he expresses his conviction that the disaster cannot be attributed to any lack of zeal or military skill in the general, and his keen sense of the loss his service sustains in the imprisonment of so loyal and capable a commander, ending with the words: "His Majesty hopes that your lordship, being a person of so much honour in yourself, and having been upon all occasions of good service, so solicitous to use your prisoners with much civility, that those in whose power you now are, especially the Commander-in-Chief, will take care that you shall be treated as a person of honour."

After his release Lord Astley never drew sword again. Indeed, he was an old man when the wars began. He retired to the house of his nephew and son-in-law, Sir Edward Astley, where he remained until 1649, when he removed to Maidstone, in Kent, to an estate left him by a kinsman. There he died at his house, " The Palace," in the year 1651, aged seventy-two years. He had married a German lady, Agnes Imple, and left Isaac Astley, his eldest son, who succeeded him in his titles and estates. Bernard, his second son, had been fatally wounded at the siege of Bristol in 1645, and three other sons had also died unmarried during their father's lifetime. His only daughter, Elizabeth, married the son of his eldest brother, Thomas Astley, of Melton Constable, in Norfolk. As in his public life Astley was beloved and highly esteemed, so also in his private life. He enjoyed the friendship of Prince Maurice of Orange 'and of Elizabeth, Queen of Bohemia, while her sons felt for him a deeper respect and reverence than perhaps for any other man.

Clarendon, as usual, with a few firm strokes portrays the man : " Sir Jacob Astley was an honest, brave, plain man, and as fit for the office he exercised of major-general of the foot as Christendom yielded, and was so generally esteemed, very discerning and prompt in giving orders, as the occasions required, and most cheerful and present in any action. In council he used few but very pertinent words, and was not at all pleased with the long speeches usually made there, and which rather confounded than informed his understanding ; so that he rather collected the ends of the debates, and what he was himself to do, than enlarged them by his own discourses, though he forbore not to deliver his own mind."

Astley was no politician, philosophical doctrines con-

cerning " the liberties of the people " had no meaning
for him ; he stood, a simple soldier, for King and country,
and when duty called, though neutrality might well have
been excused on the score of advancing years, he unhesitatingly obeyed. No cant of " honour " could
hinder him from doing his duty to the end ; he was his
master's servant, and as such bound to obey his commands without question. Thus the difficult work in
Wales was undertaken without demur, when, through the
mismanagement of others, to make it a success was a
practical impossibility. Again, though Rupert spoiled
his plans, and may therefore have been thought by some
to have caused the disaster of Naseby, Astley let fall no
word of complaint or reproach. He was a thorough Saxon
in that courage which despises danger, not because none
is seen, for it was met with open eyes; in that dogged
valour which holds out till resistance is no longer possible ;
as well as in that calm, even cheerful, facing of the
worst when the worst had befallen his country, his
master, and himself. In truth a man who " stood four-
square to all the winds of heaven."

A life, it may be said, which has left no mark on the
history of the time. It is nevertheless on men such as
Astley, with their devotion to duty, their loyalty, courage,
simplicity, and honesty of purpose, that the very existence of a nation depends.

PRINCE RUPERT

AFTER THE PAINTING BY VAN DYCK

THE CHAMPION OF THE BLOOD
ROYAL

PRINCE RUPERT

PRINCE RUPERT, the most perplexing, and at the same time perhaps the most picturesque figure in the Civil Wars, is a character of vast importance in that time of storm and stress. From first to last he championed the King's cause as a soldier, and much of the success and much of the failure of that cause was due to him. A man of striking personality, he made many friends and many enemies, and to understand his character we must not look to the plaudits of the one or the abuse of the other, for their accounts are flatly contradictory. To his enemies he was " Rupert the Devil," to his friends the most gallant and generous of princes. Clarendon, who was neither friend nor enemy, but a most careful observer, wrote of Rupert and his career : " He who too affectedly despises or neglects what is said of him, or what is generally thought of persons or things, and too stoically contemns the affections of men, even of the vulgar (be his other abilities and virtues what can be imagined), will in some conjuncture of time find himself very unfortunate. And it may be, a better reason cannot be assigned for the misfortunes which that hopeful young Prince (who had great parts of mind as well as vigour of body, and, incomparable personal courage) underwent, and the kingdom by it, than that roughness and unpolishedness of his nature which rendered him less patient to hear, and consequently less skilful to judge of those things which should have guided him in the discharge of his important trust."

This independence of judgment and action, this " roughness and unpolishedness " may be largely attributed to the circumstances of his upbringing, therefore a short summary of his youth must necessarily preface any account of his career as a King's Champion.

His mother, Elizabeth, daughter of James I, was married to the Protestant Prince Frederick of the Palatinate when Germany was on the eve of that great upheaval the Thirty Years' War. To Frederick the Protestants of Bohemia turned as a refuge from the rule of the Catholic King Ferdinand of Austria—to Frederick the crown was offered, and he accepted it, urged thereto by his ambitious wife, who declared that she would " sooner eat dry bread at the table of a King than feast at the board of an Elector." Frederick was all unfitted for the task involved, which was the leadership of Protestant Germany against the united forces of the Emperor and Spain. The last happy days of the Elector vanished with the departure from Heidelberg for Prague, where he was crowned King of Bohemia on 3 November, 1619, his wife's coronation following three days after. Within a month Prince Rupert was born, the third son of his parents, his baptism being made the occasion of a great political gathering. The triumph of the Palatinates was short-lived ; speedily the Imperial army arrived before Prague, the looked-for help from England had not been forthcoming, for James I held that his son-in-law had acted unwisely in accepting

ELIZABETH, QUEEN OF BOHEMIA

FROM THE PAINTING BY MICHIEL JANSZ VAN MIEREVELT IN THE NATIONAL PORTRAIT GALLERY

a crown which was legally the property of another, and the German princes held aloof, waiting to see which way the wind blew. Frederick and his little army were overwhelmed at the battle of the White Mountain, and he and his Queen fled from Prague. The fugitives at first took refuge with Frederick's brother, George William of Brandenburg, but their welcome not being of the warmest, they repaired to the Hague, where Maurice, Stadtholder of Holland, gave them shelter and support. Here, then, was passed Rupert's childhood. The family of Frederick and Elizabeth was a large one, but popular and gifted as the latter was, she apparently lacked the supreme gift— that of motherliness. Certainly she was but little with her children, and her sons grew up knowing but little of a woman's gentle influence. Of all her sons Rupert needed that influence most and possessed a nature which would best have responded to it. His instincts were generous, even chivalrous, but he was of a proud, independent nature; in the rough-and-tumble of a large family, in which the mother's influence was but little felt, those independent characteristics were intensified, instead of being modified and subdued to his nobler qualities. Rupert therefore always remained a child of nature.

Though the father and mother had little direct influence on their children's character, the one through the exigency of affairs, the other because her tastes lay in other directions, they took great care that their education should not be neglected. Here again Rupert struck out a line for himself. He would devote no attention to the classics, but living languages and all things military attracted him, and in the latter he became so proficient that at eight years of age he is said to have handled arms as well as an experienced soldier !

In 1632 Frederick the Elector Palatine died. He had learnt that the King of Sweden had interfered on his behalf in German affairs, and won the battle of Leipzig, and was on his way to join his forces, when he succumbed at Maintz to a fever caught in the summer campaign. He was only thirty-six years of age, but had never recovered from the shock of the death of his eldest son Henry, who had been drowned on his way from Amsterdam. Elizabeth was now left with ten children, and with no means for their support Charles I and the Stadtholder Henry, who had recently succeeded his brother Maurice, were her best friends, so long as the one was able and the other lived to help her. Of her children all had the gift of personal beauty, all had strong wills, and their unusual circumstances had developed in them that disregard of the opinion of others which, in Clarendon's view, was the fatal cause of Rupert's failure in England.

Holland was still at war with Spain and the Spanish Netherlands. Much against his mother's wishes, Rupert joined in the first two campaigns waged by the new Stadtholder in the years 1633–4 He returned covered with glory, having won golden opinions from all for his conduct as a soldier.

During the winter of 1635 Rupert accompanied his elder brother Charles to England. The object of the visit was to obtain help in money and troops to enable Charles, who was now eighteen, to make good his title to the Palatinate. In this country Rupert soon became exceedingly popular, and spent probably one of the happiest years of his life. The lad's beauty won all hearts, and his manner seems to have grown more natural and attractive amid congenial surroundings. His love of music and art drew him to his uncle, whose Court was the most cultured and artistic in Europe, while the Queen was especially fond of him and endeavoured to make him a Roman Catholic. This, and other plans for the future of the young Prince, one to send him as organizer and ruler of a new colony to be founded in Madagascar, alarmed his mother, who wished Rupert to become a soldier and help his brother to regain the Palatinate. As also the English Puritans were willing to give the Elector money, the King to lend ships, and young English nobles to give their services, the object of the visit of the two young princes was attained. They left England for the Hague in June, 1637, and so loath was Rupert to go, that, hunting with the King immediately before his departure, he wished that he might break his neck, so that he might leave his bones in England!

Rupert now joined the Stadtholder's army, then engaged in the siege of Breda. Here he met many Englishmen with whom he was to serve again in later years, notably Astley and Goring. For the former he entertained a very great affection and respect, which he never lost. After the surrender of Breda, Rupert returned to the Hague to aid the young Elector in gathering troops for the proposed expedition into Germany. With the help of Lord Craven, the English nobleman who for many years, until, in fact, his property was confiscated by Parliament, was the main support of the Palatinate family, a tiny army was gathered together and provisioned. There were, in all, three regiments of cavalry—one of guards, the other two dragoons—and a small force of artillery. Count Königs-mark was in command, with Rupert as colonel of one regiment, Lord Craven of another. It was hoped to obtain the co-operation of the Swedes, but the expedition was ill-timed. None of the Protestant princes would move, and as there was then a cessation of hostilities, the Swedish general contented himself with sending General King with a detachment of troops. Altogether the Elector's army now numbered some four thousand, to meet the whole of the Imperial forces ! The plan of the Elector was to march to the Southern Palatinate, because of its loyalty, but Hatzfeldt intercepted him with a complete army comprising eighteen thousand foot besides cavalry and dragoons. The little army fought manfully, but was overwhelmed by numbers. The young Elector and General King fled, Rupert and Lord Craven were captured. For some weeks Rupert was detained prisoner at Warrendorf, then he was sent to Lintz, a fortress on the Danube, where he remained for three years. Charles I and others made many efforts to obtain his release, but in vain. The Emperor tried by various means to win him to the Imperial side and to Roman Catholicism, but his loyalty was proof against every inducement. At first his captivity was very strict, until he was visited by the Archduke Leopold, who interceded for him. From this time his imprisonment was merely nominal; he received much hospitality from the nobles of the surrounding country, and was allowed to absent himself on parole for as many as three days at a time.

In 1641 Charles I succeeded in arousing the interest of the King of France in the case of his young nephew, and himself sent an ambassador to the Court of Vienna to intercede for him. The Emperor was not disinclined to release Rupert, who had won his respect and liking by his persistent and unselfish loyalty; he was, moreover, influenced in his favour by the Empress and the Archduke Leopold Eventually, therefore, Rupert returned to the Hague on the promise that he would not again take up arms against the Emperor.

In February, 1642, the young Prince arrived in England to thank the King for effecting his release. At the moment the country was on the verge of civil war. Henrietta Maria was about to set out for Holland with the Princess Mary, and Charles, fearing that Rupert's presence might precipitate a crisis, begged him to accompany her. August, 1642, however, saw Rupert once more in England. The war had actually begun and his uncle required his services, which it was his pleasure as well as his duty to render. His birth and education, his loyalty to and love for his uncle, his tastes and feelings, all urged adhesion heart and soul to the Royalist party. Of the high political and religious matters in dispute Rupert recked little. His uncle, the King, was opposed and threatened by a rebellious people, that was enough for him. His conduct compares favourably with that of his brother Charles, who, almost at the same moment, was hurrying from England to avoid choosing between the two parties, lest he should choose the losing side, and so prejudice his own chances of English help for the recovery of the Palatinate.

Rupert was now just twenty-three, and at the height of his youthful beauty, the very ideal of a Cavalier. Tall and vigorous, yet graceful in bearing, his countenance, though marked by impetuosity, expressed great firmness, but was softened by the gentle expression of the eyes,

11

and the " womanly dimple " in the cheek   With Rupert
came his younger brother Maurice.   On their way they
only just escaped capture by the Parliamentary fleet,
but reached Tynemouth in safety.   After three days'
delay, caused by a fall from his horse which dislocated his
shoulder, Rupert joined the King at Leicester Abbey.
Here the Prince was made General of the Royal Horse,
which at that time consisted of some eight hundred men.
The next day, 22 August, the Royalists set out for
Nottingham, where the Royal Standard was to be
set up.

The King's position was peculiarly depressing. Wilmot
had failed to relieve Coventry, the royal army was small,
comparatively few had evinced any enthusiasm for the
cause, and not only was it small in number, it was also
unarmed, undisciplined, and untrained.   Moreover, of
professional soldiers there were at present but few,
and jealousies were already rife among these.   The
ardour of the young Prince was not, however, easily
damped; his hopeful zeal soon communicated itself to
Charles, and, more important still, to the men the Prince
was in the future to lead in battle.   Rupert was altogether
a soldier, and had very many of the qualities necessary
for a successful general—practical knowledge of the
newest and best tactics, great skill in strategy, undaunted
courage and resolution which inspired his men and led
them on to victory in many a dashing charge, rapidity
of movement so that he seemed to be in all places at once,
generosity in the hour of victory. These were the qualities which gave the King the superiority in the early
part of the war.   There are, however, other qualities
indispensable for permanent success—prudence and
foresight, caution and patience, that versatility which

enables a leader to vary his tactics according to the
varying resources of the enemy—and these qualities
Rupert lacked. His characteristics sufficed as long as
the enemy was raw and undisciplined, but when experience had taught able generals the secrets of his success
and suggested methods of meeting them, the dashing
cavalry leader was at a loss—he could only repeat tactics
now become useless. It is also to be remembered that
he had extraordinary difficulties to encounter. In-
sufficiency of troops, lack of training, arms, and money
he could and did triumph over; but the jealousies of
courtier soldiers, the hindrances put in his way by
statesmen, his own inability to see any but the military
side of the struggle, which caused such lack of harmony
between him and many of the King's most devoted
followers—these were difficulties beneath which he, in the
end, sank overwhelmed. Many of these hindrances were
due to Rupert himself; he was constitutionally unable
to brook contradiction, was haughty and overbearing
in manner to his enemies, and could see no good in any
proposal made by them, while he was perhaps over-ready
to listen to those whom he loved. Then too he was a
foreigner, and that was sufficient to render him obnoxious
to many Englishmen, and he was at no pains to conciliate
the good opinion of any. Most fatal of all his enmities
was that of Digby, for he had the King's ear when,
from the exigency of circumstances, Rupert was far
away, and many plans were spoiled, many undertakings
ruined by the interference of that plausible riddle.
By the rebels Rupert was nicknamed "The Robber,"
though they too plundered the enemy when occasion
offered or necessity seemed to require; but, as Mr. Gardiner
acknowledged, he never enriched himself by one penny,

and, considering the school of war in which he had been trained, Rupert was singularly free from the vices of the professional soldier.

The setting up of the standard at Nottingham was a gloomy affair. The day was stormy, there were so few supporters for the King that Sir Jacob Astley feared lest he should be captured in his sleep, so defenceless was his position against any sudden attack of the enemy in force. Moreover, the standard itself was blown down in the night—an evil omen to the superstitious! The King was determined to make one more effort for peace, and opened negotiations. As a soldier Rupert opposed this proceeding because it hindered recruiting. Yet it had a good effect; the people realized that the whole onus of the war did not rest with Charles, that he had a true desire for peace, and it brought many volunteers to his standard. Meanwhile Rupert made the most rapid excursions in every direction in search of men, money, horses, and arms. To him a Roundhead was an enemy of the King, and his horse must be commandeered to furnish a mount for a Cavalier; a Puritan town must likewise yield contribution of money. Thus, appearing before Leicester, he demanded two thousand pounds. The inhabitants rendered five hundred pounds but complained to the King, who, fearful of alienating any of his subjects, repudiated the action of his impulsive nephew.

On 13 September the King left Nottingham for Derby, and on the 17th reached Stafford, where Rupert rejoined him. It was decided to make Shrewsbury the headquarters of the royal army, therefore it was advisable to form a line of communication along the Severn as far as Bristol. With that object in view Rupert was sent to occupy Worcester. Here he found Byron, who had come from London with treasure for the King. Essex was thought to be in pursuit, and, in fact, he had left Northampton for the west on the 19th. Rupert therefore sent a challenge to the General of the Parliament to a pitched battle on Dunsmore Heath on 10 October, with the object of settling the dispute in one engagement; or, if that did not meet the views of Essex, that he would give the Prince satisfaction in a private duel. This remarkable letter ends on a note of deep sincerity:

" I know my cause to be so just that I do not fear— for what I do is agreeable both to the laws of God and man, in the defence of true religion, a King's prerogative, an Uncle's right, a Kingdom's safety. Now I have said all, and what more you expect of me to be said, shall be delivered in a larger field than a small sheet of paper, and that by my sword and not by my pen."

It was found impossible to defend Worcester, so Rupert and Byron determined to occupy Shrewsbury. Byron was to advance with his treasure, Rupert to cover his march. The Prince desired to meet the enemy and rode out to the south in search of adventure. Seeing no sign of the rebels he took his troops into a field near Powick Bridge to rest. Almost immediately he spied a troop of horse approaching. There was no time for thought. Rupert threw himself on a horse and gave the order to charge. His officers followed, and with the men in the rear attacked the enemy as they advanced along the lane. The assault was so sudden and fierce that, though the Puritans were a strong body and fully armed, while their opponents had barely had time to seize their swords and mount, they gave way and fled in panic. Some fifty of their number were slain, six or seven colours taken, and many horses. On the Royalist side some half-dozen were killed, though most of the officers, with the exception of the Prince, were wounded. The Royalists gained considerable prestige by this victory; it gave spirit and confidence to the King's supporters and correspondingly disheartened the Roundheads. There was one who, however, was but little pleased at Rupert's success, and that was his brother Charles, who wrote to the Parliament in apologetic and sympathetic terms, and also published a manifesto, in the names of his mother and himself, disclaiming all responsibility for or sympathy with Rupert's actions.

The Prince now fell back on Ludlow, Worcester being occupied by Essex on the 24th. There is a story, characteristic of Rupert, which tells how he met a wandering merchant on his way to Essex's camp with apples for sale. For a piece of gold this man lent his clothes and stock-in-trade to Rupert, who entered the enemy's camp, sold his apples, gleaned much valuable information concerning the strength of the forces, and thereupon returned, telling the apple-man to ask the soldiers of the camp how they enjoyed the apples Prince Rupert sold to them!

Rupert reached Shrewsbury on 26 September, and was speedily joined by the King, who summoned thither all his available forces, his object being to march direct to the capital, the seat of disaffection, and crush the rebellion at its source. This plan of concentrating all the Royalist forces on the centre was very possibly Rupert's. If successful, it would probably end the war at a blow. The King's army now consisted of six thousand infantry, fifteen hundred dragoons, and some two thousand cavalry; there was practically no artillery.

At Nottingham a force of eight hundred had constituted the Royalist cavalry, and the increase in that force was due almost entirely to Rupert's energy and skill. As May, the Parliamentary historian, declared, this Prince was " like a perpetual motion, in a short time heard of in many places at great distances." Also the strength of Rupert's cavalry lay, not only in numbers, but more largely in the confidence and enthusiasm with which their leader had imbued them. They knew that he was to the enemy " very terrible," and that knowledge was to them an inspiration and a guarantee of success so long as they fought under his banner. In this very enthusiasm there lay an element of danger. Their charge in its fire and dash was irresistible ; but, victory attained, the enemy repulsed, their zeal carried them beyond control ; they did not realize that an army was not composed of cavalry alone. At such moments not even Rupert was able to keep them in hand, and so what might have been certain victory was often turned into defeat.

The Royalist army set out on 12 October. It was arranged in three divisions : Rupert, with the cavalry, was to form the advanced guard; the King, with the main body under the General, Lord Lindsey, marched as the centre; Digby, with a brigade of infantry and some horse, was to bring up the rear. Essex was uncertain of the King's intention, and his uncertainty was increased by the movements of the Royalists, who first occupied Bridgenorth, then marched on Wolverhampton and thence to Birmingham. This last move revealed the King's objective. The Londoners, in a panic, set about preparing for the defence of their city, while Parliament ordered Essex to march at once. He left Worcester for Stratford-on-Avon on 19 October, on which day the

King was at Killingworth. The 22nd saw the two armies within six miles of each other, Charles at Edgeworth, Essex at Keinton. The former was utterly unaware of the proximity of the enemy. He had no thought of immediate fighting—in fact, he had sent a detachment to secure Banbury, planning to give the bulk of the army a day's rest on the morrow, Sunday. It was by accident that the whereabouts of Essex was revealed. Prince Rupert had on the march detached himself somewhat from the rest of the Royalist forces. On the 17th he had summoned Coventry, but the town remaining obstinate he set out on the 19th to rejoin the main body. On 22 October he advanced towards Wormleighton, sending out Lord Digby with a body of four hundred horse to reconnoitre. That gentleman discovered nothing, but Rupert's quartermaster, entering Wormleighton, met the quartermaster of Essex. In the skirmish that ensued twelve prisoners were taken by the Royalists, and so Rupert learned of Essex's presence at Keinton. Thus it was night when Rupert came with the news and demanded immediate audience of the King. This Falkland, as Secretary of State, refused, and after high words on Rupert's side, who recked little of the formality of a Court when important issues were at stake, met with imperturbable dignity by Falkland, the Prince was obliged to send a message, and returned without having seen the King. He had wished for a personal interview in order to impress upon the King the necessity of fighting, otherwise on arriving before London the Royalists would find themselves between two fires. Charles was, however, soldier enough to see this, and so before morning Rupert received a message from the King assuring him that he, with all the foot and cannon, would be at Edgehill " betimes " in the morning.

In the early dawn the King, with his two sons, rode to Edgehill, where he found Rupert awaiting him. Already the Prince had been freed from taking orders from any but the King, and probably Lindsey was sore at this exemption, for, if all control of the cavalry were thus taken from him, his position as Commander-in-Chief would be an empty title. Thus when, at a council of war, the bold tactics of Rupert were supported by the King in opposition to Lindsey's more cautious policy, the latter resigned his position, and, though the Earl of Forth consented to command the infantry, the real responsibility fell on Rupert's shoulders. To one of his buoyant spirit the burden was light. It was essential for the Royalists that the battle should be fought at once. Essex had all to gain by delay, the King all to lose. The army was short of provisions, the neighbourhood was hostile; at any moment reinforcements might reach Essex Hence, it was scarcely the best policy for Rupert to arrange his army on the summit of Edgehill. The position was in itself a good one, but delay being so much in Essex's favour, he was scarcely likely to attack at so great a disadvantage. Consequently the royal army was obliged to abandon its advantageous position and descend to the plain.

The arrangement of the two armies was practically identical. The infantry formed the centre, flanked on either side by cavalry. According to Rupert's plans, the burden of the day was to be borne by the cavalry, who were to charge on the enemy's flanks and carry all before them. This part of the programme was carried out with complete success. Rupert on the right wing,

Wilmot on the left, drove the Roundhead cavalry before them in headlong rout. Unfortunately the Royalists were followed in the hot pursuit by the cavalry reserve, thus leaving the infantry entirely unsupported. The Roundhead reserve of horse, in combination with the infantry, were thus able to break through the Royalist ranks, which became thoroughly disorganized. The only body that stood firm to the last was the King's own Red Regiment, and they were practically butchered by the combined forces of the enemy's horse and foot. Sir Edmund Verney, the standard-bearer, was killed, the Earl of Lindsey fatally wounded as he fought, a simple Colonel, at the head of his regiment. Rupert, meanwhile, had been either unable or unwilling to call off his men from the pursuit, and when at last he returned to the field, it was to find the Royalist army so broken that it was hopeless to attempt to rally the scattered forces for another charge. Edgehill had been a hand-to-hand fight, the artillery had scarcely been put into operation. The Royalists were left in possession of the field, for although by the next morning Essex had been reinforced, he was too weak in cavalry to attempt an assault, while the Royalists on their side feared the superiority of the Roundhead foot. The battle was therefore a drawn one ; but inasmuch as Charles had the road to London open before him the fruits of victory were his.

Rupert now urged an immediate march on London, where the panic was great. Such a step might possibly have met with success, but Charles negatived the proposition, perhaps influenced by the openly-expressed fears of some of his supporters that Rupert's cavalry might win the town at too great a cost. These charges of brutality must have caused the brave young Prince much pain, for although he was forced to support his cavalry by supplies raised from the country, there is no proof that he ever allowed wanton cruelty, and many instances of his generosity and consideration are recorded.

After Edgehill Essex had retired to Warwick, pursued by Rupert as far as Keinton, a considerable amount of arms and ammunition being taken. Charles advanced to Banbury and captured it, entering Oxford in triumph on 29 October. While Charles remained at Oxford, Rupert was here, there, and everywhere — now at Abingdon, then at Aylesbury, which town he captured, thus cutting off Essex from communication with London. He then fixed his head-quarters at Maidenhead, whence he made a vain attack on Windsor. His men are reported to have said that they would willingly follow him to fight against men, but not against stone walls. All the while he was collecting cavalry with the object of marching on London. Essex meanwhile advanced to the capital, and with Hampden at Uxbridge, Holles at Brentford, Windsor reinforced, Kingston and Acton well garrisoned, the King was nearly surrounded.

Nevertheless he left Oxford, and on 4 November reached Reading. The army of Essex was now at Turnham Green, and Parliament sent a commission to treat with Charles. The King's only preliminary demand was that Windsor should be yielded to him as a place of residence during the proposed negotiations. On neither side was a suspension of hostilities mentioned. In fact, the King in his present position could not have afforded to make such a suggestion. Not only future victory, but his present safety depended on his remaining free to advance on London should opportunity arise. Thus Rupert was sent forward to take Brentford. In spite of its strong defence, the Prince, favoured by a mist, was enabled to surprise and overpower the garrison. Necessary from the military point of view as this step was, it did infinite harm to the King's cause. The Londoners were roused to great indignation. Essex was at once reinforced by the train bands, and took up the command of his troops at Turnham Green. Thus the King's advance was checked, and he was forced to evacuate Brentford and give up the attempt on London. Rupert was recalled, and most admirably he managed the difficult retreat in face of the Roundhead army. Though under a heavy fire, he stood his horse in the water by Brentford Bridge and cheered and encouraged his men over the dangerous passage. Not until the last man had crossed the river did he stir from his post of danger.

The winter was spent by the King at Oxford, waiting for the Queen's arrival from Holland with supplies of money and arms. His position was one of no small danger; the defences of the town were inadequate, and Essex was known to be at Windsor preparing for an advance upon it. Rupert, to whom the failure of the attempt on London must have been a keen disappointment, spent the interval in scouring the country for supplies of all kinds for the royal army. Inaction was a sheer impossibility to him. During this period the plans for the coming year were formulated. In view of recent successes in the north and west, the plan of concentrating all the Royalist forces on the centre was abandoned in favour of a new scheme. The King, with Prince Rupert's cavalry, of which Essex rightly stood in some awe, was to hold in check the main body of the enemy under that general. Meanwhile, Newcastle, as soon as should be feasible, was to march on Essex from the north through the

Associated Eastern Counties. Hopton, marching from the west, was to seize the banks of the Thames and so paralyse the trade of the capital. This triple attack on the Parliamentary centre was excellent strategy should circumstances permit of its being carried out, and it has generally been conceded that the idea was Rupert's.

During these winter months the movements of that Prince were decidedly erratic; he was indeed a "perpetual motion." In January, 1643, he planned an attack on Cirencester in conjunction with Hertford, which, for the moment, failed. In the next month, however, the Prince made a successful feint on Sudeley Castle, drawing the garrison from Cirencester to its relief. This accomplished, Rupert and Hertford simultaneously attacked the town and captured it. This was a prize of great value to the King; it laid open the road to Wales, to be in the future Rupert's recruiting ground. It was at this period that the Parliamentary attacks on Prince Rupert became most bitter and vindictive, and he deemed it wise to publish a vindication of himself. One Roundhead publication branded him thus: "O ungrateful viper, far worse than that in the fable! . . . The Commons of England will remember thee, thou flap-dragon, thou butter-box, whose impieties draw like the powerful loadstone speedy vengeance on thy cursed head!"

The Prince next planned an assault on Bristol, two citizens having agreed to open the gates to his troops. The plot was, however, discovered, and for the present Bristol remained in Roundhead hands. The news of Rupert's march on Bristol had determined Essex to open the campaign, but his speedy return—within a week—delayed the enemy's forward movement.

By the end of March, news of the Queen's arrival at York reached the King, and it was resolved that Rupert should meet and escort her to Oxford. The project was a bold one, for the intervening country was for the most part Roundhead. Moreover, Essex would be sure to seize the opportunity to march on Oxford. Nevertheless, early in April Rupert set out with an army of twelve hundred horse and six hundred foot. The news of his march brought appeals for aid from the Countess of Derby, then sorely beset in Lancashire, and from Capel for help against Brereton in Cheshire. Rupert made his way straight to Birmingham, a strongly fortified town which, from the first, had shown strong sympathy with Parliament. The town was assaulted and taken. Accusations of extreme cruelty have been brought against Rupert concerning his treatment of this town, but it would appear that the burning of some houses was the sum total of the damage, and that Rupert gave orders that the fires should be promptly quenched. Moreover, there is no doubt that the soldiers had received extreme provocation from the inhabitants.

Lichfield next defied Rupert's summons to surrender, but by a clever use of miners from the district the moat was dried, bridges made, and a mine—the first ever made in England—was sprung in the walls. The result was the surrender of the town, the garrison being allowed to march out with the honours of war—an indulgence scarcely deserved by their commander, who had so far degraded himself as to bring a calf dressed in linen to the font of Lichfield Cathedral and there sprinkle it with water, in mockery of the Sacrament of Baptism.

During this siege the Prince had received an urgent appeal from the King. Essex, as was to be expected, had taken prompt advantage of Rupert's absence and was marching on Reading. Unfortunately the governor, Sir Arthur Aston, had been disabled, and when Rupert, two days after the capture of Lichfield, met the King at Caversham, there was practically no hope of saving the town; the utmost to be achieved was the saving of the garrison. The second in command, Colonel Fielding, not aware of the King's approach, had made a truce with the attacking party for the purpose of treating, so when the relief party appeared he was unable, in honour, to make a sally. Consequently, the Royalists were forced to retire and the town surrendered. Fielding was afterwards condemned to death by a court-martial, but Rupert persuaded the Prince of Wales to intercede with the King and he was pardoned.

Early in June, Essex, who still hesitated to attack Oxford, withdrew from Reading to Thame, his object being to protect Buckinghamshire and to intercept the Queen in her march from the north. The scattered position of his troops was a great temptation to Rupert, and Hampden, who favoured an immediate attack on Oxford, warned Essex of the danger. That the danger was real, Rupert soon proved. Hearing that a convoy was marching towards Essex with some £20,000, he determined to intercept it, marched in the night from Oxford to Tetsworth, so on to Postcombe, and at one o'clock a.m. surprised and took Chinnor before the Roundhead soldiers knew of his approach. Unfortunately the noise of the firing defeated Rupert's main object; the convoy was warned by it and made a détour. Finding that he had missed his aim the Prince retreated leisurely towards Oxford, the enemy in pursuit. Finally they attacked his troops, whereupon he secured his retreat by sending a party to hold the bridge over the Thames. Then he lined a lane leading to it with dragoons and leisurely retreated, leaving his opponents to make the attack.   When they fired upon his men, however, Rupert exclaimed, " This insolence is not to be borne," forgot his newly - acquired caution, and, jumping the hedge which separated him from the enemy, rushed upon them.   They gave way before the fiery charge, Hampden fell in the struggle, and the battle of Chalgrove Field was won.   Within a space of forty-eight hours Rupert had made a circuit of as many miles with a mixed body of cavalry and infantry, captured two outposts, fought and won a battle, captured many prisoners and horses, slain large numbers of the enemy, including their general, and all with the loss of twelve men !

Meanwhile the Royalists were so successful in the north that the Queen was able to make her way as far south as Newark, and Rupert was again commissioned to meet and escort her to Oxford.   It was essential to keep his troops between the Queen and Essex, who was bent on preventing the junction.   On 1 July Rupert reached Buckingham, and so vigilant was he that Essex was kept always on duty and his men were said to be " wearied of their lives."   The following incident is characteristic of his methods.   One morning, in the midst of shaving operations, Rupert heard a noise.   Rushing out he found his men attacked by a party of the enemy. Half-dressed as he was, he quickly charged and scattered them, then calmly returned to the completion of his toilet !

Finally, by skilful manœuvring, he gave Essex the slip and met the Queen at Stratford-on-Avon, where for a night they were guests of Shakespeare's granddaughter

at New Place. On 13 July husband and wife met at
Edgehill, and the next day entered Oxford. Within
four days Rupert had found other occupation. The
atmosphere of the Court was certainly not at this time
congenial to him. Digby had become bitterly hostile.
He had fought splendidly at Lichfield, but quarrelled with
the Prince soon after, and, whether the injury was given
or received by him, he never forgave Rupert, and unfortunately his influence with the King and Queen was
rapidly increasing. From this time he was a perpetual
thorn in Rupert's side. The King's Privy Council was
another trouble. Rupert, purely a soldier, could not
stand the interference of civilians, and more especially
the interference of those who did not wish, for political
reasons, to see the King's cause absolutely triumph.
Therefore he was always happier away from Oxford,
although his troubles contrived to follow him to the most
distant parts of the kingdom.

Rupert's next objective was Bristol. The success of
Hopton at Lansdowne and Roundway Down, which had
forced Waller to quit Bath and retire to London, left
that city open to attack. The western army under Hopton,
Hertford, and Prince Maurice was to co-operate with
Rupert. On 23 July the siege began. The Somerset-
shire side of the town was to be the work of the victors of
Roundway Down. Rupert was stationed on the Gloucestershire side. The first assault was made by the Cornishmen, but as the ground was unfavourable and the defence
there strongest, the attack was repulsed with loss.
Three days after a combined assault was planned, and
this, largely through Rupert's courage and resource, was
so far a success that his troops entered the suburbs of
the town. The Royalists believed their task far from

complete when Fiennes, the Governor, offered to surrender. Thus, within an incredibly short space of time, the second city and port in the kingdom had fallen into Royalist hands, and its possession gave them the key to the whole of South Wales as well as access to the Western Sea. For his surrender Fiennes was court-martialled by Parliament and sentenced to death, a sentence afterwards remitted. He knew it to be impossible to make a successful defence, and not being a soldier, judged it better to make a timely surrender rather than by a hopeless struggle to lose many precious lives. As the outgoing garrison left the city they were attacked by some of the Royalists, probably because they were carrying out more than the articles of surrender warranted. Fiennes himself exonerated Prince Rupert and his brother from any share in this, declaring that they did their utmost to prevent it, themselves beating back the offenders with their swords.

This success was followed by an unfortunate dispute between the Prince and Lord Hertford; indeed, the quarrel was so bitter that Charles was obliged to journey to Bristol to heal the breach. Rupert was certainly to blame in the matter; he showed himself lacking in tact, that consideration for the feelings of others which was a most necessary quality in dealing with a noble who was no soldier, indeed, but who served his King in that capacity only from a strong sense of duty.

The capture of Bristol seemed to Rupert to pave the way for that combined attack on London which was the objective of this year's campaign. Unexpected difficulties arose. Newcastle found himself both unable and unwilling to march south; his followers desired first to capture Hull. Hopton, though willing, was unable to lead his Cornish-

men out of the West Country while Plymouth remained
in the enemy's hands. Thus Rupert's strategical plan
was, for the time, abandoned, and the siege of Gloucester
undertaken. The King has been much blamed for this
decision, but the question is whether it would have been
wise to march on London leaving Gloucester unconquered
in the rear. Also, the local armies of north and west
would not bear coercion. Had the siege of Gloucester
been successful, as the Royalists quite expected it would
be, or had the King defeated Essex in a great battle
after raising the siege, his situation would have been
infinitely more favourable for either an attack on London
or negotiations for peace.

In the actual siege of Gloucester Rupert took no part,
either because he disapproved of the step, or because,
in the opinion of the King's advisers, too many lives
had been lost in the capture of Bristol. He did, however,
endeavour to prevent the advance of Essex through
Gloucestershire; but his cavalry alone were insufficient
to contest the progress of a whole army. Charles was
therefore forced to raise the siege. His retreat was only
temporary; he could not have fought before Gloucester
save at a disadvantage. On the Cotswolds he hoped to
win a complete victory, for he would be between the
enemy, already short of provisions, and London, he
himself being in easy communication with Oxford.
Essex's only hope lay in immediate victory. Rupert
therefore advised the King to postpone the fight, but to
keep well between the Roundhead army and London.
Then began a war of manœuvre, and Essex at first gained
the advantage. Making a feint of advancing north by
Worcester or Warwick he gave the Royalists the slip,
turned south, captured Cirencester, and then hurried

to gain the road leading by Hungerford and Newbury to London. Charles at once pursued and was able to gain Newbury first, where fighting at once took place. The field was hotly contested, and victory might have been to the Royalists had Rupert waited to attack the Round-heads as they filed through the narrow lanes, instead of at once attacking the reserve on Enborne Heath. The London train-bands stood firm even against Rupert's furious charge, and though finally forced to give way, the retreat was in good order. Deserted by the cavalry, the Royalists were unable to check the advance of Essex at all effectually, and, when night fell, the Roundheads had certainly gained ground. Rupert's mistake might have been retrieved on the following day, but the am-munition was exhausted, and Charles, judging discretion the better part of valour, retreated to Oxford, leaving the London road open to Essex. The Royalist losses had been severe. Falkland was slain, and three hundred men of the Prince's brigade.

With the capture of Bristol Rupert's star had reached its zenith; it now began steadily to decline. Never again was he to win the glorious victories of the earlier days. He seems to have begun to realize that peace might have to be made, and a peace wherein the King, as the losing party, must give way. In any case, when the two lords, Holland and Bedford, dissatisfied with the proceedings of Parliament, came to Oxford seeking reconciliation with the King, Rupert influenced his uncle to receive them. In this he was opposed by the Queen, who from this time, supported by Digby and Wilmot, consistently set herself against his proposals. Rupert began to find his position at Court almost unbearable. Charles still believed in his nephew, but he adored his wife, and his position, between the two, was scarcely enviable. The Prince was, however, but little at Court. Ever active, he took Bedford, recovered Cirencester, and made himself master of Newport Pagnell. This last was a most important piece of work. If held it would prevent all communication between London and the north, and would be a menace to the Eastern Association, but Essex advancing towards it in force it was abandoned in October.

During the winter months the King was conducting negotiations with the Irish, which resulted in the Cessation; Parliament with the Scotch. Up to the present, though the King had not been strong enough to take London, the advantage of the war rested with him; the coming alliance of the Scotch with Parliament was to entirely alter the balance of the two parties.

Early in 1644 the Prince was made a peer with the title of Duke of Cumberland and Earl of Holderness. He was also made President of Wales, and here he was, as usual, indefatigable. His special work was to superintend the bringing of arms, ammunition, and men from Ireland, but he also established garrisons for the King in every strong place possible, personally visiting and organizing them. The defeat of these Irish troops at Nantwich and the threatened descent of the Scotch upon the north led to fervent appeals for Rupert's presence from Newcastle, in the north from the Countess of Derby in Lancashire, and from the distressed garrison of Newark in the north-west. Newark came first. This brave little garrison had declared it could starve, or it could die, but one thing it could not do, and that was open its gates to the rebels. Early in February Rupert was in Shrewsbury collecting troops. This done, he marched by way of

Chester to Newark. The relief of Newark was accomplished on 22 March, but from lack of troops it was impossible for Rupert to march to Newcastle's assistance at once. The body that had relieved Newark had been mainly drawn from garrisons in the district, and had now to be returned. He therefore turned back to Wales to raise a fresh army. The position in the north was serious. The Fairfaxes had made themselves masters of almost the whole of Yorkshire. Newcastle's army was small, he had but little of the strategist's skill, while Lord Eythin, his military adviser, was a commander of the old methodical school. He was forced to quit Sunderland and fall back on Durham. The need for Rupert's inspiring presence was hourly felt. Just at the moment when Rupert, by superhuman efforts, had contrived to gather together an army with which to undertake the relief of the Countess of Derby, still holding out at Lathom House, and of Newcastle, by this time besieged in York, came an urgent summons of recall to Oxford.

The Royalist position, after the defeat of Cheriton, was a dangerous one. Prince Maurice was still in the west, occupied in the siege of Lyme. The King's army at Oxford was too small to encounter the allied forces of Essex and Manchester, which, he feared, would fall upon him. He therefore desired Rupert's presence and the support of his army. This would have been to leave the north at the mercy of the Scotch and the Fairfaxes; therefore the Prince hurried to Oxford to sketch out a plan of campaign. The King was to garrison strongly all the towns round Oxford, which would effectually check the plans of Essex, whose army would be unable to advance leaving so many garrisons in the rear, while the position would be too extensive to be

taken even should Manchester and Waller combine
with Essex. At the same time, Rupert and Maurice
would each be free to carry out his appointed task. With
considerable modifications this plan was adopted;
the ring of fortresses round Oxford were, however,
abandoned, consequently Essex marched on the city.
The King, nerved to make an instant decision, did the
best thing possible—he marched out of the town, leaving
only a small force behind him. He had thus set himself
free to make rapid movements in whatever direction
seemed most suitable. Essex and Waller thereupon
separated their forces. Manchester had remained in the
east, first to capture Lincoln, then to join in the siege of
York. Charles then determined to attack the two
Roundhead armies in turn, and the battle of Cropredy-
Bridge against Waller was fought on 29 June.

In the meantime Rupert had set out for the north.
On 16 May he reached Shrewsbury to join his army and
to gain, if possible, fresh recruits. His object was first,
not the relief of York, but of the brave Countess of Derby.
Not merely the Prince's chivalry conduced to this decision,
but the reflection that the relief of Lathom House would
bring Lancashire once more under the sway of the
Earl of Derby, and thus a way of retreat from Yorkshire
would be secured in case of disaster. On 25 May Stockport was seized ; then Rupert fell upon Bolton, to defend
which its commander, Rigby, drew off the besieging force
from Lathom House. Within ten days all Lancashire
was overrun. On 1 June Rupert was reinforced by a
considerable body of troops under Goring, and with very
little difficulty he captured Liverpool He then resolved
to make straight for York. On 30 June he reached
Knaresborough. There was already friction between

the different commanders in the Parliamentary camp, and the siege of York was at once raised. Some attempt was made to bar Rupert's passage to York, but the manœuvring of the royal army was superior to that of the Parliament, and the Prince crossed the Ouse and halted outside York. Newcastle was apprised of his arrival and requested to join the royal army on the next day. " Prince Rupert had done a glorious piece of work," wrote a Parliamentary soldier. " From nothing he had gathered, without money, a powerful army, and, in spite of all our three generals, he made us leave York." The besieging army had retreated to Long Marston, seven miles outside York, and were preparing to retreat to Tadcaster, when they discovered, to their great surprise and delight, that Rupert was preparing to fight. They therefore returned to Marston Moor. Many things conduced to Rupert's decision to fight, which, in the event, proved such an unwise proceeding. Already he was sore at heart ; news of the intrigues against him at Court followed him wherever he went. Moreover, he had practical proof of their success in the difficulty he experienced in getting sufficient supplies of stores and ammunition. Newcastle counselled delay,' and this was in itself almost sufficient to decide the Prince in the opposite direction. For men of Newcastle's calibre—in war—Rupert had a strong contempt, though the fact that the northern army had been raised and maintained by the Duke should have caused his opinion to be at least considered. Last, and most weighty reason of all, was the letter that Rupert had received from the King on his march to the north. Considered in the light of after events, the letter does not altogether justify Rupert's action, but it was distinctly ambiguous, and he always considered that it contained a distinct order to fight under any circumstances, for, to the end of his life, he carried it on his person.

"If York be lost," the King had written, "I shall esteem my crown little less; unless supported by your sudden march to me and a miraculous conquest in the south, before the effects of their northern power be found here. But if York be relieved, and you beat the rebels' army of both kingdoms which are before it, then I may possibly make a shift (upon the defensive) to spin out time until you come to assist me. Wherefore I command and conjure you, by the duty and affection which I know you bear me, that all new enterprises laid aside, you immediately march, according to your first intention, with all your force to the relief of York. But if that be either lost, or have freed themselves from the besiegers, or that for want of powder you cannot take that work, that you immediately march with your whole strength directly to Worcester, to assist me and my army; without which, or your having relieved York by beating the Scots, all the successes you can afterwards have must infallibly be useless unto me. You may believe that nothing but an extreme necessity could make me write thus unto you."

This letter was written before the King's success at Cropredy Bridge, but it was a most unusual thing for Charles to issue definite orders to Rupert, and it seems a probable conclusion that Digby had criticized the Prince's exploits in Lancashire, hinted that he did not mean to advance on York till York was lost, and that he was really aiming at the Crown, and so thoroughly worked upon the King that he hastily wrote this ill-constructed letter to urge instant advance on York.

That his fear was lest York should fall before Ruperto
arrival is shown by his injunction that should that city
" have freed itself from the besiegers " the Prince was to
return without waiting to fight the rebels. Why then,
having himself relieved York, did he fight? Certainly
Newcastle alone had shown himself unable to cope with
the Scotch, but Rupert might have reinforced him
with some of the troops gathered from Lancashire;
also, if Rupert had returned south or made a diversion
into the counties of the Eastern Association, Manchester
and Cromwell at least must have left the north. These
considerations, as well as those urged by Newcastle—
the want of agreement among the Parliamentary forces,
the expected reinforcements for the Royalists—Rupert
was in no mood to consider ; he was at the time incapable
of calm judgment, he dwelt only on the King's words :
" Without your having relieved York by beating the
Scots, all the successes you can afterwards have must
infallibly be useless unto me." Moreover, he had never yet
met the cavalry he could not scatter as chaff before the
wind.

The turmoil of his mind is illustrated by his disposition
of the troops. Here again the calm, clear judgment of a
great general on the eve of a momentous battle was
wanting. He arranged his battle as for an immediate
attack on the edge of a wide ditch, but when the line
was prepared it was evening, and as the surprised Lord
Eythin said, too late to fight. This delay gave the enemy
an advantage. Cromwell at least saw that, arranged
as the Royalist army was, instant attack was its only
salvation, and that attack was not being made ! The
Roundhead generals would have been mad to let such an
opportunity slip. Their army was stationed on the edge

of a slope. Baillie, with the Scotch infantry, formed the centre ; on his left were the Eastern Association cavalry, led by Cromwell, supported by Scotch dragoons and horse ; on his right were the Fairfaxes with their cavalry. Behind were the reserve of Scotch infantry and cavalry. The Royalist formation was equally simple. Lord Eythin commanded the infantry in the centre ; on his right Rupert faced Cromwell ; on the left Goring faced the Fairfaxes.

As the Royalist commanders were preparing for the night's rest which they anticipated, the enemy's horse and foot were upon them, Cromwell's horse being first across the ditch. For the first time Rupert's horse gave way before the combined efforts of Cromwell and Leslie, fleeing for their lives as they had so many times caused the enemy to flee. Rupert's flight gave Crawford his opportunity. While Baillie attacked in front Crawford was able to take the unprotected Royalist infantry in flank ; but in spite of this double attack they did not break into flight, but fought on until succour came from the right. Here Goring's cavalry had put Fairfax to flight as well as the Scotch reserve behind him. Some of Goring's troops who did not share in the pursuit turned to the support of the hardly-pressed Royalist centre, and it now looked as though it would be the Scotch who would have to give way. Moreover, Goring's cavalry would soon return from the pursuit. Leven fled, but Baillie maintained the fight until Cromwell, returning from the pursuit of Rupert, and hearing from Fairfax of the disaster of the right and that threatened to the centre, gave his powerful aid to the Scotch general. Himself meeting Goring, he sent David Leslie to deal with the Whitecoats, Newcastle's veterans in the centre;

thus Baillie's task was lightened, and he was able to
scatter the remainder of the Royalist infantry. Staunch
to the death, Newcastle's Whitecoats were cut to pieces;
scarcely any left the field alive. Thus the Parliamentary
victory was complete, and it was due to Cromwell's
defeat of Rupert. Had the Prince been successful, the
battle would have been won all along the line, the north
would have been the King's, and the balance of the war
again turned decidedly in his favour.

" Sayes General King, ' What will you do ? ' Sayes ye
Prince, ' I will rally my men ! ' Sayes General King,
' Nowe what will you, Lord Newcastle, do ? ' Sayes
Lord Newcastle, ' I will go into Holland ! ' " Each was
as good as his word. Newcastle left the country, the
Prince departed to put such order into the affairs of the
north as he could, and to gather together the remnants
of the defeated army, and with it march south as speedily
as might be. Besides the pain of defeat, Rupert had to
bear the pain of loss—his dog " Boy," his faithful companion since the days of his imprisonment in Germany,
was killed in the battle. Rupert's star had declined;
never again would his name strike such terror into the
hearts of the enemy as it was wont to do—never again
would the serene self-confidence of his boyhood and
young manhood, which had been such an element in his
success, be his. From this time on the conviction of
ultimate failure for the cause which he had made his own
became stronger in his mind. The Prince left York
with about six thousand men, and moving south through
Lancashire, the way of retreat he had prepared, he
reached Shrewsbury about 20 July, having left Goring
in the north as Newcastle's successor.

During August and September the Prince occupied

himself in gathering recruits, waiting for ammunition from Ireland, and discharging his duties as President of Wales. At the end of September he joined the King at Sherborne on his return from his successful encounter with Essex at Lostwithiel. Here it was arranged that Rupert should set the defences of Bristol in order, and then return to the King. This was done, but the Prince did not arrive in time to prevent the second battle of Newbury. The winter he spent partly at Bristol, partly at Oxford with the King, who had returned there in November. He was made Commander-in-Chief in place of Lord Brentford, an able soldier, but now grown old and deaf. Prince Maurice replaced his brother as President of Wales, but the exchange was not fortunate. The Prince was disappointed that the Treaty of Uxbridge came to nothing—he realized, perhaps better than anyone save the King himself, how hopeless the Royalist position was, in spite of the victories of Montrose, in face of the growing power of Cromwell.

Early in the spring of 1645, Rupert was again recruiting in Wales in preparation for the King's last campaign. The war had become much more bitter. To the Roundheads every Irishman was a Papist and a foreigner, and as such to be exterminated without mercy. The brutal order had been given by Parliament that every Irish prisoner was to be hanged out of hand. After the capture of Shrewsbury, which was surprised by the Roundheads in February, thirteen Irish prisoners were accordingly hanged. The Prince soon put an end to this inhumanity. Of his next batch of prisoners he caused thirteen to be hanged, and sent a message to the enemy that in future for every one Royalist prisoner hanged two Roundheads should suffer. The lesson would seem to have been a sufficient one. The Prince's object at this time was the relief of Chester, but this he was unable to accomplish, though Beeston Castle was relieved. In May, he was summoned to Oxford by the King. The Royalist army then only numbered eleven thousand men, so Goring, who since Marston Moor had been high in favour, and was then in the west, which he was fast detaching from the Royalist cause by his carelessness and insubordination, was ordered to join the King's main army in preparation for the new campaign. The Royalist advance out of Oxford had already been checked once by Cromwell, who had deprived them of their supply of draught horses. On 7 May, the King was at last ready to leave Oxford. A Council was held at Stow-in-the-Wold, and here the proposed plans were debated. It was necessary to support the besieging force at Taunton, to prevent a union between Fairfax and the Scotch, to relieve Chester, to recapture Yorkshire. Two plans were put forward. That the King should first march west with Goring, thus securing Taunton and keeping Fairfax occupied. The other that he should march to the north, relieve Chester and beat the Scotch before Fairfax could join them and while they were still weak in numbers, part of their forces having been detached to oppose Montrose. The latter plan was favoured by Rupert and the Northern horse, now with the King's main army and commanded by Sir Marmaduke Langdale—the former by Digby and the civilians generally. Both plans had one weak point— Oxford, the base of operations, was left open to attack and would be utterly unable to stand a prolonged siege. Unfortunately the King tried to follow both plans, and it was decided to send Goring, with full powers, to the west to withstand Fairfax, now believed to be marching

on Taunton. His orders were to prevent the relief of
Taunton and then return to the King with all speed.
Unfortunately, Goring had attained his desire, supreme
command in the west, and had no wish to capture Taunton,
and by joining the King become merely a subordinate
again. The King meanwhile proceeded north with the
main army. The first-fruits of this northern march were
soon seen. Brereton promptly raised the siege of Chester, ·
and this changed the King's immediate objective ; he
abandoned his march on Chester and turned towards
Leicester, which he captured on 27 May. News was
now brought that Fairfax, having relieved Taunton,
was beleaguering Oxford, and it was hotly debated
whether the King should go on his way, or turn and
relieve Oxford. It was decided to return, but very soon
it became known that Oxford was in no danger, Fairfax
having retired, and the northward march was resumed.
The objective was not, however, decided. Digby advised
an attack on the eastern counties, Rupert held firm to
his original plan. Unfortunately he did not keep such
a watch on the enemy's movements as was essential.
None of the Royalists seem to have even surmised
Fairfax's intentions when he left Oxford, and from the
first Rupert had expressed contempt for the New Model
Army. Thus Fairfax, now joined by Cromwell, was able
to advance within eight miles of Daventry, the King's
head-quarters, without arousing the slightest suspicion
of his proximity among the Royalists. When his presence
was at last discovered it was decided to persist in the
northern march, but at Lubenham the King learned that
the enemy was too close for battle to be avoided. Rupert
still counselled retreat, reinforcements, he urged, could
be obtained at Leicester and Newark, it would give

Goring a chance to come up. This counsel was overruled, it was decided to draw the army up a long hill
running south of Harborough.

Astley, in command of the foot, intended that the
battle should be fought here, for an army acting on the
defensive it was an excellent situation. The King's
sole chance of victory lay in acting on the defensive, for
in numbers his army was far inferior to the enemy.
When joined by Cromwell, Fairfax commanded an army
of at least 13,600 men, Charles could not muster eight
thousand. It was due to Rupert that this advantage of
position was lost. With a party of musketeers he rode
out to discover the position of the enemy and found them,
as he thought, in full retreat. That which he thus mistook
for retreat was a movement of the Roundhead army from
one of the lower ridges to the top of the Naseby plateau,
and had been ordered by Cromwell as it afforded a better
position   Rupert at once ordered the Royalist army to
take up its position on an eminence called Dust Hill,
facing the plateau. The Prince was thus stationed on the
right wing facing Ireton, Astley with the foot faced Skip-
pon, Sir Marmaduke Langdale faced Cromwell's Ironsides.
Rupert as usual began the fight, and, as so often before,
drove Ireton's horse before him, and as before he pursued
too far, though on the day of Naseby he did not wait
to plunder the baggage, but returned to the field. His
return was too late. Cromwell on his side had driven
the discouraged northern horse before him, but detained
a large part of his force from the pursuit to support the
Parliamentary infantry. The fight in the centre was most
hotly contested, and had Rupert returned in time to
support the Royalist foot, victory might still have been
to the King. Unfortunately it was Cromwell who left

nothing to chance, and who put fresh courage into the flagging Roundhead foot. Even then all was not lost. Charles called upon the reserve to attack and would himself have led them to the charge, but the Earl of Carnwath interposed at the critical moment and the opportunity was lost. The reserve turned and fled, carrying the King with them. Thus unprotected, the infantry had no chance against overpowering numbers. Rupert returned to the field to find a defeated army which it was impossible to rally, and in time only to join in the retreat to Leicester. Naseby was decisive. The King was never again able to put a complete army in the field, for even could he have collected and armed the men, it would have been impossible to officer them, no less than five hundred officers having fallen into the victor's hands at Naseby.

From Leicester Charles himself went to Raglan, Rupert to Bristol. From Wales the King hoped to reach Montrose, but was foiled by the Scottish army, which effectually barred his way. The victory of Kilsyth inspired him to raise the siege of Hereford, which was surrounded by the Scotch, and in this he was successful. The end of August found him again in Oxford. During this period Rupert was using all his influence to induce the King to make peace. As a soldier the Prince saw that the King's cause was absolutely hopeless; he was depending solely on isolated fortresses with no army in the field. His efforts after peace, however, were entirely futile. He wrote to the Duke of Richmond, one of his few friends at Court: " His Majesty hath now no way left to preserve his posterity, kingdom, and nobility but by treaty. I believe it a mere prudent way to retain something than to lose all." Charles'

13

reply was uncompromising, though Rupert found it incomprehensible. " As for your opinion of my business, and your counsel thereupon, if I had any other quarrel but the defence of my religion, crown, and friends, you had full reason for your advice ; for I confess that, speaking as a mere soldier or statesman, I must say there is no probability but of my ruin ; yet, as a Christian, I must tell you that God will not suffer rebels and traitors to prosper, nor this cause to be overthrown ; and whatever personal punishment it shall please Him to inflict upon me must not make me repine, much less give over this quarrel ; and there is as little question that a composition with them at this time is nothing else but a submission, which, by the Grace of God, I am resolved against, whatever it cost me, for I know my obligation to be, both in conscience and honour, neither to abandon God's cause, injure my successors, nor forsake my friends. Indeed, I cannot flatter myself with expectation of good success more than this, to end my days with honour and a good conscience, which obliges me to continue my endeavours, as not despairing that God may yet, in due time, avenge His own cause—tho' I must aver to all my friends that he that will stay with me at this time must expect and resolve either to die for a good cause or, which is worse, to live as miserable in maintaining it as the violence of insulting rebels can make him. I desire you earnestly not in any case to hearken after treaties, assuring you, low as I am, I will not go less than what was offered in my name at Uxbridge."

At Bristol the Prince had occupied himself in storing provisions and making the fortifications as secure as possible, in fact, he promised the King that the town could be held for four months. He was soon to be called upon to make good that promise, for Fairfax had captured Bath and Sherborne. The importance of Bristol to the Royalists cannot be overestimated; if it were taken, in the present position of the King's affairs, the reduction of the whole of the west must almost inevitably follow. On 1 September Fairfax summoned Rupert to surrender, and before three weeks had passed, on the first serious assault, the Prince consented to make terms. It was little wonder that Charles was filled with anger and dismay at the news. It seemed to confirm the accusations of Digby, which, although repudiated by the King, had doubtless unconsciously impressed him. Nevertheless, to military men the surrender could not have been a surprise. The city was utterly unable to stand a protracted siege, and no relief seemed near. The fortifications were weak and so widely scattered that the small garrison was insufficient to defend them. The castle might indeed have been held by a stubborn general, but it would have entailed great loss of life, and innocent citizens would have suffered, all to no purpose. The Puritan Colonel Butler, writing to the Parliament, testified : " On my word he could not have held it, unless it had been better manned."

At Oxford, whence the King had set out to attempt the relief of Chester, Rupert found a letter from the King dismissing him from all his offices and bidding him seek employment beyond the sea. Of all the wounds Charles was called upon to suffer, this defection of Rupert's, as he regarded it, seems to have hurt him most, probably because the blow was to love and trust. What Charles did in thus dismissing the Prince unheard, and also in his subsequent arrest of William Legge, Governor of Oxford, Rupert's friend, was harsh and unjustifiable, yet his own words show how deeply he was hurt. " Nephew," he wrote, " though the loss of Bristol be a great blow to me, yet your surrendering it as you did is of so much affliction to me that it makes me not only forget the consideration of that place, but is likewise the greatest trial of my constancy that hath yet befallen me ; for what is to be done, after one that is so near to me as you are, both in blood and friendship, submits himself to so mean an action ? " To his son Charles sent a message : " Tell my son that I shall less grieve he is knocked on the head than that he should do so mean an action as is the rendering of Bristol Castle upon the terms it was."

Rupert refused to leave his uncle's service until he had been heard in his own defence, and cut his way through to Newark, whither the King had repaired after his failure at Rowton Heath. Here a council of war was held, and Rupert was exonerated from any cowardice or dereliction of duty in the surrender of Bristol. Unhappily, the cloud between the King and his nephew was not thus easily dispersed. When Charles, having decided to leave Newark for Oxford before the Roundhead officers, Poyntz and Rossiter, should be upon him, announced his intention of taking Willis, then Governor of Newark, and a personal friend of Rupert's, with him, the storm broke. Willis, with Prince Rupert and Gerard, demanded a personal explanation from the King. All three lost control of themselves, forgot the respect due to their sovereign, and accused him of being led by Digby in all things. Charles was very angry and refused to give them any satisfaction. Rupert, with Maurice, then rode to Belvoir Castle, whence they endeavoured to obtain a safe-conduct from Parliament wtih permission to leave the country. As they could not gain this without binding themselves never to take arms against the Parliament, Rupert at last, on the advice of Legge and other friends, humbled himself to ask the King's forgiveness. A complete reconciliation followed, and the Prince remained at Oxford until Charles left it for the Scottish army. He even offered to accompany his uncle there, but Charles declined on the ground that Rupert would be easily identified owing to " his tallness." On the surrender of Oxford special terms were granted to the two Princes, who were now allowed to betake themselves beyond the seas. In Digby's baggage, taken at Sherborne, had been found a copy of the King's letter to Rupert, answering his advice to make peace—and this did much to gain the safe-conduct for the Princes. On 4 July, 1646, the two brothers sailed from Dover, Rupert for Calais, Maurice for the Hague.

At the French Court Rupert received a warm welcome. The King had shown the completeness of his reconciliation in the letter which he wrote to the Queen : " If thou see Rupert tell him that I have recommended him unto thee. For albeit his passions may sometimes make him mistake, yet I am confident of his honest constancy and courage, having at the last behaved himself very well." The French king gave him command of all the English in France, and, when he had received Charles' permission, he fought on the French side in the Netherlands against the Spanish, where he, as usual, distinguished himself, though his wonted luck in battle deserted him, for he was struck on the head by a bullet and invalided home.

Early in 1648 there was a strong Royalist reaction in England, and part of the fleet revolted. This was put under command of Rupert, but, as the ships were only seven in number, badly fitted out and provisioned, while the loyalty of their commanders was open to question, he was not able to effect much against Warwick and Blake, leaders of the Parliament's fleet. At first, while the second Civil War was in progress, he hung about the English coast, taking a few prizes but unable to accomplish anything effectual. On returning to the Hague there was some difference of opinion as to whether the ships should proceed to Scotland to co-operate with Montrose, or to Ireland to assist Ormond. The latter course was decided upon, and in November Rupert was able to elude Warwick and reached Kinsale early in January. His fleet was not large enough to block up Dublin Harbour, and he was chiefly occupied in making prizes of English merchant vessels to supply the Royalists in France with the means of existence. Finally, he was forced to leave Kinsale, as the Parliamentary fleet was on its way to block the harbour. He now heard of his uncle's execution, and issued a solemn declaration of his intention to fight Parliament as long as he lived.

Owing to lack of men, Rupert was obliged to abandon four of his seven ships, and for three years he sailed the seas with three vessels, capturing prizes whenever possible, English, Spanish, in fact ships of any country favourable to the Parliament. Maurice accompanied him on his buccaneering expedition, the object of which was to obtain money to support his cousin and his court. In fact, Charles II was almost entirely dependent, during this period, on the success of Rupert's voyages. At last the two Princes determined to visit the West Indies, only to find, when at last they arrived there after months of perilous adventure, that the islands had declared for the Parliament. A great storm fell upon the crazy ships while they were in this neighbourhood, and though Rupert escaped, Maurice and his ship were never seen again. This was a great blow to Rupert. Maurice had been his favourite brother, and when he returned with his single remaining vessel to France he was a different man; physically and mentally, he had suffered too much for his temperament ever to regain its former poise. Exile is an evil school; it made Charles II selfish and self-indulgent, his vices had grown up as in a hot-house, his virtues were stifled. Rupert, on the other hand, was hardened and embittered by his experiences. He hid his ideals now under a veil of cynicism and indifference. That they still existed may be proved by a comparison of his life with that of Charles II and those of his Court.

For when Charles was restored, in 1660, Rupert, as a matter of course, accompanied him. His mother too spent her last few months of life in peaceful happiness in the home of her girlhood. The Court of Charles, now Elector Palatine, could be no home for either Rupert or his mother. After his return to England Rupert devoted his time to the study of science, to which he had always been much attached. In 1662 he became a member of the Royal Society, an honour richly deserved, seeing that he had, among other things, invented a new and improved kind of gunpowder. To him England also owes the introduction of the mezzotint; the process had been revealed to him by a German soldier, and would probably never have become known to the world but for Rupert's interest in the invention. The King made his cousin a member of the Privy Council and Governor of Windsor Castle. Most of his time was spent in his laboratory there, for the frivolity of the Court was utterly uncongenial to his soldier's nature.

In the wars with the Dutch Rupert held high command. With Albemarle he was Admiral of the Fleet, and gained many enemies by his exposure of the peculations of those Commissioners responsible for fitting out the Navy. In 1672, after the second war with the Dutch, he became exceedingly popular owing to his dislike of the French. He even joined Shaftesbury in opposing any friendship with that country. In spite of this association, no breath of suspicion ever touched him; he was never accused of disloyalty, he had no part or lot in Popish Plots or Exclusion Bill. From this time he took no active part in politics, but spent his time in study and sport. He had a house in London, but lived for the most part in Windsor, where he was greatly beloved for his generosity and genial friendly nature. He had been given a pension of four thousand pounds in 1660, and, being much interested in trade, he probably increased his income from that source. He was the first governor of the Hudson's Bay Company; a part of Manitoba is still known as Rupert's land. His latter years must have been lonely; Will Legge and other friends had died, Ormond was in Ireland—at Court Rupert made no friends. He died on 29 November, 1682, of fever. He had been for some years something of an invalid, the wound in his head had caused him much trouble. He left two children; a son, Dudley, who was killed at the siege of Breda, in 1686, whose mother was Frances, daughter of Henry Bard, Viscount Bellarmont. She always claimed to be Rupert's legal wife, and was received as such by his sister Sophie, but there is no record of any marriage. Ruperta, his daughter, was left to the guardianship of Lord Craven. Her mother was the actress, Margaret Hughes, to whom Rupert became attached during the later years of his life. Ruperta afterwards married Emmanuel Scroope Howe, brother of Viscount Hood.

The life of Prince Rupert may be accounted a failure, if we compare what he actually achieved with the bright promise of his youth; it may, indeed, be claimed that the cause of Charles I benefited no whit from his championship. It is, however, given to but few in this world to gain the end at which they aim. Rupert at least pursued that aim, through evil report and good report, with a singleness of purpose which is not without its heroic side when we remember the impetuosity of his character. He was prepared loyally to suffer whatever extremity of evil fortune should design for him. On the other hand, it must be borne in mind that the success of his cause would bring but little worldly gain to him; no throne awaited him, even high office in England was hardly to be anticipated; also he had not the motive of the patriot. England was not his fatherland, to be saved from the revolutionary designs of a few. In those stormy days Rupert might have used his sword to carve out a future for himself; he chose rather to devote his life to the service of Charles I from feelings of personal gratitude, affection, and loyalty. His reward was calumny and bitter invective, which exert their influence even to the present day, years of dreary wandering, the hostility of the many, the love of a few, a lonely if peaceful old age. In the end Rupert saw the triumph of the cause for which he had fought, but it did not come about through his efforts, and he saw the Court, which under Charles I had been the glory, now under his son, become the shame of England. He might well have been bitter, but time softened those harder features of his character which exile had fostered, for Campbell, writing from hearsay of Rupert's last years, said: " In respect of his private life he was so just, so beneficent, so courteous, that his memory remained dear to all who knew him ; this I say of my own knowledge, having often heard old people in Berkshire speak of him."

LUCIUS CARY, SECOND VISCOUNT FALKLAND
AFTER THE PORTRAIT BY VAN DYCK AT WARDOUR CASTLE

·A CHAMPION OF THE CONSTITUTION

LUCIUS CARY, VISCOUNT FALKLAND

FALKLAND lives for all time in the pages of Clarendon. Indeed, it may well be thought that the historian of the Civil War said the last word concerning that friend whom he so worthily commemorated. Nevertheless, no list of the King's supporters would be complete without him, for just as Rupert typifies the soldier, Newcastle the courtier, and Montrose the pure loyalist, so Falkland is the representative of that body of men who followed the fortunes of the King from a strong sense of duty. He and they felt that peace was the end, above all others, to be pursued—by fighting at first, if need be—but the sword to give place to arbitration at the first opportunity. In the unfortunate position of seeing clearly the strength of the arguments urged on either side, Falkland could not find happiness in devotion to a cause as could Hopton and others like him. Nevertheless, he believed constitutional government to be bound up with royalty; so, tortured by doubt and indecision, he yet held fast to duty, which alone bound him to the King, and at last gave his life for a cause whose strength had not enabled him to blind his eyes to the inevitable consequences of its failure or its victory. He dreaded both alike: failure, which would destroy the constitution of Church and State; victory, which he believed would give the King that despotic power which, in his early Parliamentarian days, he had opposed with patriotic fervour.

Born in 1610, Lucius Cary was the eldest son of Henry Cary of Berkhamsted and Aldenham, in Hertfordshire, a descendant of the Carys of Cockington, in Devonshire. His mother was Elizabeth, daughter of Sir Lawrence Tanfield, Chief Baron of the Exchequer. When Lucius was ten years of age James I created his father Viscount Falkland, of the county of Fife, in Scotland, and two years later he was made Lord Deputy of Ireland. Thus Lucius became a student of Trinity College, Dublin, and the religious bent of his mind was probably determined by his education there. It certainly counteracted the influence of his mother, who had become a Roman Catholic, for he, almost alone of her children, refused to follow her lead in that direction. Later he probably studied at Oxford. When only nineteen he succeeded to his grandfather's estates, the manor of Great Tew, with the priory, rectory, and demesnes of Burford, in Oxfordshire. At this period he seems to have been ambitious of a military career and to have obtained command of a company, for it is recorded that the command being transferred by the King's order to Sir Francis Willoughby, the young Cary challenged his rival to a duel. The result was ten days' imprisonment in the Fleet, from which he was released on his father's intercession.

The literary proclivities of this friend of poets had already shown themselves, and to literature he probably now turned for solace in his disappointment. He had the friendship of Ben Jonson, Suckling, Carew, and others of that merry band whom we now characterize as the

" Cavalier Poets." At the age of twenty-one he fell in love with and married the sister of a friend, Lettice, the daughter of Sir Richard Morison, of Tooley Park, in Leicestershire. As the lady was portionless Lucius incurred the anger of his father, who had hoped for a marriage from which more worldly advantage would have accrued. As a consequence of this quarrel he set out for Holland to seek military employment, but no opportunity of advancement arising, he returned to his home at Great Tew, there to resume his poetical and theological studies.

In 1633 his father died and he succeeded to the title. His wealth was not thereby increased, as the paternal estate was heavily mortgaged. He was, at about the same time, made one of the gentlemen of the Privy Chamber to Charles I, but his life was spent practically in retirement. These years between his marriage and the outbreak of civil war were probably the happiest of his life. He was rich enough to be able to enjoy the society of his friends and to do them kindnesses ; he had abundant leisure to devote to the study of the Fathers and to theology in general. The poet friends of his youth gradually gave place to more serious members of the University, who came to Tew not only for rest of body, but for refreshment of mind by contact with Falkland's intellect and wit. The friendship of Chillingworth, Sheldon, and other divines dates to the later years of this period. Though the poets were still welcomed and their company and conversation enjoyed, the growing seriousness of Falkland's mind found more pleasure in association with men of " like mind." Suckling in his " Session of the Poets " notes this change in the literary tastes of his friend :—

" But he was of late so gone with divinity
   That he had almost forgot his poetry,
   Tho' to say the truth, and Apollo did know it,
   He might have been both his priest and his poet."

The expedition against the Scotch in 1639 apparently revived his love of a military profession. At any rate, he took part in it, and his attitude in the Short and Long Parliaments towards the questions involved would effectually forbid the conclusion that he joined in the expedition from sympathy with its object. The affection still felt for him by the poets, his youthful friends, is shown in Cowley's poem written on this occasion :—

" Great is thy charge, O North.   Be wise and just:
   England commits her Falkland to thy trust."

In 1640 Falkland was returned to the Short Parliament as a member for Newport, Isle of Wight. The happy days of irresponsibility were over, the cares of state in a period of unwonted stress were in the future to press heavily on his shoulders. His artistic temperament with its yearning after the ideal, his philosophical training which had taught him ever to balance the good and evil on both sides, unfitted him for the conflict. At first his sympathies were entirely with the popular leaders. And this was natural, for in the Short Parliament that cause showed at its best. Moreover, owing to the circumstances of his youth, he had some prejudice towards the King and Court. Clarendon vividly describes the impression made on Falkland by his first Parliament: " From the debates, which were there managed with all imaginable gravity and sobriety, he contracted such a reverence for Parliaments, that he thought it really impossible they could ever produce mischief or inconvenience to the kingdom, or that the kingdom could be tolerably happy in the intermission of them. And from the unhappy and unreasonable dissolution of that Convention he harboured, it may be, some jealousy and prejudice to the Court, towards which he was not before immoderately inclined."

Thus in the Long Parliament Falkland definitely ranged himself on the popular side. In the integrity of the leaders of that party he had a most fervent belief, and with many of their aspirations he most cordially sympathized. Thus, though a lover of the Church, he was no lover of the Bishops, and so, thinking the attacks made on their lordships to be made solely in the interests of the Church, he at first approved the policy of depriving them of their seats in the House of Lords. In this he found himself in public opposition to his friend Hyde, who had a deeper insight into the aims of the Bishops' avowed enemies. Again, he believed Strafford to be dangerous to the peace of the kingdom, but in his speech on the question of the Impeachment—the first occasion on which he addressed the House—Falkland urged that a Committee should be appointed to investigate the charges brought against him, before an Impeachment was voted. He also spoke against Ship-money as being an unlawful stretching of the King's prerogative.

Six months elapsed and Falkland's attitude had changed. In October, 1623, the second Bill for depriving the Bishops of their votes was brought into the House. Falkland now opposed it. In the interval the Root and Branch Bill had been promulgated, and Hyde must have had many opportunities of convincing his friend of the true aims of the popular leaders. Not the welfare and reformation of the Church was intended, but the sweeping it away. Thus in his speech concerning Episcopacy we find Falkland urging that, " since the greatest danger of mutations is that all the dangers and inconveniences they may bring are not to be foreseen ; and since no wise man will undergo great danger but from great necessity, my opinion is that we should not root up this ancient tree, as dead as it appears, till we have tried, whether by this or the like lopping of the branches, the sap which was unable to feed the whole may not serve to make what is left both grow and flourish."

Falkland may have been influenced in his action in drawing back from the popular party by the knowledge of the Grand Remonstrance which was then in preparation. He certainly spoke against it. Thus by the end of 1641 Falkland had definitely thrown in his lot with Hyde and those patriots who stood for the ancient Constitution in Church and State, against the Extremists who desired the overthrow of the one and a radical weakening of the other.

When the King returned from his untimely visit to Scotland, on 25 November, 1641, he found a Royalist party formed out of the Ecclesiastical one he had left. To increase the reaction in his favour caused by the publication of the Grand Remonstrance, he was urged to choose Ministers from among the Constitutional party, and his choice fell upon Hyde, Falkland, and Culpeper. At first Falkland held back : he had no personal love for the King ; he had a great dislike for the Court party, especially for those who surrounded the Queen ; he was distrustful of his own powers. Moreover, he was sensitive and dreaded lest his abandonment of the popular party should be ascribed to a desire for office. Eventually, however, he yielded to the urgent representations of Hyde, and in the vain hope that he might be able to reconcile the contending parties, he accepted office as Secretary of State. Culpeper was made Chancellor of the Exchequer; while Hyde, for the moment, refused office, believing that he could render the King more effectual service if he were not actually one of his Ministers. The three friends met constantly at Hyde's house, for Charles had promised to do nothing without consulting them, and the historian pays a great tribute to his friend, saying that he and Culpeper would often have differed violently, being that they were both hot-tempered, but that Falkland kept the peace.

Had Charles kept the promise made to the three friends, it is possible that, even at this eleventh hour, civil war might have been averted. Unfortunately, when the reaction in his favour was at its height, he was led into the rash attempt to seize the five members, of which the three knew nothing, and thus all the ground that had been won during the last two months by the violence of his opponents and his own regard for legality was lost.

From this time to the actual outbreak of war Falkland's hope of conciliating parties must have grown fainter. Opinions grew ever more irreconcilable. The attempted arrest of the five members was followed by outbreaks of violence in London. The King's adjournment to Hampton Court, the demand by Parliament of the control of the Militia, the Parliamentary condemnation of the Kentish petition in favour of the Church and against the Militia Ordinance, the presentation of the Nineteen Propositions which would have transferred the entire sovereignty from the King to Parliament, the refusal of Hull to admit their King within its walls—all these events followed one another in rapid succession. They formed the subject of remonstrances and answers between King and Parliament, a " paper war " which filled the months with activity for Hyde, Falkland, and Culpeper—to whose lot it fell to compile the King's share of these wordy documents.

From the first Hyde had been with the King at York. Falkland and Culpeper soon joined him. The matter had now gone beyond the arbitrament of the pen; even Falkland was forced to acknowledge that the sword must intervene, that a show of force must be made. His reluctant conversion to this point of view is illustrated by the fact that he contributed twenty horses for three months to the support of the King. Yet to the last he strove for peace. On the advice of his counsellors, the King sent an overture for a treaty to his Parliament, a second and a third before Nottingham was left, but all were rejected save on terms impossible of acceptance. Falkland was himself entrusted with the delivery of the King's final overture to the Houses of Parliament. It was to the effect that both sides should withdraw the accusations of treason which each had brought against the followers of the other, and that he, the King, would then take down his standard and would agree to a " thorough reformation of religion." The only conditions on which the Commons would consent to treat were that the King should forsake all those whom Parliament had already declared or should in the future declare to be delinquents ! The knowledge of this did much to increase the King's army, which now rapidly filled. War was inevitable. In September, melancholy answer to Falkland's striving for peace, he was expelled from the House of Commons.

From the moment of the actual outbreak of war Falkland seems to have changed. His was probably

never a very optimistic or joyous nature. His love for
deep theological studies, his learned conversations,
entertaining and stimulating though they were to those
whose interests resembled his own, are proofs of this.
Nevertheless he had been a quietly cheerful man, with
a fund of humour all his own, or the poets of the
time would not have sought his society. Now the whole
face of the world was changed for him. The issues at
stake between King and Parliament, instead of being
debated with that calm reason and sober judgment which,
Falkland had felt, could not fail to produce a basis of
agreement, were to be left to the decision of the sword.
War would probably mean the victory of one or other
extreme, not what he desired—a compromise, in which
the best on both sides would be welded together, the
evil or the unnecessary be cast aside as dangerous and
cumbersome. In whichever direction he gazed disaster
for his most cherished ideals seemed certain, hence day
by day his melancholy increased. It is small wonder that
the purely military party, led by Prince Rupert, was
obnoxious to and utterly misunderstood by him, just
as the position of Falkland was absolutely incomprehensible to the soldiers. To strike for victory and the
recovery of the King's prerogative was the aim of the
soldier ; to strike for victory merely as a vantage-ground
from which to propose terms of peace the aim of the
councillor. To the mind of the latter the absolute victory
of the King would have been almost as disastrous as
the victory of Parliament ; the former would mean the
absolute supremacy of the King and the dominance of
Bishops, the latter the absolute supremacy of one section
of the Parliament and the domination of Puritanism.

Falkland represented that body of opinion in England

which desired that the King should rule with the advice of his Parliament, that is, of the gentlemen of England, but who had no desire to see his prerogatives curtailed, no wish for important social changes. In Church matters he and they believed the government of the Church by Bishops to be a convenient and ancient form, but not at all of the *esse* of the Church; they had opposed the teaching of Laud with might and main. On the other hand, they disliked Puritanism because of its narrowness and intolerance, its determined suppression of independence of thought, judgment, and action. In the Church, as they would have liked it to be, practically all forms of dogmatic opinion would be tolerated.

That civil war would secure the triumph of such opinions as these was unthinkable. Falkland's growing melancholy, his instance in efforts for peace, is thus explained, as is also his eagerness in the fray when fighting was toward. Victory in the field would mean overtures for peace; in the excitement of battle harassing doubts were stifled; by overmuch display of zeal he could silence those who otherwise would hint that his continually expressed longing for peace arose from lack of personal courage.

Falkland, being Secretary of State, naturally held no high command in the army; thus his actual share in the battles was confined to serving more or less as a volunteer. As Secretary of State he had a high conception of the dignity of his office, and this was shown by his rebuke to Prince Rupert, who, having refused to receive a message from the King through his Secretary, was told: " In neglecting me you neglect the King." Between Charles and his Secretary there was no great personal sympathy. Charles was cultured and deeply religious — both his culture and his love for religion took a different direction from those of Falkland. He loved art rather than literature ; his religion was experimental rather than philosophical. Their ideas on Church government were fundamentally opposed. Charles certainly held Bishops to be *jure divino ;* the Church and her divinely appointed order must be preserved together with those prerogatives he had received from his predecessors, and which he felt it a sacred duty to hand on intact to his successors. To save his own life he would betray neither, though to save the one he might be tempted to compromise on the other.

It was this attitude to religion that accounts for the fact that Charles could hold to his faith when all hope of victory had departed, when death for himself was certain. He had fought his fight ; the immediate issue he was content to leave in God's hands, confident that his cause, which to him was God's cause, would eventually triumph, certain that the future of his country was assured, black as the future must have looked from the human point of view. Falkland, no more melancholic in temperament than Charles, lacked this vital faith—perhaps breadth of view does not make for intensity of conviction—therefore he welcomed death, which, he believed, would hide from him the downfall of his country.

In spite of this vital difference on religion, which would be an effectual bar to sympathy between the two men, since neither understood the position of the other, Charles held his Secretary in great esteem, as a man of undoubted loyalty and absolutely devoid of self-seeking.

The three friends and advisers of the King, Hyde, Falkland, and Culpeper, were with the Royal army on its march towards London ; thus Falkland came to take part in the battle of Edgehill. They were all three quartered with the General, the Earl of Lindsey, at Culworth, but on reaching the scene of action Hyde was bidden to take charge of the Prince of Wales and the Duke of York during the engagement. Falkland and Culpeper both took part in the battle, Culpeper fighting under Rupert on the right wing, Falkland with Wilmot on the left, " who," says Clarendon, " in all such actions forgot that he was Secretary of State, and desired to be where there would probably he most to do." The King's cavalry on both wings got the advantage, but the foot were beaten. Therefore Falkland urged Wilmot, on return from the pursuit, to attack the enemy's reserve of horse, led by Sir William Balfour, in order to render their victory decisive; but he was so confident that the day was the King's that he replied, " My lord, we have got the day, let us live to enjoy the fruits thereof." Whether such an attack as Falkland desired would have swept the enemy from the field may be doubted, considering that Rupert did not think it wise to renew the conflict. The battle therefore remained indecisive. The King secured his road to London, but he had not put Essex to flight.

At the time of the advance on London the futile negotiations for a treaty were conducted by Falkland, who also issued the declaration explaining the King's advance on Brentford. At Oxford, in the early spring (1643), negotiations for peace again occupied the thoughts of the King's Council, of whom Falkland was one of the chief members. Though an absolute deadlock was the only result, each side holding firmly to its proffered terms, which were absolutely incompatible, we can well imagine how Falkland strove to prevent the breaking off of negotiations. The King would not be likely to recede from his terms when his arms were victorious in the west and affairs in the north were making favourable progress. Moreover, the Queen landed in England in February, and her influence was all against peace.

Through the spring and summer the King's cause steadily gained ground. In the west the successes of Hopton culminated in the combined attack on Bristol, which yielded to Rupert's forces and the western army in July. In the north Newcastle had effectually broken the power of the Fairfaxes by the victory of Adwalton Moor. Disaster was, however, imminent. The plan of campaign for the year—the acting from the circumference on the centre—had perforce to be abandoned. Newcastle sat down before Hull, the King before Gloucester. The failure of these two sieges meant for the time the failure of the King's plans.

Falkland was present at the siege of Gloucester, and it was now that his friends began most clearly to see the great change that the war had wrought in him. His high hopes of ending the war at an early stage—by successful negotiations or by a striking victory—had by this time vanished. He realized that the war was not to be speedily brought to a close—the forces arrayed on either side were too evenly matched for that. Also the war had inflamed the passions of the opposing parties. If anything, opinions were more irreconcilable now than in the opening days of the struggle. The forces making for peace grew daily weaker.

In the day Falkland threw himself with despairing ardour into the work of the siege. So careless was he of his person that Hyde more than once wrote to him urging caution, that it was not the business of a Secretary of State to be found in the posts of greatest danger. It was in action that Falkland drowned thought. The nights he passed in theological discussions with his friend Chillingworth, who tried to bring his unusual knowledge to bear on the affairs of the siege. He " had exchanged his pen for a sword and his academical habit for a military cloak, and came down from Oxford to superintend the construction of the machines which were framing with all possible dispatch in the quarters of the Earl of Forth by Lanthony. They seem to have been but just completed when the siege was raised, and they fell into the enemies' hands. The men of Gloucester derided them as ' imperfect and troublesome,' and abused the contriver of them ; but had they been brought into action and employed with skill and resolution, there is still room for doubt whether they might not have been found more formidable than they appeared."

Though, in the words of an old author, Falkland " disputed as tranquilly and abstractedly in the neighbourhood of guns and drums as though he had been in his mansion at Tew," yet that his spirit was deeply oppressed by the prospect of a long-continued war was apparent to all—for he would in an interval of silence suddenly ejaculate " Peace, peace ! " He was conscious that his deep and irrepressible desire for peace might be falsely interpreted, and this was his excuse to Hyde for so rashly adventuring his life, " that all might see that his impatiency for peace proceeded not from pusillanimity."

He was soon to give the final proof of this. Gloucester was relieved by Essex on 7 September, 1643. The King then hastened to Newbury in order to bar the road to London, and here, on 20 September, was fought the first battle of Newbury. Like many people of somewhat melancholic temperament, Falkland probably had a presentiment that the fight would be his last ; he explained his desire for clean linen by saying that he might fall in the battle, that he was " weary of the times and foresaw much misery to his country, and did believe he should be out of it ere night." Moreover, on that morning he received the Holy Communion. Hyde had written urging him to be more careful of his person, but, rash as ever in action, he fell in attempting to force a gap in a hedge when unsupported by the rest of the horse. Byron, in whose company Falkland rode that day, describes the manner of his death. The royal foot was hard pressed by the enemy, and the support of the horse was called for. Byron rode up with his two regiments and found the Roundhead foot drawn up in a place surrounded by a quickset hedge, in which there was only a small gap big enough for the passage of one horse at a time. Byron, giving orders for the widening of the gap, had his horse shot, and while he called for another, Falkland, impatient of delay, plunged through the gap. He and his horse were immediately killed. Through the opening thus made Byron charged with his horse, at first with no success, but on the third attempt routed the enemy in that part of the field.

Prince Rupert sent a letter to Essex asking for the bodies of Falkland, Captain Bertie, and Serjeant-Major Wilshire. When Falkland's body was recovered, not without some difficulty, it was taken to Oxford and thence to Great Tew, where he was buried. Whitelocke, the chronicler of the Parliament, thus comments on his death : " His death was much lamented by all that knew him, or heard of him, being a gentleman of great parts, ingenuity, and honour, courteous and just to all, and a passionate promoter of all endeavours of peace betwixt the King and Parliament."

He left two sons, Lucius, who died in Paris in 1646, and Henry, who inherited the title and estates of his father but few of his characteristics. His wife, Lettice, survived him for some few years, which she devoted to the care of her children and household and to works of mercy.

Falkland's most important literary work was theological, a refutation of the Roman claims entitled, "A Discourse on Infallibility." He also wrote poems, the best known being an eclogue on the death of Ben Jonson. In the judgment of later writers Falkland was "not a good poet though a great wit. He writ not a smooth verse, but a great deal of sense." His religious opinions have been a matter of some controversy. From his friendship with Chillingworth and his known leaning to Latitudinarian views, he has been accused of Socinianism, but this can scarcely be maintained in face of the facts of his life. He attended regularly to religious duties, and though his studies and philosophical tendencies caused him to regard ceremonies and forms of government as accidents and not essentials, he never lost his hold on orthodox doctrine. The testimony of Duncon is sufficient proof of this—he wrote an account of the life of Lady Falkland, and incidentally furnishes much information concerning her husband, and if Falkland had been a follower of Socinius he would certainly not have won the whole-hearted approbation and esteem of the sequestered Church of England priest.

It is not, however, as a poet, theologian, or statesman that Falkland will live. It is the man as depicted by him with whom he had "an entire friendship" for thirteen years that will for ever stir the imagination and hold the interest of his fellows. · " In this unhappy battle was slain the lord viscount Falkland : a person of such prodigious parts of learning and knowledge, of that inimitable sweetness and delight in conversation, of so flowing and obliging a humanity and goodness to mankind, and of that primitive simplicity and integrity of life, that if there were no other brand upon this odious and accursed civil war than this single loss, it must be most infamous and execrable to all posterity. *Turpe mori, post te, solo non posse dolore.* Thus fell that incomparable young man, in the four and thirtieth year of his age, having so much despatched the business of life that the oldest rarely attain to that immense knowledge ; and the youngest enter not into the world with more innocence ; and whosoever leads such a life need not care upon how short warning it be taken from him."

A CHAMPION OF ADVENTURE
GEORGE, LORD DIGBY

IN common with other supporters of the King, George, Lord Digby, was found on the popular side in the earlier years of the dispute between Charles I and his Parliament. This attitude was probably due to his sense of the treatment meted out to his father by Charles, owing to his opposition to Buckingham.

John, first Earl of Bristol, had been employed by James I on many embassies to Spain, but quarrelled with Buckingham, and was, by his order, committed to the Tower. It was this incident which brought the young George, then aged twelve, into prominence. His father determined to appeal to the House of Commons for redress and to make that appeal through his young son. The course was altogether successful, and Digby displayed on that occasion many of those qualities which were afterwards to bring him so much influence and power. Even at that early age his manner of presenting the petition, and the apt words with which he accompanied the action, foreshadowed two of his most prominent characteristics : his absolute self-confidence, and his persuasive skill as an orator. Later, on the accession of Charles I, the elder Digby's hostility to Buckingham was so marked and so resented by the young King that no writ for Parliamentary attendance was sent to him,

GEORGE, LORD DIGBY

FROM AN ENGRAVING BY GOLDAR AFTER THE PAINTING BY VAN DYCK

and on 1 May, 1626, he was charged with high treason and other offences. He retaliated by preparing articles of impeachment against Buckingham, but the King dissolved Parliament.

It was in this year 1626 that the young George Digby, who, being born at Madrid, 1612, had hitherto been educated on the Continent under his father's direction, was entered at Magdalen College, Oxford, where he was a pupil of the famous Peter Heylin. He had a great variety of natural talents, and learned without effort. He took his degree of M.A. in 1636, and travelled in France before returning to his father, who was then living in retirement in Dorsetshire. For the next few years his time was spent chiefly in study ; he was well versed in classics and philosophy, and to theology he also devoted some attention, for to this period must be ascribed the attack on the Church of Rome, which he addressed to his Romanist relative, Sir Kenelm Digby. He was returned to the Short Parliament as member for the county of Dorset, and at once attached himself to the party hostile to the Court. The cause of this was not solely filial devotion— he had also a personal grievance. Shortly before he had quarrelled and fought with a courtier, and as the duel took place within the precincts of Whitehall, Digby was seized and imprisoned.

In Parliament he soon made the value of his alliance felt, and was returned again to the Long Parliament by his former constituency. His ambition and sense of his own powers soon led him to take a prominent part in debates. His eloquence was of a very high order. He was skilled in the choice of words best fitted to wound opponents, so that his polished darts, launched with the most charming grace of manner, never failed to reach their mark, when the rude, rough weapons of other leaders of the popular party failed. Thus, by his speeches against the Court, he came to be admitted into the innermost councils of the party. He spoke frequently, his first great speech being to move the appointment of a Select Committee to frame a remonstrance to the King on public grievances. This speech, in its simplicity and felicity of expression, was a revelation to the House. One passage has often been quoted : " It hath been a metaphor frequently in Parliament, and, if my memory fail me not, was made use of in the Lord Keeper's speech at the opening of the last, that what money Kings raised from their subjects, it was but as vapours drawn up from the earth by the sun, to be distilled upon it again in fructifying showers. The comparison, Mr. Speaker, hath held in this kingdom of late years too unluckily. What hath been raised from the subject by these violent attractions hath been formed, it is true, into clouds, but how ? To darken the sun's own lustre, and hath fallen again upon the land only in hailstones and mildews, to batter and prostrate still more and more our liberties, and to blast and wither our affections, had not the latter of these been kept alive by our King's own personal virtues, which will ever preserve him, in spite of all ill-counsellors, a sacred object both of our admiration and love."

This eloquence was welcomed by the popular leaders as especially effective in debates on Church matters For Digby could express a deep devotion to the welfare of the Church in simple heartfelt language, and at the same time direct the most subtle attacks on her leaders These were far more effective than the undisguised hostility of the Puritan members of Parliament, not only to the leaders, but to the Church itself. It was small wonder, therefore, that such a man should soon find himself deep in the counsels of the party with whom he had to all appearances irrevocably thrown in his lot. So certain were the popular leaders of his adherence, that he was made one of the Committee for the management of the prosecution of Strafford, on whose destruction Pym and his followers were determined. In the early stages of the trial Digby showed no sympathy with the great Earl; in fact, one authority states that "it has even been said that the charge of high treason against that great man would have been abandoned but for the excitement produced by the close reasoning and the polished bitterness of Digby's invectives."

What circumstances or considerations really led to Digby's sudden change of front during this historic trial will probably never be ascertained—he took no one into his confidence. Whether, indeed, the change was due to any other cause than the caprice which apparently dominated his actions at certain periods of his life is doubtful. Perhaps, having attained a position of dominance in his party, he felt impelled to seek "other worlds to conquer." One apologist states that he was disgusted with the methods of the popular party and unsatisfied with the evidence brought against Strafford, but such scruples of conscience are hardly consistent with the character of the man. It is, however, possible that at some point in the prosecution he was seized with the conviction that the evidence against Strafford was weak, and as he had no personal animus against the Earl, he impulsively acted on that conviction, and that the spirit of adventure led him on to the abandonment of his party. Whatever the cause, his zeal against Strafford showed a growing coolness, and when the Bill of Attainder was brought into the House of Commons he threw off all pretence and spoke openly against the evidence on which that Bill was chiefly founded. The point then brought against Strafford as evidence of his treason was the witness of the elder Sir Henry Vane, that at a Privy Council meeting the Earl had recommended the bringing over of an Irish army to subdue " this country." The truth of this statement rested at first solely on the accuracy of Vane's memory; later, however, the Commons admitted as evidence Vane's notes of the meeting which had been abstracted from his father's papers by the younger Vane. When this accusation was brought forward, Strafford so ably defended himself, and exposed with such skill the weakness of the prosecution that the suspicions of the House were aroused. To give point to those suspicions the Earl was followed by Digby, who, in a witty speech, declared himself " not only unsatisfied in the matter of law, but more unsatisfied in the matter of fact." It was thought that Strafford could not so skilfully have repulsed the attack of the prosecution had he not known beforehand of the evidence to be brought forward. Suspicion became certainty when it was found that the notes produced by the younger Vane were missing from among the papers of the prosecution. Every member of the Commission was examined, but all, including Digby, affirmed their innocence. Several years later, after the battle of Naseby, the King's cabinet was taken, and among the papers it contained, these notes, in the Lord Digby's hand, are said to have been found. The only reason for doubting the truth of this story lies in the incredibility of such condemnatory evidence being preserved, and for so long.

From this time Digby was an especial object of hatred to the leaders of the popular party. For a little time he continued in Parliament and spoke against the Covenant and in support of the Bishops, none of which proceedings tended to allay the hostility of the Commons. His offence was beyond forgiveness and that this was so was soon attested. His speech against the Bill of Attainder was condemned to be burnt, his name was posted at the head of the list of those called " Straffordians, or enemies of their country." Digby's surrender to the Court was seen to be complete when on 9 June he was made a Baron and next day admitted to the Upper House. On the same day he was expelled from the House of Commons.

Digby now became one of the most trusted advisers of the King. Nor is this surprising in view of the attractiveness of his personality, the persuasiveness of his speech, and his readiness to undertake any enterprise, no matter how difficult. In fact, one of his greatest faults as a counsellor was, as Clarendon observes, his thinking " difficult things too easy," and this made him very dangerous to Charles, who, owing partly to his lack of self-confidence, was especially attracted by that quality in others. Digby also displayed at times much acumen in discerning character, and this he showed when, by his advice, Charles promoted Falkland and Sir John Culpeper to his Council, the former with the office of Secretary of State, the latter as Chancellor of the Exchequer. He would also have preferred Hyde at the same time, but he declined office, thinking he could best serve the King's interests in Parliament. The King promised at this time to do nothing without consulting the three friends. Unfortunately, Digby seemed fated ever to follow up an especially praiseworthy step by one especially culpable. At this moment the King seemed to be recovering much of his lost ground in the affections of his people, and this was due in large measure to the wisdom of his action in appointing Falkland and Culpeper, men respected by all, to positions of trust, and to his conciliatory attitude generally. His behaviour stood then in marked contrast to the factiousness of the popular party, who had lost ground with moderate men by the issue of the Grand Remonstrance, and who now, not content with the exclusion of the Bishops from the House of Lords, on their protest had cast twelve of their number into prison on a charge of high treason. All moderate men were disgusted by such violent action, and had the King been patient, following the advice of Falkland and Hyde, all might still have been well.

At this critical juncture Digby came forward with a proposal that the King should impeach the five most prominent leaders in the Commons, Pym, Hampden, Hazelrigg, Hollis, and Strode, and Lord Kimbolton in the Lords, and that he should go himself in person to the House to arrest them. Such action amounted to a breach of privilege and caused popular sympathy to turn from the King, for, together with the proposed appointment of Sir Thomas Lunsford to command the Tower, also on the advice of Digby, it gave the Commons, in the eyes of the people, ground for their distrust of the King.

The peculiarities of Digby's character are nowhere more clearly shown than in his conduct throughout this affair. In the House of Lords, when the King's Attorney read the accusations of high treason brought against Lord Kimbolton and the five members, none showed

more astonishment than Digby; indeed, being seated
next to Kimbolton, he whispered to him that the King
was badly advised to take such a step, he must find out
who had inspired it! Yet later, on the King's failure to
secure the persons of the accused members, he offered
to go in person with a few trusty followers and seize them
wherever they might be. Possibly he could not bear that
Kimbolton should suspect him, in his presence, of such
foolish advice, and especially against him to whom he had
always professed friendship, though away from him he was
prepared, impulsively as ever, to carry out what he had
himself proposed. His offer was, however, refused;
the King was determined to act legally; such a *coup
d'état* did not appeal to him.

The result was that the Lord Digby was discredited in
the eyes of all. Those who had previously been his
friends, notably Hyde and Culpeper, could not forgive
him that he had, behind their backs, advised the King
to such a foolish proceeding, and their anger became
greater when he induced the King to go next day to the
Guildhall and there justify his conduct, which exposed
him to the insults and reproaches of the crowd. The
people as a whole also regarded Digby as the author of
these unpopular actions, so that he was at this time
perhaps the best-hated man in the kingdom.

Early in January, 1642, the King withdrew to Hampton
Court, and shortly afterwards Digby, suddenly timid,
left the country. The immediate cause of his flight was
the step taken by Parliament in ordering the sheriffs to
suppress all unlawful assemblies with the trained bands,
a step which was directed against Digby in particular.
For, immediately upon the King's withdrawal to Hampton
Court, Digby had been sent on a message to Kingston-on-

Thames, where he met Colonel Lunsford, and " to the terror of the King's subjects," he journeyed thither in a coach and six with, presumably, outriders. This action was reported to the Commons, and by them construed into an unlawful assembly and the levying of war. Hence the order to the sheriffs, which seems to have revealed to Digby the extent of his unpopularity ; for almost at once he received the King's permission to leave the country and betook himself to Holland. The motive of this flight was no feeling of cowardice. Whatever his faults, Digby never lacked personal courage ; but he seems for once to have realized that his presence was only adding to the King's difficulties, since the Commons assumed that all His Majesty's actions were prompted by him. Moreover, were he impeached those difficulties would be incalculably greater, since Charles would, of necessity, stand by his servant. Very soon after his arrival in Holland, Digby wrote to friends in England. His letter was intercepted and handed over to the Commons, who made no scruple of opening it and detaining both the letter and an enclosure to the Queen ; presuming also to recommend the King to see that his wife held no further intercourse with the Lord Digby, or " any other fugitives and traitors." Certain expressions in these letters gave great offence to the leaders of the popular party, so great, indeed, that the Commons reverted to the Kingston business, making it a pretext for indicting Digby of treason before the House of Lords. The Peers proved unwilling to carry on the impeachment, which was, in any case, mere waste of time, since the accused person was not to be apprehended.

From the time of the King's leaving London for Hampton Court and Windsor events moved quickly.

The Militia Ordinance, the appointment of Sir John Hotham to the governorship of Hull by the Commons, the journey of the King to York, the refusal of Hotham to admit him within the walls of Hull, were followed by what is known as "The Paper War," when the King and the Parliament issued Remonstrances and Answers ; each setting forth in detail the grievances demanding remedy, of which the only result was to show clearly that there were certain points on which agreement could not be arrived at without a resort to arms. In these Remonstrances and Answers Digby is frequently mentioned, especially as the author of the letter advising the King to "betake himself to some strong place where he may avow and protect his servants," advice which, the Commons declared, the King had followed when he attempted to enter Hull.

Meanwhile, Digby's restless spirit had tired of the comparative inactivity of life in Holland, although, since the Queen's arrival, he had been of very much help to her in the work of collecting arms and ammunition to send to the King at York. He therefore disguised himself as a Frenchman and made his way to York. Charles and his advisers, the latter of whom, at least, did not as yet despair of coming to terms with the Parliament, found his presence somewhat inconvenient, since, should it become known to the Commons, it would prejudice any negotiations between them and the King. Therefore Digby was quickly dispatched, with Ashburnham and others, to Holland, to hasten the supplies from the Queen, which were daily expected. Hardly had they set out in a little bark than they met the "Providence" with the supply of arms and ammunition from Holland. Letters were handed to Digby, who was now in doubt as to

whether he should continue his voyage to Holland or
return to York with the " Providence." He delayed
so long that the Parliamentary fleet appeared in sight.
The " Providence " got safely into harbour, but the
bark with Digby and Ashburnham on board was captured
The former with great presence of mind at once assumed
his rôle of French passenger and, on pretence of sea-
sickness, remained below, which gave him the opportunity
to destroy all compromising letters. The prisoners were
conveyed to Hull, and so well did Digby play his part,
that Sir John Hotham, before whom at his own request
he was brought, had no idea of his identity. Nevertheless Digby felt his predicament to be hopeless. Too
many people knew of his presence on that bark for him
to be able to keep up the deception for any length of
time, and Hotham was one of his most bitter enemies.
Once in the hands of Parliament he could not hope for
his life. Therefore he resolved on a bold step. He
revealed his identity to Hotham, throwing himself on
his mercy, relying, as he said, on his feelings as a gentleman not to betray him into the hands of his enemies.
And, surprising fact to those acquainted with Sir John
Hotham's character, the ruse succeeded. Digby had
imputed to him a virtue which he did not possess, and
he was either too ashamed or too much taken by surprise
to do other than accept the situation. It is, however,
possible that Hotham was by no means sorry to give
the King and his party cause for gratitude to him. His
position at Hull was somewhat invidious ; he was not
entirely trusted by Parliament—in fact, his son was joined
with him in the command of that port in order to make
it certain that he would not repent his former action
and hand over Hull to the King. On Hotham disclosing

some of his fears to Digby, the latter at once improved the occasion, giving such rosy and entirely imaginary prospects of the King's immediate success and of the absolute discomfiture of Parliament, that he prevailed upon Hotham to declare that if the King appeared before Hull with troops he would surrender the town. Armed with this delusive hope Digby was dispatched to York, and the King did, in consequence, reconnoitre Hull in some force, but only to find that Hotham was either powerless or unwilling to fulfil his promise; whereupon the train-bands called together for this object were dismissed, and the King returned to York.

Thus Digby's zeal had for its sole result a decrease of respect for the King's judgment, since his advisers and followers, knowing nothing of the reasons which determined his march upon Hull, could only condemn a warlike expedition undertaken with apparently so little reason and abandoned for still less! Throughout the career of this remarkable man a like fate followed him; his advice ever brought disaster on his royal master, yet he never brought maturer judgment to bear on his loyal impulses. From first to last Digby was an opportunist, and an opportunist who failed, as all gamblers must, sooner or later, whether they gamble with dice or fate.

Digby now appeared openly with the King at York, and on the declaration of war raised a regiment of horse. For a time, therefore, he took part in the military operations of the Civil War. He behaved himself with much gallantry at Edgehill and was with Prince Rupert at the siege of Lichfield, where he was wounded in the thigh in an assault upon the town, in April, 1643. It was not likely that two men of such high spirits as Prince Rupert and Digby should long agree ; very soon they quarrelled. Digby threw up his command in high dudgeon and returned to Court. The relations of the two men were never happy, and many of the future difficulties of Rupert can be traced to the hostility of Digby, whom the Prince certainly never condescended to placate, and who easily persuaded himself that Rupert's plans and actions were contrary to the King's best interests. He now joined the army as a volunteer, and was present when the Prince routed the enemy at Auburn Chase in the attempt to cut off the retreat of Essex from Gloucester, after his successful relief of that city. Here Digby met with one of those marvellous escapes of which his history is full. He was wounded in the face by a pistol discharged so near to him that the powder caused his face to bleed and temporarily blinded him ; yet he received no other hurt, so that it was thought that the bullet must have dropped out of the pistol before the shot was fired. We have no record of Digby's share in any other military event in the early part of the war, and on the death of Falkland, in September, 1643, Digby succeeded him as Secretary of State.

A more unfortunate choice could scarcely have been made, for Digby could never agree with Culpeper, Hyde, or any other of the more sober and moderate counsellors of the King. He was ever for extreme measures, cared nothing to maintain the Constitution, but only to bring about, by any means, a victory for the King's cause. He was the partisan of the Queen and of her policy of foreign alliances and negotiations with the Irish. He could see none of the disadvantages which such a course would entail—the alienation of the moderate section of the people from the King's cause, the plausibility it would give to the wildest and most unfounded accusations of the Parliament. It seems incredible that the man who, in the beginning of the Long Parliament, could speak so eloquently on the rights of Parliament and people, should now have absolutely no regard for either. A middle course was always impossible to him, he must be at the one extreme or the other. His opinions were not the result of sober judgment, though he knew well how to give every appearance of calm deliberation to his most unconsidered schemes, and he could meet every objection with such plausible arguments that the King, who was always ready to rely on anyone who had great self-confidence, was most easily persuaded by him to courses which his own judgment would never have approved. There was another and even more fatal objection. Digby could not act in concert with other councillors, for the reason that he never disclosed to them his whole mind upon any matter, reserving some fact or agreement which might have changed the whole aspect of the matter under discussion. " Nor did he act thus," says Clarendon, " from jealousy or distrust of those with whom he was connected, or from a contradiction to their opinions and judgments, with which he was most ready to comply. Indeed, upon any debate he was more easily persuaded to depart from his own inclinations that was almost any man who was ever known who possessed such an extent of understanding." " The reservation proceeded only from an opinion that his concealing something which was unthought of by the rest would, in the sequel, add greatly to his own credit and reputation."

The inconvenience likely to arise from being associated with a man of such disposition as joint advisers to the

King is readily perceived. A certain course of action would be decided upon, when, owing to some new fancy of the Lord Digby's, who imagined in his self-esteem that the matter was not worthy of mention to his colleagues, since they would be bound to see the wisdom of his action, an entirely different line of policy would be adopted. Thus there could be no certainty, no steadiness in the policy of the King, and it is to this fatal flaw in Digby's character that we can trace much of the inconsistency of the King's actions and policy—an inconsistency freely labelled as duplicity by supporters of the Parliament. Had Charles been a strong man, certain of himself on every point as he was only on one, Digby's influence would have had no such pernicious effect. The King had, however, the fatal weakness of being able to see the good to be obtained from every suggested course of policy, together with an inability to weigh the comparative merits of each. He was thus the prey of the one who last obtained his ear, and in most cases this was Digby or the Queen. There was only one point on which neither Digby, Jermyn, nor even the Queen could move him: under no circumstances would he surrender to the enemy his sword, his friends, or, above all, his Church.

During the next two years Digby was ever with Charles, and his influence can be traced in many of the King's actions, military as well as political. The most hopeless projects seemed most to appeal to Digby's adventurous spirit, and no failures discouraged him from advocating and even attempting new and more daring plans. He was in favour of the bringing over of the Irish troops; he was one of the few supporters of Montrose and Antrim when the one begged to be allowed to go into Scotland

and raise forces there, the other to be sent to Ireland to raise troops to co-operate with Montrose in the Highlands.

Again, late in the year 1644 he himself opened secret negotiations with Major-General Browne, governor of Abingdon, hoping to induce that sturdy Roundhead to yield the place to the King. Browne led him on by pretended compliance for long enough to enable the fortifications to be strengthened sufficiently to withstand a Royalist attack. Digby's belief in himself and his powers of persuasion were so great that he never once suspected a trick until he was met by open defiance. Moreover, he did not profit by the experience, for in the next year he wrote letters to General Leven, of the Scotch army then in England, with the hope that he might be induced to co-operate with the Royalists and Montrose. Leven merely sent the letters to Parliament, and vouchsafed no answer to their author.

Digby's serene optimism never failed; however grave the disaster might be that befell the King's cause, there was always a fresh source of relief to be tested, till that too failed in its turn. The successes of Montrose were to Digby overwhelmingly more important than the disasters which the King's arms encountered at home. He refused to consider the possibility of failure, and thus, when the Royalist army in the west, led by the utterly unprincipled, unreliable Goring, was growing daily weaker, when Bristol was on the point of surrender, the King's own army at Hereford being far too small to attempt relief, with this gloomy outlook Digby could write enthusiastically to the Prince of Wales, after describing the victories of Montrose: " These things, sir, are things rather like dreams than truth, but all most certain. God is pleased to point out the way by which he will bring upon the rebellion of both kingdoms the judgments that are due upon it, having already brought so heavy a vengeance upon that which hath been the origin of all our misery. You see from what a low condition it hath pleased God to bring His Majesty's affairs into so hopeful a one again, as that if, while Fairfax's army is entertained before Bristol, your Highness can but frame a considerable body such as may give His Majesty leave, with the forces he hath together, to play the fairest of his game in these countries and northward, for the assistance of Montrose with horse, or, at least, for the withholding Leslie's army of foot from him, I see no cause to doubt, but that upon the whole matter, His Majesty may conclude the campagna more prosperously than any, and with fairer foundations for a mastering power of next year than ever."

On the very eve of the fall of Bristol, Digby wrote with enthusiasm of the hopes of the King—that his army would be recruited from Shropshire, that Fairfax's army then besieging Bristol was in sore distress, that Goring was on the march towards that town. " I must confess," he wrote, " that these miracles, besides the worldly joy, have made me a better Christian by begetting in me a stronger faith and reliance upon God Almighty than ever before, having manifested that it is wholly His work, and that He will bring about His intended blessing upon this just cause by ways the most impossible to human understanding, and consequently teach us to cast off all reliance upon our own strength." The fall of Bristol could not dash Digby's hopes ; he now placed all reliance on the King joining with Montrose. Goring was to join the King, troops from Ireland to take his place in the west, a junction to be effected with Montrose, and the Scotch army annihilated. This successfully accomplished,

London would be at the King's disposal and the war at an end. Such were the pictures of the future, conjured up by Digby's vivid imagination, and not even the successive disasters of Rowton Heath and Philiphaugh were sufficient to quench his faith. He urged upon the King to persist in the northward march, insisting that Montrose had not been utterly defeated, he had quickly recovered and beaten Leslie. It was in vain that Willis and others urged the King to collect all his Midland garrisons and, thus reinforced, join Goring in the west, Digby and the King were resolved. It may be that Digby was anxious to avoid a meeting with Prince Rupert, who had been dismissed by Charles on the fall of Bristol, had even—and this must have been at Digby's instigation —been accused of treachery in that surrender. Rupert was hastening to lay his cause before the King, and, though the Secretary of State may well have convinced himself that the Prince's conduct was treacherous, Rupert would not be good to meet when still smarting under the sense of injustice.

At this juncture news came of the failure of Montrose to recruit his army, and even Digby was forced to see that for the King to march north was entirely out of the question. So when a proposal was made that Langdale, with the horse, should attempt to redeem the King's pledge to Montrose, Digby welcomed that leader's suggestion that he should be in command of the expedition. To stay at Newark and face Rupert was beyond even the assurance of Digby. He was an adept at self-deception, but he had never been able to convince himself that the Prince believed in his asseverations of friendship— which, however, he probably meant when he made them. On the other hand, he had thoroughly convinced himself that Rupert was a traitor, since he had endeavoured to prevail upon the King to come to terms with the rebels.

Once again, then, Digby found himself at the head of a body of troops, bound on an enterprise certain to appeal to his love of adventure and hazard. At first it seemed that he would be successful, but at the crucial moment, when victory was apparently within his grasp, by a mere accident it was snatched from him. The defeat of Digby and Langdale at Sherborne was due to no fault of either— their plans had been skilfully laid. The enemy failed to flee in the direction expected of them, and were mistaken for retreating friends ! Consequently Digby's reserve fled before the conquered foe, and Langdale, deprived of support, was unable to hold his own. To continue their perilous march into Scotland with a tiny disorganized band of men was to court certain failure. Nevertheless, the two leaders persevered in their intention till they found themselves hemmed in by the Scotch army in front and the northern levies behind. Digby was at last convinced of the hopelessness of the attempt to reach Montrose, and, characteristically, at once turned his mind to fresh projects. Setting sail for Ireland, he wrote to the King that he went to attend to the raising of troops for England.

In Ireland he found Glamorgan entering upon negotiations with the Roman Catholics, and granting such terms as he knew well the King had never sanctioned. He therefore proceeded to indict him before the Council, saying that the King's authority, upon which Glamorgan claimed to be acting, "must be forged or surreptitiously gained, as it is certain that the King would never grant to the Irish the least piece of concession so destructive to his regality and religion." Certainly Digby might claim to know the King's mind on such matters, for he had done his best, though in vain, to persuade Charles to allow the Scotch to believe that he would eventually grant the establishment of Presbyterianism in England. The Council, on this accusation, committed Glamorgan to prison, and the concessions he would have granted were repudiated by the King.

Digby remained in Ireland for some few months, and managed to convince himself that an Irish army was all ready to enter into England, and only awaited the leadership of the Prince of Wales Accordingly, June, 1646, found him in Paris urging the Queen to persuade the Prince to set out for Ireland. She was not inclined to listen to any such proposition. All her hopes were centred in France, and she was eager for her son's presence in Paris. Digby was quickly won over to her point of view, and crossed to Jersey to urge the Prince to join his mother, his argument being that the Scots would do nothing but through France, and that nothing could be done in France without the Prince. Digby was so far successful that the young Charles decided to go to Paris, though his faithful counsellors, Hyde, Capel, and Hopton, refused to accompany him.

In Paris Digby was treated with the deference he loved ; his opinions were invited, and apparently deferred to. He imagined that the instructions given to the French ambassador, who was to negotiate between Charles and the Scotch, were from memoranda drawn up by himself ; in reality, the ambassador had received his instructions from Mazarin. As a matter of fact, neither had a chance of success, as the King utterly refused to accept Presbyterianism, and the Newcastle propositions therefore came to nothing.

In July Digby returned to Ireland, bent on trying to accomplish the peace which was to land Irish troops in England, but neither he nor Ormond was able to cope with the various parties to the negotiations, and the Irish peace failed. Digby fled to France with some difficulty. He was one of those excepted from pardon by the Houses, and so was forced to remain in exile until the Restoration. Mazarin continued to show him attention, and when in the war with the Frondeurs he commanded a troop of horse, largely composed of English gentlemen, and distinguished himself in that service, he was rewarded with a lucrative monopoly. An incident in the war won him great favour with the impressionable French. He was challenged by an unknown officer of the Frondeurs to single combat, but as he rode out to the meeting he was treacherously fired upon by his antagonist's troops and severely wounded.

On the death of his father, Digby became Earl of Bristol, and at about the same time Charles II bestowed the Garter upon him. Enjoying a large income from his monopoly and reputed a miser, Digby seems to have given way secretly to the most excessive license and extravagance, so that he very soon found himself practically penniless. One story that is told of him probably belongs to this period. In common with many others, Bristol paid court to a well-known Parisian beauty. She had formerly shown favour to a certain young Abbé, who, finding his attentions no longer welcome, expressed his discontent to the lady. She, much offended, complained of his conduct to her acquaintances. The Earl of Bristol, hearing of it, kidnapped the Abbé and sent him, securely guarded, to the lady with a note intimating that, if he did not abase himself to her satisfaction, he should be returned to the writer, who would see that justice was administered. The lady was highly incensed at this unwarrantable interference in her affairs, and desired the officer in charge of the Abbé to signify to his master that in future she did not desire him to guard her reputation or to meddle in her concerns !

When the Earl found himself at the end of his resources his ambition awoke. In 1650 Mazarin, owing to factions at Court, was obliged to leave Paris. He had become much attached to Bristol, whose attractions were undeniable, and recommended him to the Queen Regent. Forgetting all gratitude, wild dreams of filling the Prime Minister's place filled Bristol's ambitious soul, and he was so unwise as to take the Queen into his confidence. Mazarin's exile was not, however, a long one, and, being informed by the Queen of the Earl's intrigues, he at once resolved to dismiss him from all employment at the French Court. He did not do this at once, but waited for a fitting opportunity, which arrived when a treaty was made with Cromwell, when it was easy to cause Digby to believe that the Protector had made it a condition of coming to terms.

Digby's sense of importance was thereby flattered, and, being dismissed with a handsome present, he turned his mind to new schemes for his own glory and advancement. Spain was the El Dorado to which he now looked, and although at Bruges, where he had joined Charles II, all his friends dissuaded him from the course which he contemplated, he would listen to none of them. Confident in his own powers, he set out for Spain. Nor was he disappointed. His reception was cold enough to discourage any less assured person. Don Juan received him most coldly; the Spaniards hated all they knew

16

of him, his every characteristic being exactly opposite to their national predilections. Nevertheless, by his inimitable talents he very soon brought about a complete *volte face.* Determined not to take offence, he joined cheerfully in every discourse, and by his learning and charm of manner won first Don Juan—who was especially attracted to him by his skill in astrology—and by degrees his officers. His share in the recapture of St. Ghislain from the French completed the conquest; he was soon able to return to Charles II with news that Don Juan advised His Majesty to send an agent to the Spanish Court, which was well disposed towards him. Later, in 1658, he accompanied Charles II into Spain, and the chief minister, Don Luis de Haro, was so much attracted by him that he persuaded him to accompany him to Madrid, where he promised that he should be taken into the service of the King of Spain. This he did, and remained in that country till the Restoration. During his sojourn in Spain he became a Roman Catholic, probably not from conviction, but because he saw no prospect of a Stuart Restoration, and therefore believed that his future years might be spent in Spain. This step was some disadvantage to him when the Restoration eventually took place, for though Charles II received him cordially, he was given no high office in the State. This disappointment he attributed to Clarendon, and another rebuff which he sustained, concerning the King's marriage, he also laid at the same door. He had advocated a marriage alliance with a member of the Medici family, and Charles allowed him to go to Italy to secure information concerning the lady. He returned to find that Charles' marriage with Catherine of Braganza was an accomplished fact.

The Earl of Bristol made yet another attempt to obtain pre-eminence in the King's favour, by intriguing to form a King's party in Parliament. The plan was discovered, and Charles, as usual, threw over his adviser, who was, however, clever enough to clear himself before Parliament. He did not forgive either Charles or Clarendon, and in 1663 brought forward a charge of treason against the latter, which only recoiled on his own head. The Peers rejected his accusation with scorn, and Charles issued a warrant for his apprehension. Forced to flee, Bristol remained in hiding for two years, when he induced the Duchess of Cleveland to effect his reconciliation with the King. His public career was, however, ended; he retired into private life to waste the not inconsiderable fortune bestowed on him by Charles II in gaming and making unnecessary additions to his estate. One final piece of inconsistency must be recorded of this complex character: his last public act was to vote for the Test Act of 1673. On 20 March, 1676, he died at Chelsea, leaving a son and two daughters.

His career may best be summed up in the words of Lord Orford: "He was a singular person, whose life was one contradiction. He wrote against Popery and embraced it; he was a zealous opposer of the Court and a sacrifice for it; he was conscientiously converted in the midst of his prosecution of Lord Strafford, and was most unconscientiously a prosecutor of Lord Clarendon. With great parts he always hurt himself and his friends; with romantic bravery he was always an unsuccessful commander. He spoke for the Test Act, although a Roman Catholic, and addicted himself to astrology on the birthday of true philosophy."

THE CHAMPION OF SCOTLAND
THE MARQUIS OF MONTROSE

THE first Marquis and fifth Earl of his line; Montrose came of a distinguished family. The Grahams had, in early days, married into the Royal Family, furnished leaders of the national movements under Wallace and Bruce, as well as distinguished Bishops to the Church. His grandfather had risen to considerable eminence, being High Treasurer, Chancellor, and finally Viceroy of Scotland. His father, John, Earl of Montrose, had the tastes rather of a country gentleman than those of a State official, though he too had been President of the Council. On the distaff side Montrose was descended from the Ruthvens, his mother being the sister of the necromancer head of the family. It is said that she consulted with witches at the time of his birth, and was told that her son would trouble the country, a prophecy not reassuring in view of the past records of the wild Ruthvens. Montrose probably spent his youth between the three family estates of Kincardine in Perthshire, Mugdock in Stirlingshire, and Old Montrose in Forfarshire, and grew up proficient in all manly exercises of the time.

In the year 1626, when he was fourteen years of age, his father died, and he was left to the joint guardianship of various relations, but the care of his education was probably in the hands of the Lord Napier, though Sir

THE MARQUIS OF MONTROSE
FROM THE PAINTING BY HONTHORST IN THE POSSESSION OF THE EARL OF DALHOUSIE

William Graham, of Claverhouse, and Patrick Gordon, of Inchbrakie, were also men to whom he turned for advice and support in later years. Already, since the age of twelve, he had had a separate establishment in Glasgow for the purpose of study. Shortly after the death of his father Montrose was sent to the University of St. Andrew's, where, although he lived a merry, somewhat irresponsible life, he yet acquired such a love of study that in the intervals of arduous campaigns in later years he turned for solace and refreshment to books, which he must have learned to love in these early days. It was during his University career that he met and loved Magdalene, daughter of Lord Carnegie, afterwards Earl of Southesk. He was but seventeen at the time of his marriage in 1629. Very little is known of the bride, though for the next three years the home of the young married couple was made at Kinnaird Castle. Marriage probably sobered the very youthful bridegroom, for the only record we have of the next three or four years is that he studied to such purpose as to become, in the exaggerated language of the chronicler, " not merely a great master, but a critic of the Greek and Latin."

In 1633 Montrose set out for the period of foreign travel without which no nobleman's education could then be deemed complete. His romantic temperament and love of arms were probably strongly aroused by his residence abroad in that time of " Sturm und Drang," when the exploits of Gustavus Adolphus were the theme of every tongue. During this period Montrose studied great men and their actions to some purpose. When he returned to Scotland, at the age of twenty-four, he was at the zenith of his youthful beauty. Heylyn, in his life of Laud, thus describes him : " He was of a middle stature and most exquisitely proportioned limbs, his hair of a light chestnut, his complexion betwixt pale and ruddy, his eye most penetrating though inclining to gray, his nose rather aquiline than otherwise. As he was strong of body and limbs, so he was most agile, which made him excel most of others in those exercises where these two are required." It is, however, Patrick Gordon who points out more clearly than any of his biographers the secret of his charm, which seems to have been felt by most of those with whom Montrose came into contact. After describing his personal appearance, he goes on : " Of a staid, grave, and solid look, sparkling and full of life, of speech slow but witty and full of sense, a presence grateful, courtly, and so winning upon the beholders as it seemed to claim reverence without suing for it ; for he was so affable, so courteous, so benign as seemed to scorn ostentation and the keeping of state, and therefore he quickly made a conquest of the hearts of all his followers, so as when he list he could have led them in a chain to have followed him with cheerfulness in all his enterprises ; and I am certainly persuaded that this his gracious, humane, and courteous freedom of behaviour, being certainly acceptable before God as well as men, was it that won him so much renown and enabled him chiefly in the love of his followers, to go through so great enterprises, wherein his equal had failed, although they exceeded him far in power, nor can any other reason be given for it but only this."

This charm was not, however, felt by all, and this was probably due to the fact that Montrose possessed the defects of his qualities. A magnanimous, sanguine temperament looks for appreciation and sympathy ;

from most of his equals and all inferiors this was forthcoming. There were, however, many men of his age
and time, superior and equal to Montrose in rank, who
were jealous of his attractions and abilities, and when
met with suspicion Montrose was at no pains to conciliate. To such men his manner was haughty and
unapproachable, to such " his carriage, which was not
ordinary, made him seem proud." This stiffness towards
rivals almost certainly arose from vanity and self-
consciousness. In spite of such petty defects, his sublime
self-forgetfulness in devotion to the cause which he
espoused raises him for all time above the men of his age.
None on either side can approach him in his utter lack
of self-seeking, in that lofty idealism which caused him
to believe that to strive for a good cause must inevitably
exalt men even of base character; that all, like himself,
must lose sight of self in the hour of success, and unite,
however varied their ambitions, to support and strengthen
the monarchy which they were destined to rescue from
destruction. This was Montrose's vision of the future.
Idealistic, in truth, but an idealist, even when his ideals
seemed shattered, has consolations, for he lives in the
future, and the cause he now sees overthrown must some
day rise triumphant. Present failure is a passing incident;
in God's own time, good—his good, no other exists for
him—must be dominant. Of such stuff are heroes made,
and Montrose was the one hero the Civil Wars produced.
To no other was it given to overlook present actualities
and stake all on a vision of the future. This is the secret
of Montrose's desperate enterprises, and, too, the secret
of their frequent success. Self-confidence is half the
battle, and Montrose had not only self-confidence,
but, what was of more importance, confidence in the

ultimate issue of the struggle, the final triumph of the cause for which he lived and died. It was this supreme confidence which inspired his men on occasions when annihilation would have seemed their only prospect. Cardinal Metz, who knew Montrose personally, estimated him truly when he said : " Le Comte de Montross, Ecossois, et chef de la maison de Graham, le seul homme du monde qui m'ait jamais rapellé l'idée de certains héros que l'on ne voit plus que dans les vies de Plutarch, avoit soutenir le parte du Roi d'Angleterre dans son pais, avec une grandeur d'âme qui n'en avoit point de pareille en ce siècle."

At the age of twenty-four the possibilities of Montrose's character were naturally not discernible by the multitude, although his devoted biographer relates that his " resolute undaunted spirit " began to appear even in childhood " to the wonder and expectation of all men." The discerning eye was lacking in Charles I when Montrose, at the invitation of the Duke of Hamilton, appeared at the English Court. For some reason Montrose failed to please the King. It has been said that Hamilton, apparently his friend, was jealous, and prejudiced Charles against the young Earl. Whatever the cause, Montrose returned from Court disappointed. Yet the trend of affairs in Scotland should have caused Charles to secure the loyalty of a young, ardent, and impressionable man. Charles was not, however, worldly-wise, neither was he a skilful dissembler.

Montrose returned to Scotland to find a raging aristocracy, a discontented and rebellious clergy, and a people who, influenced by their leaders, were already convinced of a conspiracy threatening their most cherished institutions. The train for the explosion had long been laid, and within the last year Charles had himself applied the match. In the first years of his reign he had attempted to carry out a reform which he knew had been near his father's heart, but for which James had not found the times expedient. At the time of the Reformation in Scotland the Church had been despoiled. Two-thirds of her property had been alienated to the laity; Knox had with difficulty secured one-third, a bare pittance, for the maintenance of the Presbyters who succeeded the Catholic hierarchy and priesthood. This gross injustice Charles proposed to remedy, but, as in England, though the nobles cared but little what form of religion was professed, when it became a question of restoration of Church property it was " Hands off ! " The opposition was vigorous, for the nobles stirred up the clergy and people by skilfully assuring them that this was but the first step—an attack on their religion and forms of worship would certainly follow. Charles thereupon wisely withdrew his proposition, but appointed a Committee to inquire into the possibility of the restoration of the tithe to its original purpose—the maintenance of religion. In this he had the support of all honest thinking men ; for not only was the proposal just in itself, it would also free the people from a most grinding tyranny. The nobles were accustomed to collect their tithe when and how they pleased, often forcing tenants to leave their crops standing until they had taken their due, and delaying that until the crop was ruined. Thus the Tithe Bill was carried ; but the hostility of the aristocracy was naturally not allayed thereby, though they were for the present forced to submit. They had aroused the suspicions of the Presbyterian clergy, the train was laid, the least unwise action on the part of the King would be sufficient to set it alight.

This was the moment that Laud chose for the issue of a Book of Canons, and this was followed by the promulgation of the new Liturgy in 1637. These two actions brought clergy and nobles together. Deliberately they set to work to organize resistance, to stir up the people to withstand this, as they represented it, wilful and deep-laid scheme to deprive them of religious and political liberty. Moreover, the Puritan party in England were only too ready to urge the Scotch to revolt. Baillie, the historian of the Covenant, acknowledges that the Presbyterian nobles and clergy were equally to blame with Charles and his advisers for the violent outburst that soon convulsed Scotland, in that " they put idolatry, Popery, superstition in sundry things which are innocent of these things." The agitation was controlled by a faction headed by the noblemen Rothes and Loudon, with Archibald Johnston the lawyer. The fanatical outburst in St. Giles's Cathedral on the occasion of the first attempt to use the new Liturgy was certainly engineered, and well served the purpose of its promoters—to excite the passions of the more phlegmatic portion of the population. To inflame such as were as yet unaware of any cause for revolt was the next step. Scotland was divided into districts, and certain ministers were commissioned to visit these, to agitate and to organize the resistance they advocated. In none of these preliminary proceedings had Montrose any share. He first appeared at a great' Convention which met in November, 1637, after he had been in Scotland for more than a year. It would not, therefore, appear that in joining the movement he was influenced simply by motives of spite and injured vanity, or he would have become a member at the earliest possible moment. On the other hand, it would be rash to assume that disappointment with his reception at Court had no part in his decision. Human nature is complex, and few people act invariably from single motives. Baillie writes that " the canniness of Rothes brought Montrose in," and Rothes probably knew how to play on all the varied strings of the human heart.

At this Convention, that Committee of sixteen, representing the four Estates of the Realm, was appointed, which was later to usurp to itself, most unconstitutionally, all the functions of government. So important was the " capture " of Montrose deemed, that he was one of the four selected noblemen. The motives of the faction were, however, by no means single ; it was not alone the position and ability of Montrose that dictated their choice. The "canny" Rothes had probably well estimated the character of the man. As one of the inner circle he would believe himself to be aware of their every design ; in reality much would be hidden from him. Thus not only would he be less likely to suspect ulterior motives and work against them, as they knew that he inevitably must were he aware of the full extent of their plans, but also the suspicions of the moderate men would be lulled to rest, they would feel themselves secure in the certainty that no treasonable design would ever receive the sanction of Montrose.

Then followed the promulgation of the Covenant, and Montrose was one of the first to sign it. Ostensibly this was a mere renewal of a Confession of Faith which James had signed in his youth, and to which had been added by the same King a bond for the maintenance of the true religion and of the King's person. A new obligation was now interpolated, that of defending each other even against the King himself. Copies of this Bond were quickly dispatched for signature all over the country, and "such as would not sign it were accounted little better than Papists." Of these, however, Lord Napier was one. With rare perspicacity he perceived what might come of such a movement, and here for once he differed from Montrose. It is possible that the latter in his youthful enthusiasm and self-confidence may have dreamed of controlling and guiding the movement—his loyalty to the King it is impossible to doubt. With Lord Napier, he believed Charles to be misguided. Both deprecated his latest actions, but while the one feared any form of open resistance lest a flood be loosed impossible to stem, the other, never easily persuaded to turn aside from a path deliberately chosen, deemed the Covenant a means of convincing the King that the religion and liberties of a people are sacred.

By various means and from various motives the greater number of the people were quickly persuaded to subscribe to the Covenant. The inhabitants of one district alone held aloof, and that the district under the sway of the Earl of Huntly, chief of the Gordon clan. He had utterly refused to have part or lot in the Covenanting doings, and Aberdeen, the chief town in that part of Scotland, was the only one of importance to contemn the Covenant. Accordingly Montrose, with Henderson and other ministers, was sent to exercise his influence, but the mission was fruitless.

Meanwhile the King had sent the Duke of Hamilton as his representative to negotiate with the Scotch. The whole country was practically in a state of rebellion; a War Committee had been appointed, and a regular contribution, which was, properly speaking, a tax, levied on the people. In face of this Charles was prepared to make certain concessions, but nothing was to be promised till the Covenant was rescinded. Negotiations on such terms were bound to end in failure, for the Scots on their side made large demands, viz. the abolition of the Liturgy, the Book of Canons, and the Court of High Commission ; the summoning of a free General Assembly and a free Parliament, together with the maintenance of the Covenant. The deadlock was not likely to be removed by Hamilton's diplomacy. He wrote to the King that an appeal to force was inevitable, and at the same time gave the Covenanters every reason to doubt his sincerity and that of his master. As a culminating stroke of policy he committed what was undoubtedly an act of treachery towards his sovereign. Having spoken in public as the King's representative and issued his ultimatum—withdrawal of the Covenant as a necessary preliminary to the discussion of points in dispute, he privately told the leaders of the movement that they had only to persist in their demands to obtain all that they desired ! Montrose was one of those to whom this amazing confidence was made, and it seems to have created in his mind some suspicion of double-dealing on Hamilton's part. He told Bishop Guthrie that he should look carefully to his steps in future.

The failure of Hamilton's preliminary negotiations was followed by more concessions on the King's part. A General Assembly should be called, the hated Liturgy should be done away with as well as the Book of Canons and Court of High Commission, the articles of Perth should be suspended, and the Bishops subjected to the authority of the Assembly. These concessions came too

late. The demand now was for the entire abolition of
Episcopacy, and when the General Assembly met, in
November, 1638, with Hamilton acting as the King's
representative, it was quickly seen how far the movement
had advanced since the time of its inception.

The very constitution of the Assembly itself was a
declaration of war. For the first time, and utterly
contrary to all constitutional precedent, laymen had been
admitted. Hamilton protested against this innovation,
for together, nobles and clerics would be certain to prove
an impossible nut to crack. The protest was vain,
therefore Hamilton had no choice but to declare the Assembly illegal. In spite of this dissolution it continued to
sit, and passed a series of Acts which overthrew Episcopacy altogether and established Presbyterianism as the
religion of Scotland. In all these proceedings Montrose
took a leading part, so that Hamilton was able once
more to confirm the prejudices against the Earl which he
had before implanted in the King's mind. In a letter to
the King, written immediately before his dissolution of
the Assembly, he declared: " For the Covenanters I
shall only say this, in general they may all be placed in
one roll, as they now stand. But certainly, sir, those that
have both broached the business and still hold it aloft
are Rothes, Balmerino, Lindsay, Lothian, Loudon,
Yester, Cranston. There are many others as forward in
show, amongst whom none more vainly foolish than
Montrose."

The victory of the Covenanters brought them in a
new ally. Argyle, who had hitherto held aloof, now
declared his adhesion to the Covenant, and was from
henceforth to be its leading spirit. Of this man his own
father is reported to have warned Charles in earlier days :

" Sir, I must know this young man better than you can do ; you may raise him, which I doubt you will live to repent, for he is a man of craft, subtilty, and falsehood, and can love no man ; and if ever he finds it in his power to do you mischief, he will be sure to do it."

Both sides now prepared for the inevitable conflict. Before the Covenanters could regard themselves as masters of Scotland they must subdue Huntly. To arguments in words he had already replied : " My house has risen by the Kings of Scotland, has ever stood for them, and with them shall fall, nor will I quit the path of my predecessors ; and if the event be the ruin of my sovereign, then shall the rubbish that belongs to it bury beneath it all that belongs to mine." The argument of force was now to be applied. Huntly had been appointed by the King Lieutenant in the North; but on Hamilton's advice was bidden only to act on the defensive and not to act at all without his order. The command of the enterprise to be undertaken against Huntly was given by the Covenanters to Montrose, with Alexander Leslie as his Lieutenant. This Leslie, of the House of Rothes, was but lately returned from service under Gustavus Adolphus, and on him had devolved the work of organizing the Covenanting army and of drawing up a plan of campaign.

Montrose, by his rapidity of movement, outmanœuvred Huntly, who was moreover hampered by the orders of Hamilton. The city of Aberdeen was treated with great consideration. Beyond the imposition of a fine and the acceptance of the Covenant, the inhabitants found themselves practically unmolested. Terms were arranged between Huntly and Montrose. Unfortunately, when the latter returned to Aberdeen he found the

Covenanting Council there reinforced by new leaders, who decided that he had been far too lenient and sent for Huntly to Aberdeen under promise of a safe-conduct. This promise was violated, and Huntly was conveyed to Edinburgh by Montrose. He had previously warned Huntly that he had only one voice, and the very curtness of his announcement of the Council's decision to Huntly was probably adopted to hide his very natural shame at being forced to take part in so dishonourable an action. On his refusal to take the Covenant, Huntly was imprisoned ; his eldest son, Aboyne, released on parole, broke it and remained in the north to take up the leadership of the Gordons.

Hamilton now arrived in the Firth of Forth with a fleet bearing three regiments of English soldiers. He felt himself far too weak to oppose the ably organized Covenanting army under Leslie, and took refuge in negotiation. Aboyne had hastened to the King to solicit aid in men and money for the projected rising of the Gordons, and Charles, seeing the importance such a diversion would have, sent instructions to Hamilton to help Aboyne to the utmost of his power. Meanwhile the Gordons had risen prematurely, and instead of going himself or even sending troops to their aid, Hamilton dispatched two of his three regiments to the King at York, where they were comparatively useless. Thus, on the arrival of Aboyne with the King's message, Hamilton could only express regret and aid him with a few soldiers from his sole remaining regiment, one or two guns, and a leader who earned for himself in the subsequent actions against Montrose the unenviable title of " Traitor Gunn." It is hard to reconcile Hamilton's conduct with his professions of loyalty. Even now, if he had made vigorous use of his English troops and co-operated with Aboyne, the forces of Leslie now to be dispatched to the Borders might have been considerably weakened ; instead he proceeded south to join the King at York, leaving Aboyne to do the best he could.

To Montrose had been entrusted the work of suppressing the northern nobles, and Aberdeen had again fallen into the hands of the Covenanters, led by Earl Marischal. Montrose was in time to save the town from plunder, much to the discontent of the Covenanting leaders, and also of his own followers, many of whom deserted when they found their expectations of rich booty so grievously disappointed. Aboyne now appeared, gathered together an army of some four thousand, and gave Montrose battle in the open near Stonehaven. The result was a rout of the Royalist infantry, though, owing to the steadfastness of his body of cavalry, Aboyne was enabled to cover the retreat and fall back on Aberdeen. Once more, this time after some stiff fighting, Montrose captured that most loyal city, and again he showed his clemency. This time he had the greatest difficulty in overbearing those who wished to give Aberdeen up to destruction, but his determination triumphed even against the direct commands of the leaders of his party.

Immediately on this success came news of the Pacification of Berwick, that treaty or truce whose terms were, as Hallam declares, " unsatisfactory and indefinite, enormous in concession, yet affording a pretext for new encroachments." Baillie hints that the Scotch were anxious for the treaty, not being secure of their own party, especially Montrose, though so far he had certainly shown no signs of defection. In accordance with the

terms of the treaty Montrose disbanded his army. He
had already shown Scotland his worth. Lightning
activity, resource which could turn what looked like certain defeat into glorious victory, clemency in the hour of
triumph—these are qualities of a great general, and these
Montrose was destined to display time and again, though
in other service than that of the Covenanters. Montrose
now proceeded to Berwick to take his part in celebrating
the peace to which his efforts had largely contributed.
From this period his loyalty to the Covenant began to
waver, and this was due to many causes—his renewed
belief in the sincerity of the King's promises concerning
religion, his dislike of the actions of the Parliament
which soon met in Scotland, and which proceeded to
make changes revolutionary of the Constitution and
destructive of any semblance of the royal power, and his
suspicions of Argyle, whom he now perceived to have aims
other than those of the Covenant which he had engaged
to defend.

The great difference between Argyle and Montrose at
this juncture was, that whereas the former saw clearly
that the old order was changing and resolved accordingly
to mould the new to his own ends, Montrose believed in a
restoration of the old form of Constitution free from
tyranny of sovereign and subject alike. The one was an
opportunist, the other an idealist.

The summoning of the Assembly which Charles had
agreed in the Pacification to consult on all disputed
ecclesiastical questions was the signal for fresh strife.
The King summoned the Bishops to attend as heretofore,
and this the Scots took as a breach of his promise concerning the settlement of religion. Accordingly, though
the royal fortresses were restored, the promise to dis-

band the army and abolish the Tables was not carried out. Charles was furious and summoned the leading nobles to answer for their conduct. Only six appeared in answer, but Montrose was among them. Very naturally the King refused to trust himself in Scotland, whose leaders would not trust him, and the Parliament met without him.

The first trial of strength between Argyle and Montrose was now to take place. The enforced absence of the Bishops necessitated a reconstruction of the framework of Parliament. The King proposed that Presbyterian ministers should take the place of the Bishops. Both Argyle and Montrose opposed this. The latter desired that the King should nominate nobles; Argyle, who feared many of the nobility, and aimed at substituting his own authority for that of the King, carried a motion that each of the four Estates should nominate members. Thus while his influence was to be paramount in Parliament in the future, that of the King was utterly overthrown. The opposition of Montrose to this and to certain attacks on the prerogatives of the King caused him to become "suspect" by that party, which, under Argyle's leadership, was fast becoming a mere faction. This is shown by the paper which Montrose found one morning affixed to his door bearing the words " Invictus armis verbis vincitur "—in reference to his alleged subversion by the King during his recent visit to Berwick. Certainly Montrose had begun to draw back, he had even begun to define his ideal Constitution and to believe that Charles might yet, with the help of a loyal Scotland, realize that ideal. He did not believe in the rule of subjects, but in the just rule of one person advised by his nobles. Just as little as he believed in the rule of subjects did he believe

in a state controlled by clergy, hence his opposition first
to Charles' attempts to enforce Episcopacy and the
rule of Bishops, and now to the dominating influence
of the Presbyters. Still he was not sure of his
ground. He had no following, no proof of Argyle's
intentions, only suspicions. He still hoped to control
the faction and outwit Argyle ; to declare too soon for
the King might ruin all, precipitate the very crisis which
he wished to avoid. This is the secret of his remaining so
long in the ranks of the Covenanters. Not until he was
thoroughly convinced that their aims included the
substitution of Argyle as Dictator for Charles as King
would he abandon the cause which he had so enthusiastically supported. Even then, though morally convinced,
he could not act alone. He waited, hoping to collect
evidence and then act in an open constitutional manner.
By his delay he gave Argyle the victory for the second
time. The difficulties in his way were, however, very
great. During the early months of the Parliament he had
written once or twice to the King, and Baillie, in a letter
written during October, 1639, speaks of rumours concerning the defection of Montrose, Marischal, Sutherland,
and others. Yet he, with other members of the Conservative party among the Covenanters, was made a
member of the permanent Committee of Estates, and
agreed to a resolution that in future the castles of
Edinburgh, Stirling, and Dumbarton shall be given over
to the charge only of Scotchmen, who may, indeed, be
appointed by the King, but only with the approval of
Parliament.

Probably, nay certainly, it was not without protest
and serious misgiving that Montrose agreed to this and
other revolutionary proposals. The faint hope that each

new demand was the extreme limit beyond which the
Covenanters would not advance, the dread that if they
went into open opposition the last barrier to the over-
throwing of the monarchy would be removed, such
considerations alone kept Montrose and his party within
the ranks of the Covenanters. It is possible also that
they may have desired that Charles should learn his
lesson, that he should see the determination of the Covenanters and realize the expediency of abiding by his
pledged word.

During the prorogation of Parliament Argyle went to
subdue the loyal north, which he did with considerable
inhumanity. Montrose now began to hear whispers of
certain radical changes in the government of Scotland.
Various proposals were current ; in some the scheme
was to partition the country, in others to appoint Argyle
as Dictator over the whole country. It required very
little imagination to discover in each of these proposals
treason to the King and the ultimate settlement of
Argyle as chief ruler of the country. They could therefore
only be abhorrent to Montrose, and he at once set to work
to undermine Argyle's plans. The vague form in which the
schemes were propounded made open denunciation
useless. Montrose therefore determined to form a
counter bond of all those who, while loyal to the declared
objects of the Covenant, were at the same time loyal to the
monarchy. Thus the Cumbernauld Bond came into
existence. It was signed by all the nobles of the Conservative party and also by others, such as Mar, governor
of Stirling Castle, Almond, second in command of the
army under Leslie, and Erskine. Such names as these
prove that the Bond could not have been subversive
of the Covenant, as the enemies of Montrose afterwards

declared, though they were very careful that the public eye should never peruse one word of its " damnable " contents. While thus forming a league in opposition to the secret machinations of Argyle, Montrose decided that he must bide his time, collect further evidence, and when Charles should be in Scotland presiding over Parliament, he would prepare articles of impeachment against Argyle. The success of this plan depended on absolute secrecy, and for this Montrose's open nature was unsuited ; moreover, he had reckoned without Argyle and his faithful henchman, Archibald Johnston.

Montrose as yet then showed no disposition to leave the Covenanters. While busy collecting signatures to his bond, he was also employed in collecting troops to join the army now about to cross the Borders ; he was, in fact, the first to cross the Tyne into England. Nevertheless, Montrose was in no sense of the word playing a double game ; with the aims of the Covenanters, so far as he understood them, he was in complete sympathy. He believed that they had formulated all their demands, and were now only concerned with enforcing them ; he believed, too, that the proposals which he had planned to circumvent emanated only from " the indirect practising of a few." While he was convinced that Charles meant to keep his word, he agreed that the Covenanters must show firmness and resolution, or he might fancy their demands were not those of the whole Scottish nation. He was yet to learn that every concession made by Charles was only to be used by the faction as a stepping-stone to fresh demands, that the plottings of Argyle had permeated the whole Covenanting body, and that he and his friends, useful as decoys, were now to be cast aside, but in such fashion that they might be utterly discredited with both parties alike, and so be of no danger to their some time friends and allies.

The disgraceful conduct of the English army in face of the Scottish troops who occupied Newcastle, led to the reopening of negotiations between Charles and his rebellious subjects, and certain Commissioners were sent to London. Among them was Archibald Johnston. The aims of the Covenanters began now to come to light. When Charles agreed to an Act of Oblivion which should cover all past offences on either side, the Commissioners demanded that the Act should justify all the proceedings of the Covenanters, which necessarily implied condemnation of the King's own actions, and also that such of his servants as the Commissioners should designate should be exempt from the benefits of the Act. Charles in anger declared that if his servants were to be excluded, he on his part would exempt certain of the leaders of the Covenanters of whose treason he said he could produce ample proof. Upon this Archibald Johnston at once wrote to the Committee of the Estates that they should proceed against Montrose and his friends, in order that their evidence might not be forthcoming for the King, " seeing we hear it comes from Montrose." This advice did not fall on deaf ears. Montrose had already been accused of holding correspondence with the King. He at once avowed the truth of the statement, asking in what the crime consisted. This the Covenanters were unable to answer, as so far they protested fervent loyalty to the King's person. Next his Bond was produced. Montrose acknowledged its authorship, and justified his action as being for the upholding of the Covenant against the " indirect practising of a few," and not for its undoing. The Committee had declared themselves satisfied with these answers, accompanied as they were by the surrender and burning of the Bond, and he returned to the army at Newcastle. That his mind was very unsettled by these happenings is proved by the fact that he seriously thought at this time of leaving the country and joining the army of the Prince Palatine.

When Archibald Johnston's information arrived, Montrose was again summoned before the Committee and interrogated concerning the accusations of treason he had made against Argyle. This information was not the only ground of the Committee's action. Since the burning of the Bond, Montrose had talked to various persons of his reasons for forming that Bond within a Bond, of his suspicions of Argyle, and of his future plans for the overthrow of that nobleman's ambitious schemes. There were not wanting tongues to report these conversations to the leaders of the Covenanters. Montrose frankly confessed his doubts concerning Argyle's intentions, and challenged him to prove their falsity. Argyle knew that the time was not ripe for the public disclosure of schemes towards which he was as yet only feeling his way, so denied all knowledge of them. Montrose thereupon named his authorities. John Stewart, who had heard Argyle in conversation speak of the necessity of removing the King from power, was one of these; Lord Lindsay, who had spoken to Montrose concerning the Dictatorship, another. James Stewart, in face of Argyle's denials, adhered to his story; but Lindsay, while acknowledging the gist of the conversation with Montrose, denied that he had spoken of Argyle as Dictator. John Stewart was lodged in prison and, in fear of his life or from promise of reward, confessed that he had invented the treasonable speeches of Argyle, and also disclosed the fact that copies of them had been dispatched to the King by a messenger from Montrose, Walter Stewart. The Committee hastened to waylay this Walter Stewart, and obtained from him a letter from the King to Montrose. In itself this contained no matter treacherous to Covenant or Covenanters. It was merely an answer from Charles to a petition from Montrose, begging him to come in person to Scotland and preside at the forthcoming Parliament. It certainly pointed to some degree of correspondence between the two, and it would seem that Montrose had acquainted the King with his ideas on government and on the manner in which Charles should deal with present difficulties. A paper is extant containing, in Lord Napier's writing, just such recommendations as were afterwards adopted by Charles, and the very words of which he occasionally reproduced in his speech at the opening of Parliament. Thus it would appear that the King was so influenced by the pleadings and advice of Montrose that he came to Scotland on his sole solicitation, when such a course was strongly discouraged by his advisers in England.

This letter was the only proof of any " plot " on the part of Montrose and his friends. It is true that Walter Stewart afterwards spoke of and produced papers, in his own handwriting, written in some sort of cipher, in which letters and the names of animals were used to designate some persons unknown. These, as he translated them, pointed to the denunciation of Argyle as a traitor, and to the concerting of measures to be taken against him. Nevertheless, no corroboration of this evidence was obtainable. In spite of this, Montrose, Lord Napier, Sir George Stirling, and Sir Archibald Stewart were seized and imprisoned in the Castle. It was known that these four men had frequently met in the dwelling of one or other of them, and they had therefore become known amongst the Covenanters as the Plotters and Banders, though the extent of their " plotting " was to persuade Charles to come to Scotland to settle affairs peaceably.

When the King arrived in Scotland, in August, 1641, it was to find his friends in prison and the field open to his enemies. In vain Montrose and his friends demanded a public trial ; they were examined in secret and singly, though Montrose himself refused to answer when questioned in this manner. John Stewart, in his confession, had exonerated Montrose no less than Argyle from the charges brought against him. He declared that when he reported to Montrose the words of Argyle he was instructed to obtain more substantial proof, but such proof must " rather keep within bounds than exceed " a direct injunction against any form of false evidence. All the evidence that can be procured seems to point to Montrose's intention of preferring a charge of treason against Argyle, publicly, in Parliament, when he should not only be satisfied in himself that treason was intended, but have obtained such proof as would justify him in taking action. Treason put away, Montrose had no doubt in his own mind that King and Parliament would come to terms.

When Charles found himself flouted in Scotland, though outwardly he was treated with every form of deference, he was forced to agree to all the demands made upon him, save that on the question of the nomination of officers of State he would only concede that Parliament should approve his choice, not itself nominate. The Covenanters were, however, satisfied with the

King's nominations, though Argyle was disappointed of the Chancellorship which he coveted. Charles would not return to England until he had secured the liberation of Montrose, Napier, and their friends, though repeatedly entreated to leave them to their fate. Nicholas, the King's secretary, wrote to his master: " As for the Lord Montrose and the rest, some here (that pretend to understand the condition of their case) are of opinion that their innocency is such as they will not fare the worse for your Majesty's leaving them to the ordinary course of justice"; to which the King replied: "This may be true that you say, but I am sure that I miss somewhat in point of honour if they be not relieved before I go hence." During the King's residence in Holyrood Montrose had some communication with his sovereign—through the agency of Will Murray, of the Bedchamber, who was granted permission by the Covenanters to visit him, and who conveyed letters from Montrose to the King. There is small doubt that Murray was a traitor, and, as he had done before, carried to the Committee of Estates, or to Argyle, not only the reports of Montrose's conversations with himself, but the letters that passed between him and the King. These undoubtedly hinted of grave danger to Charles from unsuspected quarters, and the last contained an offer to prove the treachery of someone in close connection with him, clearly pointing to Hamilton. At this letter coincided with suspicions which had already entered the King's mind, he resolved to take counsel with some of the chief State officials, including Argyle.

Before he could do this, Argyle, Hamilton, and Lanerick his brother, suddenly fled from the capital, it was said from fear of their lives, they having learned of a plot by which they were to be seized in the King's presence, and there either killed or dispatched to a British ship lying in the harbour. The matter touched the King's honour, and he demanded an instant and public inquiry. Though not public, the result of this inquiry was declared to be that His Majesty's honour was entirely vindicated. Naturally, these secret inquests have effectually hindered any certain knowledge of the affair, which is commonly known as "The Incident." Wild rumours were at once spread that Montrose had accused these men of treason, that they were to be seized and, according to some, murdered then and there; according to others, imprisoned either to await trial or until they could be conveniently dispatched in other fashion. It was left for Clarendon, in his version of the affair, to suggest that Montrose himself offered to kill these enemies of the King! There is no hint of any such thing in Scottish documents, and, if any suspicion had attached to Montrose, it must have been seized upon by his enemies and have brought about his ruin. It is possible that Montrose urged the impeachment of Argyle and Hamilton, and that a further suggestion had been made, either by him or more desperate Royalists, that in view of the great power of the accused, their persons should be first secured. They may have argued that although, at first sight, such a step might seem to prejudice the King in the eyes of the majority of the Scotch people, if Argyle and Hamilton were proved guilty of treason, as they firmly believed would be the case, he would be completely justified.

To such an extent the "Incident" may have been based upon fact. What is certain is that the King's cause, both in Scotland and England, suffered from its failure. Argyle and Hamilton dared not face impeach-ment ; through treachery they heard of its imminence, hence their counter move, which was completely success-ful.

The King and Montrose were examined concerning the letters written by the latter, but he refused to specify any particular person as guilty of the treason of which he had spoken. The " Incident " died a natural death, a new topic of discussion being afforded by the Irish Rebellion. Argyle and his friends returned to Edinburgh declaring themselves satisfied that now, at least, no harm was intended them. The King found himself forced to fill vacant offices with Argyle's nominees, and titles were given to any who desired them. On Charles's promise never again to employ them in his service, Montrose and his friends were released, to come up for trial when called upon. No formal judgment was ever given ; it was left to the King to pronounce sentence. The Committee had attained their end. By keeping the inquiry secret, people believed the case against the accused to be far stronger than it was—there is ever something suspicious in a mystery. In his struggle with Mont-rose, Argyle, the man of cunning, had won his third victory.

Montrose had now definitely broken with the Cove-nanters, and for the same reason that Strafford before him had forsaken the Parliament after the signing of the Petition of Right. Montrose believed that the Cove-nanters had gone far enough, that Charles had granted all, and more than all, that a loyal people could desire. Therefore, when he saw that the faction were determined not to stop there, but were proceeding to strip the monarchy of all its prerogatives and even of the throne itself, he drew back. That he did not at once join the King was due to the peculiar circumstances in which he was placed, to that nobility of character which made him slow to believe his fellow-Covenanters guilty of absolute disloyalty, and to some extent to his belief in himself and his power to combat treason. In this he made a mistake. He would probably have done better to act promptly, to declare openly for the King when morally certain that the Scottish Parliament was controlled by a faction. To remain nominally in the Covenanters' ranks was to lay himself open to the suspicion that he desired to run with the hare and hunt with the hounds. As an inevitable result, he was distrusted by the Royalists and hated by the Covenanters as a renegade.

To the latter, however, he was worth a bribe. Charles, still guided by Hamilton, whom he could not bring himself to distrust, believed that the Scotch would be loyal, and that he would be able to use them against the rebels at home Montrose knew how far matters had gone between the Scotch and the English Parliament; he knew that the only possible chance for Charles lay in arming the loyal north against the Covenanting army which was being rapidly gathered together under Leslie, now Earl of Leven. Montrose could not, however, gain a hearing from the King, who adhered to his promise made to the Covenanters, but he met the Queen on her arrival in the north of England, and urged his point of view upon her. She and the King would have none of his proposals, but lent a willing ear to Hamilton, who urged diplomacy and concession, and he was dispatched to Scotland, with the title of Duke.

For more than a year the young Royalist was forced

to eat out his heart in inactivity, watching events turning
daily as his fears had anticipated, powerless to stay them.
In order that he might learn definitely the intentions of
the Scotch Covenanters, he dallied with certain proposals
made to him by Henderson. In the presence of Lord.
Napier and two or three other faithful friends, he learned
that the army, high command in which was offered to
him if he would rejoin their councils, was destined, not
for Ireland, as the King and Hamilton would fain believe,
but for service against Newcastle in the north of England.
Hamilton did his best to secure the presence of Montrose
and the loyal peers at the Convention which was about
to meet, though the Scotch had received no warrant
from the King for its election, since, according to the
Triennial Bill, it was not due to meet till June, 1644.
Montrose refused unless Hamilton would promise that
if this body should prove hostile to the King and unwilling to redeem its pledge of " allowing no diminution
of the King's just rights by themselves or others,"
that he would resort to force. This guarantee Hamilton
would not give. " I will protest, but I will not fight."
In the event he did neither, although the Convention
decided by a large majority to ally with the English Parliament. The Solemn League and Covenant was drawn
up and subscribed to by both parties 25 September, 1643.
Hamilton's diplomacy had ended in failure, and at last
the King's suspicions against him were thoroughly
aroused. His " masterly inactivity " at the Convention
caused him to be arrested on a charge of treason on his
return to Oxford, and he was imprisoned in Pendennis.
His brother, Lanerick, who had openly sided with the
Covenanters and affixed the King's seal to the order
for the levy of the army which was to fight against the

King, was likewise arrested, but contrived to escape to the Covenanters. These arrests were not due to Montrose, though he had hastened to Gloucester as early as August to lay before the King the proposals made to him by Henderson, and to urge his counter stroke. Charles had rejected his counsel then, but now, when Hamilton's failure was indisputable, he was at last willing to listen. Yet the moment had already gone—the Scottish army was in England. Such an enterprise as Montrose had projected could only be a forlorn hope at this stage, and had he been actuated solely by ambition, or had he been a man of less lofty soul, he would have refused to undertake a mission so dangerous and with so little prospect of success. He was, however, of heroic mould, and asked nothing better than the service of the King on any terms and under any conditions. He only desired a few troops to secure his passage into Scotland, where he hoped at once to raise the north and all the loyalist nobles. Montrose was given a commission as the King's Lieutenant-General in Scotland. He had declined the command-in-chief, which was given to Prince Maurice, under whose orders Montrose thus voluntarily placed himself, though, as Prince Maurice was not in Scotland, this supreme command was nominal. Montrose had asked that it might be so arranged in order to avoid arousing the jealousy of the proud Scottish nobles, whose aid he hoped to obtain.

In January, 1644, Montrose left Oxford. Charles was unable to spare a single regiment, so he was obliged to rely on whatever help the Marquis of Newcastle might be able and willing to render. Of necessity this would be but small, as that nobleman was now face to face with the Covenanting army which reinforced the Fairfaxes.

Finally, Montrose set out for the Borders with a body of one hundred badly-mounted men and two small guns. On his way he gathered together reinforcements of eight hundred foot and a small contingent of horse. In that same month of January Antrim had been dispatched to Ireland to enlist the aid of two thousand Roman Catholics, who were to proceed to the Highlands to co-operate with Montrose. The latter therefore crossed the Borders with high hopes, and, as the first-fruits of his enterprise, took Dumfries. The nobility did not, however, rise in his support, and as the local levies under Callendar were advancing against him and most of his own army deserted, Montrose was forced to retreat to Carlisle. He heard, too, that Huntly, who had risen in the north, had been promptly suppressed by Argyle.

Disappointed but not dismayed, Montrose remained in the north of England foraging for the Royalists, sending supplies into beleaguered Newcastle, even capturing the castle of Morpeth, but all the time waiting his opportunity. Rupert, on his way to York, dispatched a message to Montrose to join him there. In spite of his rapidity of motion, he failed to reach the Prince till the battle had been lost and won, which would almost seem to prove that Rupert fought Marston Moor on the impulse of the moment. With the Scottish enterprise ever in mind, Montrose begged one thousand men of Rupert, who at first agreed, but next morning withdrew his promise; every man was necessary to secure his own retreat to Wales. Montrose now realized that he must stand alone or give up his hope of raising Scotland. To make his way thither with his present following would be madness, yet he sent two of his men to spy out the land. They returned with the information that there was no news of the Irish contingent, and that the Covenant was supreme. Montrose apparently resigned himself to the inevitable, and set out on his return to Oxford.

Nothing was, however, further from his thoughts than to return with his purpose unaccomplished, nay, even unattempted. He had been created a Marquis in May, 1644, for what he had already achieved; he must put the seal on those early accomplishments. After two days' journey, having only taken the young Aboyne into his confidence, Montrose slipped away from his followers and returned to Carlisle. Leaving Aboyne there, he set out for Scotland disguised as the serving-man of two Covenanting troopers, who were in reality two of his own supporters, Sir William Rollock and Sibbald. Thus he slipped through the hostile country, though twice he was within an ace of detection. His goal was Tullibelton, on the Tay, where one of his own family held sway. For some time he lay concealed on the estate of this relative, Patrick Graham, of Inchbrakie, spending his time amongst the hills and in a little cottage in the woods, awaiting any event which should give him an opportunity to move. The news which met him on his arrival was not encouraging: Huntly had fled to the mountains; his sons, with the exception of Aboyne, were largely under the influence of Argyle, their maternal uncle; there was therefore little to be looked for from the Gordons, most important of the Highland clans. The members of the Forbes, Fraser, and Grant clans were all in arms for the Covenant with the Earl of Sutherland and Seaforth. The loyal men of Athol, Mar, Badenoch, Lochaber, and the shires more directly under the influence of Montrose, Napier, and Sir George Stirling—

Perth, Stirling, Angus, Mearns—had waited in vain for a
leader, and so were accounted for the Covenant. Practically the whole of the Lowlands stood for the Covenant,
for there the prosperous middle class, the strength and
support of Argyle, formed the bulk of the population.
There seemed, indeed, little hope in Scotland for Montrose
and his cause. Nevertheless, it was when the prospect
looked blackest that relief came. Accidentally Montrose
heard of a body of wild Irish who were plundering in
the north. He at once concluded that here at last was
the force promised by Antrim. His conjecture received
speedy confirmation in a letter which, addressed to
Montrose at Carlisle, now fell into his hands. It was
from the leader of this body of twelve hundred Scots
and Irish, himself a clansman, Alaster Macdonald,
the son of Coll Keitach, the left-handed. The opportunity
so patiently awaited had arrived: this small force
might be strengthened by Highlanders, many of whom
would be ready to champion the cause of a King of Scotland against the hated Campbell. Montrose therefore
sent a letter, as if from Carlisle, to bid Macdonald await
his coming at Blair Athol, a district where he himself
was well known.

Macdonald had landed in Scotland in July, and had
spent the intervening time in plundering the lands of his
hereditary foes, the Campbells. Hearing no news of
Montrose, and being hard pressed by his enemies, he
determined to return to Ireland, but found that his fleet
had been destroyed. As he and his troops were regarded
with hostility by most of the clans, his position would
have been practically untenable had Montrose not joined
him speedily. At Blair Athol he was received with
suspicion, and Montrose arrived, alone, save for his

kinsman, Patrick Graham, and in the garb of a High-lander, just in time to prevent the men of Athol from falling upon the nucleus of his future army.

At once the magic of Montrose's personality filled the ranks. On the publication of his commission as the King's Lieutenant for Scotland, eight hundred men of Athol, three hundred Highlanders from Huntly lands, hastened to enrol themselves under his banner. At last he found himself at the head of an army. What an army! The Irish and Highlanders were half clothed and wretchedly armed; some had broadswords or pikes, but the majority would have to content themselves with stones taken from the battlefield. With this body Montrose had to oppose three armies which had been hastily gathered together to prevent the escape of Macdonald—for, at this point, the presence of Montrose was unsuspected. Argyle was hurrying from the west to be avenged on the plunderer of his lands, a second body was being formed at Aberdeen, while Lord Elcho had gathered together the men of Fife and South Perth-shire to guard the valley of the Tay.

Montrose had long ago formed his plan of action. To strike at once and strike hard was his motto. If Mont-rose's gains now, when the tide of rebel success was in full flood, are any gauge of what his gains would have been had his advice been followed earlier, the Scottish army that marched into England might well have been one led by Montrose to the aid of the King, in which case his cause must assuredly have triumphed. Prompt in decision, Montrose set out to attack Lord Elcho. On the way he met with a body of five hundred men under the command of Lord Kilpont, who had been summoned to oppose the Macdonald. To oppose Montrose was another matter, and Kilpont joined the ranks of the King's Lieutenant. Even with this addition Montrose's army was far inferior to that of Lord Elcho, both in numbers and arms. All told, his forces numbered some three thousand men on foot; the Covenanters were between six and seven thousand strong, with seven hundred horse, while Montrose boasted three! and they but skin and bone, being the animals on which he and his companions had ridden into Scotland. In the matter of the quality of his troops Montrose had the advantage; his men were fighters born, inured to hardship, accustomed to look death in the face every day, with everything to gain by victory and but little to lose by defeat. The men commanded by Lord Elcho were townsmen born and bred, undisciplined, untrained, with no experience of danger or risk. Moreover, the spirit of confidence, cheerfulness, and determination shown by Montrose had entered into his followers. Enthusiasts, as all Celts are, they were prepared to follow their leader wherever he led.

Montrose found the enemy drawn up in a long line in the valley of Tippermuir, some three miles from Perth. He arranged his men in a long line, only three deep. They were ordered only to shoot in the face of the enemy, then to use their swords; those without weapons were to make use of stones, of which there was a plentiful supply. Taking advantage of a momentary confusion in the Covenanting ranks, Montrose gave the order to charge. The wild rush of the Highlanders and the volley of stones were too much for the town-bred soldiers. They broke and fled. Only Sir James Scott, with a body of horse, made any attempt to retrieve the disaster, and he was speedily forced to retreat. Two thousand townsmen were killed in the pursuit, some even dying of exhaustion in their panic flight. Montrose had won his first victory for the royal cause, and that although a Covenanting preacher had declared : " If ever God spake words of truth by my mouth, I promise you in His Name certain victory this day." The town was not sacked, but the arms, ammunition, and baggage of the conquered host were, of course, the lawful prize of the victors.

After a rest of two or three days Montrose marched north to meet another foe, for, as it was the habit of the Highland clans to return to their homes after each victory with the booty they had acquired, he was not at the moment strong enough to await Argyle at Perth. During the interval an unfortunate event had occurred. Lord Kilpont had been murdered in the camp by James Stewart, of Ardvoirlich, who afterwards fled to Argyle and was by him well received. Later an Act was passed pardoning Stewart on the ground that he " did good service to the kingdom in killing the said Lord Kilpont and two Irish who resisted his escape." So far had the political fury of the Covenanters led them. The cause of the murder is obscure, but whatever it may have been, the result was unfortunate for Montrose, as it deprived him of the aid of the Kilpont contingent. In spite of this defection and the temporary absence of the Highlanders, the army had improved, at least in appearance. The Irish were well clothed and armed from the spoils of Tippermuir ; also on the way through Angus and Mearns they were joined by the gentry of those districts led by the brave old Earl of Airlie, and including his two sons Thomas and David Ogilvy, and that staunch loyalist, Nathaniel Gordon. This addition was doubly welcome since it included a small force of cavalry, between forty and fifty well-armed and mounted troopers.

Thus, when Montrose arrived before Aberdeen on 13 September, he was at the head of a small but trained army of fifteen hundred foot and forty-four horse. Nevertheless, the army he had to face was vastly superior in point of numbers, consisting as it did of two thousand foot and five hundred horse. Moreover, Lord Balfour of Burleigh had the advantage of position. His men were posted on the side of a hill outside the town, and he had possession of some houses and gardens bordering a lane which led to his centre. As he also possessed far better artillery than Montrose, the outlook for the latter was black enough. The issue of the day did not, however, depend on numbers and position so much as on the skill of the opposing generals. Lord Balfour knew little of war, and those under him no more. Moreover, before the battle began the Covenanters gave the Royalists the spur of a desire for revenge. Montrose had determined to try the effect of negotiation, for Aberdeen was no Covenanting centre; but the magistrates, for the Kirk to a man, rejected all proposals, and a drummer lad who accompanied the Royalist messenger was wantonly killed. As this was already the second occasion on which the flag of truce had been violated, Montrose was filled with rage, and promised his followers the plunder of the town. With his fury at white heat the genius of Montrose was never more clearly shown. His weakest point was made the strength of his army This was arranged in the usual manner, the cavalry forming the wings; but Montrose knew that for forty-four horse to charge five hundred would be madness. He therefore interspersed his scanty cavalry with musketeers and, instead of charging, bade them wait the enemy's advance. He himself proceeded to clear the houses and gardens bordering the lane leading to the enemy's centre. His right wing was then attacked by Lord Lewis Gordon, who adopted the antiquated tactics of advancing, firing, and then retreating to reload. A second attack on the same wing was easily repulsed by the Royalists, and a third was not attempted. This failure of the Covenanters on the right cost them dear, for when a strong body of horse was within an ace of turning the weak left flank of the Royalists, Montrose was able to reinforce Nathaniel Gordon with horse and musketeers from the right, and so ensured the defeat of the whole Covenanting army. A general charge led by Montrose scattered the whole body of horse and cut the foot in pieces.

Then followed the sack of Aberdeen, which lasted for three days, and which has served to brand Montrose in the eyes of many as a murderer and barbarian from that day to this. Yet it was an isolated case. Always, before and after, Montrose personally displayed the greatest humanity and mercy, and strove, sometimes unsuccessfully it is true, to curb the excesses of his Irish and Highland followers. On this solitary occasion he seems to have made no such attempt. It was the greatest mistake of his career. It gave apparent justification to the Covenanters for their subsequent treatment of the Irish; it caused many waverers to join the Covenanting ranks; it increased the hatred of the Lowlanders; it has blinded the eyes of posterity to the great and noble qualities of the man who countenanced the sack of Aberdeen. There are many excuses to be made. Montrose had promised retaliation for a cowardly crime; his men were unpaid and, allowed to plunder, were difficult to restrain; his own fury had not had time to cool during a two-hours' battle. Nevertheless, when all allowances have been made, Montrose must bear the blame. He had proved before, and was to prove again, that he could restrain his followers; moreover, a promise made at such a time and of such a kind is better broken than kept. Argyle published a decree that a reward of twenty thousand pounds should be paid to any who should bring in the head of Montrose, and seems to have cared little what means were used to attain that end. Rollock was sent by Montrose to the King with news of his victory, and to beg for aid to enable him to keep the field. On his way the messenger was captured and sentenced to death, but life was offered him as recompense for the murder of his leader. Rollock agreed, but returned to Montrose only to reveal the shameful bargain.

Now, at last, Montrose was opposed to his great enemy, Argyle, but for the present was unable to take the field against him, much as he desired to do so. He had called in vain on the Gordons for co-operation. Macdonald had left him to recruit in the Western Highlands. Montrose therefore resolved to give the slow-footed Argyle some exercise; for ten weeks he darted hither and thither among the Grampians, keeping Argyle always two or three days' journey in the rear. Only once did they come to blows. At Fyvie Castle Montrose stood at bay, and with bullets made from the pewter vessels of the Castle, and the active aid of a young Irish Lieutenant, O'Cahan, Argyle's attack was beaten off. By November the latter had had enough of this "strange coursing." The long-continued forced marches from Aberdeen to Blair Athol, from Blair Athol back again towards Aberdeen, amid heavy rain, had weakened his forces; the Estates and others were beginning to wonder why Argyle never seemed able to catch his wily antagonist. He therefore returned to Edinburgh and threw up his commission. The road into the Lowlands now lay open before the Royalists, and Montrose, calling a council of war, proposed that the army should march south. This would force the Scottish army then in England to return, and Montrose would have redeemed his promise to the King. This proposal was not, however, to the taste of the Macdonalds and Camerons; they desired an immediate attack on their hereditary enemy, the Campbell. The Lowland officers were tired of the campaign, and deserted his banner; therefore Montrose was forced to humour the Highlanders or give up his project entirely. Sorely against his will he submitted, and turned north once more. The passes into the lands of Argyle were so difficult, that the Campbell clan had often boasted that even in summer they were impassable to an enemy. Argyle himself had declared that he would rather lose one hundred thousand crowns than that any mortal man should know the way by which an army might enter his country. It was now December, yet Montrose and his army penetrated into the rich valleys of Inverary and spoiled them as, earlier, Argyle had spoiled the Gordon lands and Athol. The chieftain fled, leaving his clan to the tender mercies of the Macdonalds. The work occupied less than a month, then Montrose turned north again, but found himself surrounded.

Facing him was Seaforth at the head of an army of five thousand men. Behind him marched Argyle with the remnants of his Highland clan and some Lowland levies, while Baillie took up his post at Perth. Montrose

had no more than fifteen hundred troops, and these
mainly Irish—the Highlanders, as usual, having taken
their plunder to their lairs. In spite of this weakness
he determined to turn and attack Argyle before Baillie
could join him. In order to surprise his enemy before he
could shirk the fight, Montrose marched by a circuitous
route over snowclad hills, instead of advancing by an easy
road through the valley. By this means he would take
his enemy in flank and prevent retreat. The troops
marched thirty miles through frost and snow, crossing
rivers and mountain peaks with little or no food, so
that on the morning of the battle we are told that Montrose
and Airlie " had only a little meal mixed with cold water,
which they eat with their knives for want of spoons."
The men had not tasted bread for two days! Nevertheless, on reaching Inverlochy they stood under arms the
whole night through to guard against surprises. Such
is the magic of a great leader.

Surprise they need not have feared, for, although
Argyle's scouts had brought word of hostile forces
among the mountain passes, it entered the imagination
—of none that these could be the army of Montrose.
Only when morning dawned and the Royalist trumpets
sounded the salute for the King's standard did they realize
the truth. Even then Argyle did not anticipate defeat.
It is true that he could not take the offensive, but his
army was superior in numbers, the men were fresh. Of
his own safety he made sure. Taking advantage of an
injury to his sword arm, he watched the fight from a
galley on the lake, leaving the command to Sir Duncan
Campbell, of Auchinbreck. He arranged his Highland
clans in the centre with a Lowland regiment on either
wing. To face these, Montrose himself led the Highlanders

in the centre, Macdonald being in command of one wing, O'Cahan of the other. The superiority of horse over infantry was soon revealed. At the first charge the Lowland regiments broke and fled, and the Campbells were then utterly unable to bear the weight of the whole of Montrose's force. They too fled, and of the three thousand troops who faced the foe seventeen hundred were slain, by far the greater number of these being Campbells, for whom Montrose was utterly unable to obtain quarter. Argyle set sail and fled; his power in the Highlands was utterly broken.

It is small wonder that Montrose was confident of the future. "I doubt not," he wrote to the King, " that before the end of this summer I shall be able to come to your Majesty's assistance with a brave army, which, backed with the justice of your Majesty's cause, will make the rebels in England, as well as in Scotland, feel the just rewards of rebellion. Only give me leave, after I have reduced this country to your Majesty's obedience, and conquered from Dan to Beersheba, to say to your Majesty then, as David's general did to his master, 'Come thou thyself, lest this country be called by my name.'" If, however, we analyse the causes of his success, there was but one factor that was permanent, and that one the genius of Montrose himself. The Highlanders, and Macdonald, had co-operated with heart and soul to bring about the downfall of their hereditary foes, it was uncertain how long they could be kept together when they marched south; their habit of returning to their native glens with the spoil of each victory would be more disastrous then, when victories must be followed up at once if their results were to be permanent. Then, too, even if they followed loyally, the very fact that they formed the bulk of Montrose's army would strengthen the Lowland opposition, since to the men of the south Highlanders were as foreigners and barbarians; the sack of Aberdeen would not be forgotten. Yet it was to Lowland Royalists that Montrose looked for aid, though their co-operation with Highlanders had been thus rendered practically impossible.

Nevertheless, it was not only Montrose who anticipated great things. His victory at Inverlochy affected affairs in England. He was now considered formidable by the Roundheads. Leven was commanded to send part of his forces, under Baillie and Hurry, to deal with Montrose; thus the Scottish army in England was weakened and the King gained an opportunity. He sent a message to Montrose that a body of cavalry, under Sir Philip Musgrave, should be sent to his aid, without which, indeed, it was a practical impossibility for the Marquis to penetrate into the Lowlands to oppose the trained and disciplined forces under Baillie and Hurry. The King's plan of seizing the opportunity to strike a blow at the weakened forces of the Scotch in the north was, however, frustrated by the activity of Cromwell.

Meanwhile, Montrose had wasted no time after his victory of Inverlochy. He promptly turned north upon Seaforth and the northern Covenanters, but this army melted away at his approach. Indeed, Seaforth himself made his peace with the Royalist leader, and joined his personal following to the forces under Montrose. The latter had had another object in view when turning northwards again; he had resolved to make one more attempt to obtain the co-operation of Huntly, the head of the Gordons. In this he failed, but at Elgin he was joined by Lord Gordon, Huntly's heir, who brought in with him a small but efficient body of cavalry, and from that day became a devoted adherent and personal friend of the Marquis. With his army thus reinforced, Montrose marched south to meet Baillie. On his way he sustained two severe losses. His eldest son, Lord Graham, a lad of sixteen, died early in March, worn out by the hardships of the campaign, and shortly after the old Earl of Airlie fell ill and was forced for a time to withdraw from the conflict. To add to the grief of Montrose, his second son, a boy of fourteen, was captured by Hurry and imprisoned in Edinburgh Castle.

Now began the war of manœuvre. Baillie was a very different antagonist from Argyle or Balfour; he determined to avoid a definite engagement with Montrose, but to wear out his patience and the endurance of his troops by keeping him ever on the defensive. Montrose thus found himself unable to force an engagement on his wily opponent, and, weary of the forced marches followed by no repetition of their early successes, the Highlanders gradually deserted their leader. The Royalist general therefore determined to give his followers some opportunity of gaining reward for their labours. Believing that Baillie and Hurry were on the west of the Tay, Montrose marched on Dundee, captured it, and delivered it up to plunder. In the midst of the sack of the town news arrived that Baillie and Hurry were marching to its relief. With his scanty following it would have been madness for Montrose to attempt resistance. On the other hand, to most commanders it would have been an absolute impossibility to call off those Highland troops from their prey. Yet Montrose succeeded, and, in the teeth of a hostile army, with his little band of less than eight hundred men, he executed one of the most masterly retreats in history.

Then began again the weary work of collecting forces. Nothing had been heard of the promised cavalry from England. Lord Gordon was dispatched to gather reinforcements from the lands of Huntly, Macdonald to the west for the same purpose. Two pieces of good fortune then arrived to Montrose. Aboyne, younger brother of Lord Gordon, cut his way through from Carlisle and joined his friend and sometime leader. News also arrived that Baillie and Hurry had divided their forces; the former was stationed at Perth, while the latter had gone north to gather together a sufficient force to fall upon the Gordon lands. Swiftly Montrose planned and acted; he slipped to the north, past Baillie, to effect a junction with Lord Gordon, and was joined on the way by Macdonald. He was now strong enough to fight, and, with the object of protecting the Gordon lands, chose Hurry as his prey. The latter was now in Inverness with a considerable following of northern Covenanters, for Seaforth had changed sides again and his example was followed by others.

Hurry now determined to lure Montrose into a hostile district, and then fall upon him at his leisure. In this he succeeded. Montrose, in pursuit of the enemy, found himself at Auldearn, amid an unfriendly people, from whom he could gain no word of intelligence. It was accident alone that prevented Hurry from completely surprising the foe. A party of his soldiers fired a volley to clear the barrels of their muskets of damp powder. The sound reached the ears of some of the Royalists, giving Montrose just enough time to arrange his troops in battle array. He knew the weakness of his forces, and so determined to take the utmost advantage of his position. The village of Auldearn is built on a slope; Macdonald and the Irish were to form the right wing, and were hidden amongst rocks, brushwood, and broken ground on the upper part of the slope. Montrose himself and the Gordon horse were to form the left wing posted behind the ridge. Of centre or reserve he had none— he "could not afford such luxuries." In order that Hurry might concentrate his attack on the right wing the Royal standard was given to Macdonald. Hurry fell into the trap, but Montrose's plan was near defeat through the weakness of Macdonald's force. At first he was driven back and defeat seemed inevitable. At once Montrose came to the rescue; before any of his followers were aware of Macdonald's difficulties, he shouted to the Gordons: "Come, come, my Lord Gordon, shall Macdonald with his Irish carry all before him and leave no glory for the House of Huntly?"—on the words dashing with his left to the rescue. The charge was entirely successful—the scale was turned; Hurry's cavalry of the right wing were driven off the field; his foot, thus exposed and thrown into disorder, were easily defeated by Montrose's infantry, while the left wing were left between Macdonald and the rest of the Royalist forces. Hurry and his horse fled towards Inverness, the infantry that had not fled were slaughtered on the field. The Gordon attack had been rendered fiercer by their desire for vengeance on the murderers of James Gordon of Rynie, who, left wounded in a cottage, had been killed by a party of Hurry's men.

This battle well illustrates the versatility of Montrose's genius. At Tippermuir he had shown that he knew how to make the best use of the Highland dash; at Aberdeen he showed that he could hold his weak cavalry in until it was possible to use it to some advantage ; Auldearn testified that, given a suitable body of cavalry, he could make as good use of it as could Rupert or Cromwell.

The battle was fought on 10 May, and meanwhile Baillie was ravaging Athol. Montrose must be able to defend his supporters, but, as usual, his army was weakened by desertions and he had a strong enemy still to meet. Baillie, near Strathbogie, was joined by Hurry and the remnant of his scattered army ; Lindsay was advancing north from the Lowlands with an army of recruits. Montrose was not strong enough to fight Baillie, so he led him many miles in pursuit, giving him no chance to fight, till at last scarcity of food forced the Covenanting general to retreat to Inverness. Montrose then marched in search of Lindsay, who had no stomach for a fight in which his raw recruits would be pitted against the Irish and Highland veterans. He therefore retired to Newtyle, and at this point, when Montrose would have forced an engagement on Lindsay, the young Aboyne suddenly deserted, carrying with him the bulk of the Gordon cavalry. The cause of this desertion is unknown ; it may have been due to Huntly's jealousy of Montrose, or to his fear of Baillie, who was now threatening his territory. Whatever the cause, his father's commands had no influence on young Lord Gordon, whose devotion to Montrose had but increased with longer intercourse.

To obtain reinforcements was imperative. Macdonald was again dispatched to the Highlands, Lord Gordon and Colonel Nathaniel Gordon to the Huntly lands to bring back the runaways. When these last arrived Montrose was ready for Baillie. This general was not in an altogether enviable position. He was not master of his

19

own camp, for he was accompanied by a committee by whose advice he was compelled to regulate his actions. As this included Balfour, Argyle, and Elcho, each of whom had been defeated by Montrose, and who therefore made the usual mistake of despising the enemy, it was hardly likely to inspire confidence in any who were soldiers in deed and not only in name. Baillie was commanded to exchange one thousand of his trained men for four hundred of Lindsay's raw recruits, but the two bodies were not to co-operate, the only course that might have been of some material use. Lindsay marched south to fall upon Athol and, thus weakened, Baillie thought it best to avoid any engagement with Montrose. Failing to induce Baillie to fight, Montrose marched south and took up his position at Alford, well knowing that the rebel general must follow in order to prevent the Royalists from entering the Lowlands. This ruse was entirely successful—Baillie followed. Montrose placed the greater part of his men behind the crest of a hill hoping to lure Baillie on to cross the river Don and some rough and boggy ground which lay below it. He would then have to charge up the hill, and, if driven back, the bog and the river would make retreat a very difficult matter. Baillie saw the danger, and would probably have refused battle if left to himself, but the committee and Balcarres, the cavalry officer, urged the attack and, against his better judgment, Baillie yielded.

Montrose had placed cavalry on each wing, the right commanded by Lord Gordon and Colonel Nathaniel, the left by Aboyne and Sir William Rollock ; each wing was supported by a body of Irish infantry, the centre Montrose himself commanded. At first the fight was very equally sustained   Lord Gordon repulsed Balcarres' first attack, but he quickly rallied. Nathaniel Gordon turned the scale by commanding his musketeers to stab or hough the enemy's horses. This had the desired effect. The enemy's left, then right, gave way and fled, and the centre, being now taken in flank, were put to rout. This great victory of Alford, fought on 2 July, 1645, was, however, clouded by the death of Lord Gordon, who was beloved by all, and was especially dear to Montrose. The body was conveyed to Aberdeen, escorted by Montrose himself with a picked guard, and buried in the Cathedral Church with all the honours possible at such a time.

This last victory of Montrose forced the Covenanters to realize that their position was desperate. The only army undefeated was Lindsay's, and Lindsay was indeed a frail reed. On 8 July the Parliament met at Stirling and levied a force of some ten thousand foot and five hundred horse from the southern counties. This body was to meet at Perth by 24 July, and Baillie was to be in command, in spite of the fact that he had tendered his resignation. He was to be guided by the advice of the same committee as at Alford, for Parliament had not profited by experience.

By the end of July Montrose was ready. Reinforcements had poured in upon him after Alford. Macdonald had returned from his recruiting expedition with a body of fourteen hundred " wild west " Highlanders; the men of Athol followed Patrick Graham to the banner of his kinsman. Aboyne had brought in a contingent of Gordons, but in insufficient numbers; he was therefore again dispatched to his native glens to procure further recruits. Montrose then advanced on Perth to harass, as far as possible, the gathering levies He encamped in

Methven Wood, and inflicted much annoyance on the Covenanters. His want of cavalry finally forced him to retreat, and the enemy revenged themselves for their losses by massacring the women, wives, and followers of the Irish, who had been left behind in the wood, a butchery to be speedily avenged. Aboyne now rode in with a strong body of cavalry; Airlie, recovered from his indisposition, again joined his leader with a contingent of Ogilvies; so that Montrose was at the head of the largest army he had yet gathered together for the King. He was eager for the fray. He knew that Lanerick was gathering a force of Hamiltons to reinforce Baillie, and was anxious to fall upon the latter before the junction was effected. Moreover, the only hope for the King's affairs lay in a decisive victory in Scotland. Naseby had destroyed the Royalist army, recruiting in Wales was growing daily more difficult, and hope from Ireland was wellnigh abandoned. Could Montrose defeat the rebel army decisively enough to make himself master of the south, he might join hands with Charles, and victory might yet be to the King.

Montrose therefore determined to fight in the south or not at all, for he guessed that Baillie's Fifeshire levies would not be altogether free from the local spirit, and would fight with less heart away from their homes. He marched south and west, crossed the Forth, and encamped at Kilsyth, on the way to Glasgow, on 14 August. Baillie had no choice but to follow. The Royalist forces were arranged on an open meadow surrounded by hills, on one of which Baillie halted his men. The advantage of position was not altogether with the Covenanter, for the slope was too steep for a downward charge to be successful, and if he resolved to act on the defensive the cat-like Highlanders would make but light work of the up-hill climb. Moreover, the slaughter of the women in Methven Wood had inflamed the Irish. Montrose was prepared for the up-hill charge ; he bade his footmen strip to the waist that they might be as lightly equipped as possible for their heavy task on a hot day ; the cavalry were told to put their white shirts over their other clothing that they might be easily distinguishable from the enemy.

Meanwhile there was discord among the Covenanting generals. Baillie at first desired to delay the fight until Lanerick, who was but a little distance away, should have time to join them. In this he was overruled by Elcho, Argyle, and Balfour, whose only fear seemed to be lest Montrose should take to flight ! Disavowing responsibility, Baillie then arranged his troops as advantageously as possible and determined to await his enemy's attack. In this again he was thwarted by the folly and overweening confidence of the committee. On their right was a long hill, smoother and not so steep as that on which they were ranged. Could they reach that they might swoop down, attack Montrose, and effectually prevent his escape. He, of course, would watch the execution of the dangerous manœuvre in the very front of his position, and quietly await their attack. In vain Baillie, supported by Balcarres, protested. All that he could do was to neutralize the danger of the movement by keeping his troops well behind the brow of the hill, to conceal their march from the foe. Misfortune dogged his footsteps. Contrary to orders, a party of soldiers broke loose from the ranks and attacked the Royalist advance guard posted on the slope of the hill and led by Macdonald. They were driven back and pursued by the fleet-footed Highlanders, who thus advanced up the hill and caught the enemy as they were executing their risky manœuvre. If the Highlanders were successful the rebel army would be cut in two. Meanwhile Montrose had grasped Baillie's design, and dispatched a body of Gordon foot to cut off the enemy at their head. These, being few in number, would have been in difficulties, but were quickly supported by cavalry under Aboyne. These also were insufficient for the task, but Airlie and Nathaniel Gordon followed with the remainder of the cavalry, while Montrose led the main body of his army to the support of Macdonald and his Highlanders. The Covenanting army, attacked at the head and in the centre, was thrown into the most hopeless confusion; there was no cohesion among the different regiments, each leader did what seemed best in his own eyes. Baillie hurried to bring his reserve of Fifeshire levies to the rescue, only to find that they had already broken and fled. It was a general *sauve qui peut*; the luckless foot were slaughtered as they fled; about one hundred lived to tell the tale. The horsemen stood a better chance, but the bog swallowed up many, while others were killed in the pursuit. Argyle once more escaped by sea, other nobles fled to Stirling, some even to Carlisle and Ireland. The rout of the Covenanters was complete. Lanerick fled to Berwick, his levies melted into air.

Scotland now lay at the feet of Montrose and his sovereign. He had fulfilled his pledge. Six armies had been raised to resist a single man; six armies had been wiped out by that one man's energy and genius. This had been accomplished in the face of apparently hopeless odds. He had entered Scotland alone, a hunted man; those on whom he most relied had failed him at every turn ; he had lacked every single material requisite of success—money, arms, the support of his fellows ; on every side he had met with treachery and disappointment. In spite of all he had persevered ; the almost divine quality of his faith in his cause had sustained his own courage and inspired it in others. No disappointment, no treachery could dishearten him ; he looked beyond the present to the end to be attained, to his superb faith failure was a thing impossible. Scotland must be freed from the yoke of avaricious nobles and self-seeking political clergy; the reign of peace and love under her lawful sovereign must be restored. As far as human eye could see, the victory of Kilsyth had achieved this end. Glasgow threw open her gates to the conqueror, Edinburgh made humble submission and set free her prisoners, among whom were Montrose's own friends and relations, Lord Napier, the Ladies Lilias and Margaret, Lord and Lady Stirling of Keir, and other near friends and kinsmen. South vied with north in loyal addresses ; nobles from all parts came to pay homage to the King's Lieutenant-Governor. In that capacity Montrose summoned a Parliament to meet at Glasgow in October.

Very soon the inevitable difficulties arose. To secure the loyalty of the citizens and farmers of the Lowlands was imperative if Montrose was to lead an army south of the Border to join hands with the King. All plundering was therefore sternly repressed ; indeed, he encamped his army at Bothwell, outside the walls of Glasgow, that it might be out of the reach of temptation. The Highlanders were dissatisfied and, with Alaster Macdonald at their head, demanded permission to retire to their homes. Under a promise of return this permission was perforce given, but the promise was never fulfilled. Aboyne also seized this opportunity to desert his leader ; although he had been rewarded by an Earldom, he chose to consider that the southern nobles who had joined Montrose were preferred before him, and returned to his father with a large body of horse and foot. The remaining Irish, Nathaniel Gordon, and the old Earl of Airlie with a small body of horse were all that were left to Montrose of the army that had won Kilsyth.

It was of great importance to Montrose that the Border lords should declare themselves on his side. Of these the most prominent were Home, Roxburgh, and Traquair, and they sent urgent messages to Montrose to join them, in order to countenance their raising of levies. The step was a dangerous one, for it was known that David Leslie had been dispatched north with all speed to prevent the victor of Kilsyth from crossing the Borders. Montrose believed that Charles or Digby would cut off Leslie, and confidently advanced south. On his arrival at Kelso he was met by Traquair's son and a few troops, with intelligence that the other two nobles were prisoners in Berwick, in the hands of Middleton. It is generally believed that they were playing a double game—that the troops they were raising were believed by Montrose to be for the King, by the Covenanters to be for them, and that their imprisonment had been at their own request. By this time Montrose must have realized that the hold of the Kirk on the lower and middle classes was too strong for him to break ; not one farmer or peasant had joined his ranks. At Kelso his army comprised his five hundred Irish foot and a body of twelve hundred horse, all nobles and gentlemen.

Traquair now recalled his son, and is generally believed to have betrayed the weakness of Montrose's position to Leslie. That general had evaded Charles, and at first marched north with the intention of cutting off the Royalist's retreat to the mountains. From some cause, perhaps by the treachery of Traquair, he changed his course and pursued Montrose into the western borders, whither he had marched in the hope of finding more support than he had done in the east.

When, on 12 September, Leslie arrived at the village of Sunderland with a body of horse four thousand strong and a considerable number of infantry, Montrose lay at Selkirk, some four miles distant, all unconscious of his approach. Occupied with dispatches to the King, to whose coming he certainly looked, Montrose left the posting of the scouts to his officers; these from time to time reported that no enemy was within ten miles. The night was dark, and when morning broke there was a heavy mist, but without treachery of some sort it would seem impossible that such an army as Leslie's could advance within a mile of Montrose's position before its coming was perceived. Such was, however, the case. When, warned at last, Montrose hurried to the field of Philiphaugh, it was to find all in disorder. Only one hundred and fifty cavalry under the staunch old Earl of Airlie and Nathaniel Gordon could be rallied to resist the charge of Leslie's four thousand, and though these were loyally supported by the five hundred Irish, they were eventually overborne by sheer force of numbers. Leslie's onrush was twice repelled, but a third attack found only some forty or fifty horsemen left. The unequal fight was over. With much difficulty Montrose was persuaded by his friends to seek safety in flight. Three hundred of the foot still stood their ground, but when two hundred and fifty had been slaughtered quarter was asked and obtained for the remainder. Whatever cruelties may be laid to the charge of Montrose's Highlanders, they did not slay women in cold blood as did the self-righteous Covenanters. Every man and some three hundred women and children who followed the camp were mercilessly slain, the few who by some miracle escaped being afterwards thrown over a bridge into the river near Linlithgow. Neither when quarter was given did Montrose ever break his word; the quarter granted to the Irish was soon retracted; every one of the fifty was murdered by the soldiers at the instance of the Covenanting clergy and nobles, who declared that the quarter had been granted not to the men, but only to the officer who asked it! Such are the tender mercies of the righteous!

The disaster of Philiphaugh—it can scarcely be called a battle—was the death-blow to Charles' hopes from the Royalist forces in Scotland, though for some time he refused to recognize it as irretrievable. Montrose, still not despairing, had hurried north to see if the King's great need would not stir Huntly to make some final effort in his master's cause. In Athol he called upon the Highlanders to renew their efforts. Advancing further north, Aboyne and his younger brother, Lord Lewis, answered to his summons. Success seemed once more within his grasp, when suddenly Huntly recalled the Gordons, without whom the project of advancing on Glasgow was hopeless. It was probably not jealousy alone that prompted Huntly's action, his own territories were threatened by Middleton and, from his point of view, it would be madness to invade the south, leaving his own lands an easy prey to the Covenanters.

It has been suggested that Montrose would have been

better advised to have co-operated with Huntly in crushing Middleton than to stake all on marching south. It is, however, an open question whether even then Huntly would have loyally supported Montrose ; certainly he had given the Royalist leader no very convincing proof of either ability or zeal in the King's cause. Moreover, Montrose felt himself in honour bound to fulfil his pledge of returning south, summoning the Parliament that he had called at Glasgow, and giving the King the opportunity at least to march north to his support. Also, there were those youthful adherents who had been captured at Philiphaugh—he must do his best to save them. Huntly was deaf to every consideration but the one—the necessity of crushing Middleton and preventing the sack of his lands. Bereft of the Gordon contingent, Montrose found himself forced to abandon his march on Glasgow. When he returned to Athol news came of the death of his wife. Very little is known of her, and she was probably more in sympathy with her Covenanting relations than with her husband. Nevertheless, Montrose attended her burial in the town of Montrose, and then returned to Athol to learn that Lord Napier, his friend and counsellor, had died during his absence.

Meanwhile rumours that Montrose had won yet another victory were current in England, and Charles would gladly have made an effort to join him. Unfortunately Montrose was still in the Highlands and two hostile armies were between him and the King—that of Leslie in the Lothians, and Leven with the Scottish army on the Tees. Charles was therefore forced to abandon his projected march. Yet for honour's sake Langdale and Digby were sent with a body of northern horse to effect a junction with Montrose. They were defeated at

Sherburn, and even Digby's sanguine mind was convinced that the plan was not feasible. He was forced to retreat to Ireland, and Charles opened negotiations with the Scottish army in England.

These occupied some months, for not only was the King determined that he would make no terms with Presbyterianism, but he was equally bent on bringing Montrose into any bargain that should be made. He seems to have estimated that hero's services at their true value, though he was utterly unable to appreciate the hostility of the Scotch Covenanters to his person. Montrose had but fought for his King, to whom the Scotch now professed the utmost loyalty; he could not understand their refusal to have any dealings with their fellow countryman. Their deeds, at least, should have convinced him. In October, at Glasgow, Sir William Rollock, Sir Philip Nisbet, and Alexander Ogilvy were beheaded with every possible contumely; at St. Andrews, Nathaniel Gordon and Alexander Guthrie met the same fate. Neither youth nor loyalty could avail to save any one of Montrose's followers who fell into the hands of the Kirk, whose leaders revelled in the blood thus shed. "The work goes bonnily on," cried one of them concerning the execution of the younger Ogilvy, a brave lad of eighteen. Lord Ogilvy alone escaped by the courage and daring of his sister, much to the wrath of Argyle.

To Montrose himself Charles wrote: "Be assured that your less prosperous fortune is so far from lessening my estimation of you that it will rather cause my affection to kythe the clearlier to you." To others he declared that: "From henceforth I place Montrose amongst my children, and mean to live with him as a friend and not as a King." The Scotch, however, would have none of

him, and when Charles joined their army at Newark the
first demand made upon him was that he should command " James Graham " to lay down arms. Though
Charles, justly incensed, replied that " he who had made
the Earl of Lothian an Earl had made James Graham a
Marquis," he found that nothing could be done till that
demand was granted. Therefore, in May, 1646, Charles
wrote to Montrose : " You must disband your forces
and go into France, where you shall receive my further
directions. This, at first, may justly startle you, but I
assure you that if, for the present, I should offer to do
more for you I could not do so much."

Montrose had no choice but to comply, and terms were
arranged with Middleton. These were that Montrose,
the Earl of Crawford, and Sir John Hurry, who had
again become a Royalist, " should be excluded from all
favour and pardon except transportation beyond seas,
on condition of setting sail before 1 September." To
the friends and followers of Montrose, with the exception
of one whose lands were already forfeit, were granted
their lives and estates " in all respects as if they had not
engaged with him."

These terms were too generous for the Covenanters,
and Montrose realized that a trap was being prepared for
him. The captain of the ship that was to take him into
exile declared that he could not be ready to sail for
several days after the appointed time. He therefore sent
his friends off on a Norwegian boat which set sail from
Stonehaven on 3 September. He himself, disguised as
the servant of a clergyman, entered a wherry in the port
of Montrose and rowed out to his friends, who were
anchored outside the harbour. He thus reached Bergen
in safety. Huntly, irresolute and fickle as he had been

from the first, now that it was too late showed signs of
resolution. He refused to lay down his arms, but as he
had none of the genius of Montrose the resistance of the
Gordons under his leadership was utterly futile. He was
seized, handed over to the Committee of Estates, and
condemned to death.

In France Montrose found himself disregarded by the
Queen and her chosen counsellors. She had been entirely
won over by the Hamiltons, who now, after the surrender
of the King to the English Parliament, led a middle
party in Scotland, opposed to the tyranny of Argyle and
pledged to the support of the Covenant and the restoration of the King. The " engagement " which ended so
disastrously at Preston might have had a far different
result had the leader of that Scottish host been Montrose
instead of Hamilton. With such an army at his disposal
Cromwell would have met his master in Montrose, who
was in every respect his equal as a soldier, in some his
superior, more especially in the power of varying his
tactics to the varying conditions and·resources of the
enemy. It is practically certain, however, that no such
host would have followed Montrose. The moderate
Covenanters had been taught by their clergy to regard
him as a renegade, and no Roman Catholic priests ever
had such a hold on the credulity of any people as the
clergy of the Kirk had on their followers. Moreover,
he had led Irish and Highlanders to make war on and
plunder the Lowland Scotch; the horrors of that warfare
were fresh in their memory; the cruelties perpetrated by
their own party, though exercised in cold blood and
therefore far more horrible, were utterly unable to obscure
that memory; indeed, they may well have served to
inflame the hatred of the Lowlanders for the defeated

party and their leader. Rather than serve under Montrose, they would cheerfully look on at the utter ruin of the cause for which they now fought.

The poverty of the welcome afforded him at the French Court drove Montrose to Austria and the Spanish Netherlands. Here he met with sympathy enough, but at that time the Emperor was in no condition to give active aid. Montrose therefore retired to Brussels, and later to the Hague, where the Prince of Wales was now established.

The news of the King's murder utterly prostrated his devoted follower. For two days he would not see or speak with any one, and from that time one single hope animated his soul, to avenge his beloved master and to restore his son to the throne. Commissioners from the Scotch Estates arrived to treat with the young King; to Montrose they were the authors of the late King's misfortunes and the cause of his death. A letter written at this time discloses his feelings :—

" MY LORD,

" I am so surprised with the sad relation of yours that I know not how to express it ; for the griefs that astonish speak more in their silence than those that can complain. And although we could never justly look for other but such a tragic effect, yet the horridness of the thing doth bring along too much of wonder not to be admired, and never enough complained of. I pray God Almighty that our young Master, the King, may make his right use every way, and in particular that rogues and traitors may not now begin to abuse his trusts, as they have done his father's, to ruin him who is all our hopes that are left and lay all in the dust at once ; their coming at this conjuncture can carry no better things. Their impudence, I must confess, is great, nay, intolerable, and it concerns all such of you who are able and faithful unto His Majesty, to make him aware that at least he may shun their villainy ; it will be no more time now to dally, for if affection and love to the justice and virtue of that cause be not incitements great enough, anger and so just revenge, methinks, should wing us on. Always being afraid rather to spoil my thoughts than express them, I shall not trouble you further in this temper I am in, but only say that I am yours, etc.,

" MONTROSE "

There were now three parties at the Hague. Of these, the Covenanters desired to force upon the young King, as the price of their support, those terms that his father had died rather than grant—that is, the acceptance of the Solemn League and Covenant which involved the establishment of Presbyterianism in England. The Engagers were the remnants of that body which had failed at Preston, and were led by Lanerick and Lauderdale. The third party was represented by Montrose, who was " of clean another temper," and he was supported by the most devoted of the late King's followers. Charles II hoped to unite the two latter parties and so avoid making terms with the Commissioners. The Engagers would, however, have nothing to do with Montrose, and no arguments or persuasions could move them. They carried their jealous hostility to such a pitch that they refused to stand in the King's presence if Montrose were also there, and protested against Wishart, Montrose's chaplain and biographer, being allowed to preach before the King. Charles, irate at such discourtesy, thereupon asked Montrose for his advice on the Covenanting proposals. His reply was read in Council on 21 May, 1649. In it he declared that to consent to the League with the Covenant would be to condemn his father's memory, and that the Covenant alone was very different now from what it had been in the time of James I. Further, he pointed out that Charles is only to be King if he will consent to their ands and ifs "—that is, " in civil matters he is to obey Parliament, in religious matters the Assembly ; to have no choice at all." Moreover, those who would now proclaim him King were still engaged in persecuting those who had committed no crime save that of loyalty. " Against all which, in my humble opinion, I know no other remedy (since the disease is so far gone as Lent physics cannot at all operate) than that contraries should be quickly applied, and that your Majesty should be pleased resolutely to trust the justice of your cause to God and better fortunes and use all vigorous and active ways, as the only probable human means that is ·left to redeem you. In the way of which (according to your Majesty's commands) I shall, I hope, be much more able than in this, to witness unto you with how much zeal and faithfulness I am

Your most Sacred Majesty's most humble and obedient
Servant,

" MONTROSE,"

Charles was not unaffected by these arguments. He may have believed that a strong Royalist party could be gathered together in Scotland. Accordingly, he declined the terms of the Scottish Commissioners, though leaving a way open for the renewal of negotiations by

22

" consenting to confirm all existing laws relative to the Church in Scotland, but proposing to refer the question of the extension to England of the Solemn League and Covenant to a free Parliament."

Montrose was appointed Lieutenant-Governor of Scotland and commander-in-chief of the royal forces, and sent as Ambassador Extraordinary to obtain aid from the northern Courts of Europe. Promises he had in plenty, performance lagged sadly behind. Sweden had been won over by Cromwell, Denmark was too weak to spare either men or money, the Emperor in not much better case. Nevertheless, by the end of August Montrose had obtained a small body of Germans and Danes, with arms and ammunition. These he dispatched to the Orkneys, where they were awaited by the Earls of Morton and Kinnoul. He himself waited to gather together another contingent and for final dispatches from Charles II, now at Jersey. From Scotland urgent messages reached him declaring that his presence was all that was needful for the Scotch, weary of the tyranny of Argyle, to arise in arms in behalf of their lawful King.

When the expected dispatches arrived they told that the King was about to re-open negotiations with the Scotch Covenanters at Breda, but Montrose was bidden to prosecute with vigour the work on which he had engaged. Yet Charles must have known that a necessary preliminary to any negotiations with the Scotch must be the dismissal of Montrose, whom they termed " that cursed man, the most bloody murtherer in our nation." He may have hoped that Montrose would win immediate success, and render any treaty with the Scotch unnecessary, or, if failure should again await him, that he might wrest his pardon from the Kirk. In that case he little knew the character of Argyle, Montrose's implacable enemy! Upon receipt of this letter, together with the George and Ribbon of the Garter, Montrose at once set out for Scotland, having dispatched his second and larger body of mercenary troops. He himself landed in the Orkneys in March, but the ships containing the troops were for the most part wrecked, only about two hundred out of some twelve hundred men reaching land safely. Disappointment awaited Montrose at every turn; when he reached Caithness he found that the Earls of Morton and Kinnoul were dead, and the Highlanders were so terrorized by the vengeance of Argyle that they dared not obey the summons of their old leader.

On his arrival Montrose had issued a declaration that he was in arms for and by the command of the lawful King, in order to enable him to obtain better terms from the Kirk, that immediately on the negotiations being concluded he was ready to lay down his arms. His banner was black, with the representation of a bleeding head, and the motto, " Judge and revenge my cause, O God ! " The Parliament took swift measures. Colonel Strachan, with a strong body of cavalry, was sent to oppose Montrose's southward march, and he was joined by the vassals of the Earl of Sutherland, while Leslie followed behind with a force of three thousand foot. To oppose these united forces Montrose had a band of some twelve hundred men all told, and was besides unaware of the strength of the enemy. Strachan's cavalry overwhelmed his few horse under Hurry and fell upon his foot before they could retreat to a more sheltered position. The fight lasted barely two hours; most of

Montrose's officers had either fallen or been taken prisoners ; he himself was grievously wounded and had his horse killed under him. Nevertheless, he fought on, determined to sell life dearly, until a horse was forced upon him by a young follower and flight thus rendered possible. He determined to retire to his garrison at Caithness, and, so indomitable was his spirit, to make, if possible, another effort to retrieve disaster. If that were not possible he might from thence escape to the Continent. With this end in view he exchanged clothes with a peasant, threw away his George and Garter and any incriminating papers. Unfortunately, neither he nor any with him knew the country, and, after wandering for two days and nights without food, Montrose at last took refuge in the house of a certain Macleod, of Assynt. A price had already been set upon his head, and Macleod made haste to inform Leslie of the presence of the fugitive in his house.

Thus Argyle had won his end and accomplished the ruin of his rival. Montrose could expect no mercy from the Kirk, nor did he anticipate aught but the worst. He had fought his fight, life had no sweetness for him except in so far as he could use it in his master's service ; to lay it down for him was the greatest honour he could desire.

Meanwhile, during his final struggle Charles had made terms with the Covenanters, and at their behest had dispatched orders to Montrose to lay down his arms and quit the kingdom. This command never reached Montrose ; he was, in fact, already a prisoner when the letter was penned. Charles had stipulated with the Commissioners that Montrose should go free if he laid down his arms. It is possible that Argyle anticipated this, and so made haste to compass the death of his rival before news of the condition should reach Scotland.

On being secured Montrose was at once dispatched to Edinburgh, his progress through the country being accompanied with every possible indignity and insult. Mounted on a pony, with feet tied beneath it, in his peasant's garb as he had been taken, he was processed through all the principal northern towns, the people, encouraged by the clergy, hooting and reviling him as he passed. It is perhaps in this, and the still greater humiliations which were to precede his execution, that the heroism of Montrose burns brightest. Well might we have felt, in the words of a modern poet :

> No sign, groaned he,
> No stirring of God's finger to denote
> He wills that right should have supremacy
> On earth, not wrong !

Many men in the excitement of conflict act the part of heroes. It is given to few to bear failure, and the expressions of public loathing and contempt consequent on that failure, with dignity. If the greatest hero is he "who does his very best and fails, yet is not embittered by that failure," then Montrose surely deserves to be accounted great. He had that larger vision of which the poet sings :

> All we have willed or hoped or dreamed of good shall exist,
> Not its semblance, but itself ; no beauty, nor good, nor power
> Whose voice has gone forth, but each survives for the melodist
> When eternity affirms the conception of an hour.
> The high that proved too high, the heroic for earth too hard,
> The passion that left the ground to lose itself in the sky,
> Are music sent up to God by the lover and the bard,
> Enough that He heard it once, we shall hear it by and by.

Before Edinburgh was reached sentence had been passed upon Montrose. He was to be " hanged on a gibbet at the cross of Edinburgh, with his book and declaration tied in a rope about his neck, and there to hang for the space of three hours until he was dead, and thereafter to be cut down by the hangman, his head, hands, and legs to be cut off and distributed as follows . his head to be affixed on an iron pin and set on the gavel of the new prison at Edinburgh ; one hand to be set on the port of Perth, the other on the port of Stirling ; one leg and foot on the port of Aberdeen, the other on the port of Glasgow. If he was at his death penitent and relaxed from excommunication, then the trunk of his body to be interred, by pioneers, in the Grey Friars, and otherwise to be interred in the Borough Muir, by the hangman's men, under the gallows."

Every detail of their triumph was planned by the Parliament. When Montrose arrived at the Watergate of Edinburgh, not now in the peasant garb, for at Dundee Leslie had allowed him to obtain clothing more befitting his rank and dignity, he was met by the hangman's cart. In this he was placed on a high chair, bareheaded, with his hands and feet tied, and the cart was driven through the streets of Edinburgh to the Tolbooth. The streets were crowded, but here was no reviling ; the people were moved to silence by the quiet dignity and serene composure of the victim, whose mien suggested a triumph rather than a march to prison and an ignominious death. On the way the procession halted below a balcony in which sat Argyle and a party of friends. If he, " who only wanted honesty and courage to be a very extraordinary man," thought to gloat over the spectacle of a cowering victim, he was disappointed.

One of the guests, the Countess of Haddington, Gordon's sister, did indeed speak bitter words, and even spat upon the man whom her dead brother had most revered. Montrose looked up and met the gaze of Argyle, who shrank back, unable to meet the clear and steadfast eyes of the man whom he had hunted to death. Montrose had never looked primarily to the world for support and favour, and afterwards declared that the intended insult was unfelt by him, that it had been " the most honourable and joyfullest journey that ever he made, God having all the while most comfortably manifested His Presence to him and furnished him with resolution to overlook the reproaches of men and to behold him for whose cause he suffered."

On arrival at the prison a deputation from the Parliament arrived to examine him. When Montrose was satisfied that the King had indeed come to terms with the Covenanters he acknowledged their right, but begged to be excused for that night, as he was tired; " the compliment they had put upon him that day was something tedious." The procession through the streets of Edinburgh had occupied three hours ! Very little rest was vouchsafed to the unfortunate prisoner. The next day, Sunday, and again on Monday, he was visited by various ministers, who recapitulated his offences in the eyes of the Kirk, and exhorted him to repentance that he might be freed from excommunication. To all their arguments he returned the one answer: " The Covenant which I took, I adhere to it. Bishops, I care not for; I never intended to advance their interest." When, unable to obtain any sign of the submission they desired, the ministers resorted to the threat that as he would die unrepentant he must remain excom-

municate, for " what is bound in earth God will bind in
Heaven," he replied : " I am very sorry that any actions
of mine have been offensive to the Church of Scotland,
and I would, with all my heart, be reconciled to the same.
But since I cannot obtain it on any other terms, unless
I call that my sin which I account to have been my
duty, I *cannot*, for all the reason and conscience in
the world."

That same day he was summoned before Parliament
to hear his sentence. He had probably been visited in
prison by some of the ladies of his family—the Lady
Keir, Lady Napier, and Lady Lilias Napier, and if so
they provided him with the clothes in which he appeared
at the bar of Parliament. He wore a suit of black cloth,
with a short scarlet cloak, both trimmed with silver,
on his head a beaver hat with a band of silver lace.
He is said to have looked somewhat " pale, lank-faced,
and hairy," which is not surprising, seeing that he had
been without food for three days before he was taken,
that he was wounded, and that he had not been allowed
the services of a barber. When his request concerning
this last point was refused, he remarked : " I would not
think but they would have allowed that to a dog."
After a recapitulation of his crimes Montrose was allowed
to speak in his defence. This he did in a short and very
dignified speech, in which he justified his opposition in
arms to the League, on the ground that their monarch
had granted all their demands so that every man could,
if he willed, have lived in peace " under his own vine
and fig-tree." He declared his hands free from the
shedding of any man's blood save in the heat of conflict,
and that in his last appeal to arms he had acted by the
command of him whom he and they regarded as their

lawful sovereign. He therefore demanded justice according to " the laws of God, the laws of nature and nations,
and the laws of this land. If otherwise, I do here appeal
from you to the righteous Judge of the world, Who one
day must be your Judge and mine, and Who always
gives out righteous judgments." This solemn appeal
was met by a volley of abuse from the Chancellor, and
Montrose was commanded to kneel to hear the reading
of the barbarous sentence pronounced against him.
No sign of discomposure was shown by Montrose during
this proceeding ; he spoke no word of reproof or appeal,
but sighed deeply and scanned the faces of those who
so malignantly triumphed over him.

On his return to the Tolbooth the ministers again
attacked him. To them he declared : " I am much
beholden to the Parliament for the great honour they
have decreed me. I am prouder to have my head fixed
on the top of the prison, in the view of the present and
succeeding ages, than if they had decreed me a golden
statue in the market-place, or that my picture should
be hung in the King's bedchamber. I am thankful
for that effectual method of preserving the memory of my
devotion to my beloved sovereign. Would that I had
flesh enough to send a portion to every city in Christendom
as a testimony of my unshaken love and fidelity to my
King and country." Then he begged them to allow
him to die in peace. The next morning, Tuesday,
21 May, he arose and breakfasted on bread dipped in
ale, and then prepared himself for execution. As he was
dressing his long hair, Archibald Johnston entered his
cell and demanded with a sneer : " Why is James
Graham so careful of his locks ? " He was answered :
" My head is yet my own—I will dress it and adorn it ;

to-night, when it will be yours, you may treat it as you please."

He was led forth to the place of execution. A gallows thirty feet high had been erected in the Grassmarket, and hither Montrose walked. No friend or relation was allowed to be near him, but he wore the same dress in which he had been sentenced, and, wrote one who was present, " he stepped along the street with so great state, and there appeared in his countenance so much beauty, majesty, and gravity as amazed all the beholders. And many of his enemies did acknowledge him to be the bravest subject in the world, and in him a gallantry that graced all the crowd, more beseeming a monarch than a peer." The place of execution was thronged ; Montrose was not allowed to address the crowd, but he made a speech on the scaffold to the magistrates and those near him, which was taken down by a boy present and preserved.

" I am sorry if this manner of my end be scandalous to any good Christian. Doth it not often happen to the righteous according to the ways of the wicked, and to the wicked according to the ways of the righteous ? Doth not sometimes a just man perish in his righteousness and a wicked man prosper in his malice ? They who know me should not disesteem me for this. Many greater than I have been dealt with in this kind. Yet I must not say but that all God's judgments are just. For my private sins I acknowledge this to be just with God—I submit myself to Him. But in regard of man, I may say they are but instruments—God forgive them. I forgive them ; they have oppressed the poor and violently perverted judgment and justice, but He that is higher than they will reward them. What I did in this

kingdom was in obedience to the most just commands
of my sovereign, for his defence, in the day of his distress,
against those that rose up against him. I acknowledge
nothing, but fear God and honour the King, according
to the commandments of God and the law of nature and
nations. I have not sinned against man, but against
God, and in Him there is mercy, which is the ground of
my drawing near unto Him. It is objected against me
by many, even good people, that I am under the censure
of the Church. This is not my fault, since it is only for
doing my duty and obeying my Prince's most just
commands for religion, his sacred person and authority.
Yet I am sorry they did excommunicate me—and in
that which is according to God's law, without wronging
my conscience or allegiance, I desire to be relaxed.
If they will not thus do it, I appeal to God, Who is the
righteous judge of all the world, and Who must and will,
I hope, be my Judge and Saviour. It is spoken of me
that I should blame the King! God forbid. For the
late King he lived a saint and died a martyr. I pray
God I may so end as he did. If ever I would wish my
soul in another man's stead, it should be in his. For
His Majesty now living, never people, I believe, might
be more happy in a King. His commands to me were
most just. In nothing that he promiseth will he fail.
He deals justly with all men. I pray God he be so
dealt with that he be not betrayed under trust, as his
father was. I desire not to be mistaken, as if my carriage
at this time, in relation to your ways, were stubborn.
I do but follow the light of my own conscience, which
is seconded by the working of the good spirit of God
that is within me. I thank Him I go to Heaven's throne
with joy. If He enable me against the fear of death

and furnish me with courage and confidence to embrace it even in its most ugly shape, let God be glorified in my end, though it were in my damnation. Yet I say not this out of any fear or distrust, but out of my duty to God and love to His people. I have no more to say, but that I desire your charity and prayers. I shall pray for you all. I leave my soul to God—my service to my Prince—my goodwill to my friends, and my name and charity to you all. And thus briefly I have exonerated my conscience."

He desired the prayers of the ministers, though he could not comply with their demands and so win the blessing of the Church; they refused to intercede for one whom they termed "a faggot of hell." He then prayed silently for about a quarter of an hour. " Then with a most undaunted courage he went up to the top of that prodigious gibbet, where, having freely pardoned the executioner, he gave him three or four pieces of gold, and inquired of him how long he should hang there; he told him three hours. Then, commanding him at the uplifting of his hands to tumble him over, he was accordingly thrust off by the weeping executioner. His last words were : " May God have mercy on this afflicted kingdom." Thus died Montrose, " the worthiest and noblest person Scotland ever bred," in the thirty-eighth year of his age, in the very prime and vigour of manhood, for no other crime than devoted loyalty to the man whom his murderers at that very moment were hailing as their King.

The horrible details of the brutal sentence were carried out, but a beautiful legend has it that the body was opened a few nights after the execution, the heart removed, placed in a silver casket, and given to the Lady

Napier, whose husband had, according to another uncle, a Covenanter, " such a preposterous love for Montrose." There is a portrait of that lady in later life with her arms resting on a casket, believed to be that which contained the heart of Montrose.

After the Restoration, in 1661, the remains of Montrose were collected and a public funeral accorded them in the Cathedral Church of St. Giles, where they still lie, now honoured by a stately shrine erected to the memory of Scotland's greatest hero by general subscription, in 1888.

INDEX

21

PRINTED BY
WILLIAM BRENDON AND SON, LTD.
PLYMOUTH

A SELECTION OF BOOKS PUBLISHED BY METHUEN AND COMPANY LIMITED 36 ESSEX STREET LONDON W.C.

CONTENTS

OCTOBER 1910

A SELECTION OF

MESSRS. METHUEN'S

PUBLICATIONS

In this Catalogue the order is according to authors. An asterisk denotes that the book is in the press.

Colonial Editions are published of all Messrs. METHUEN's Novels issued at a price above 2s 6d, and similar editions are published of some works of General Literature. Colonial editions are only for circulation in the British Colonies and India.

All books marked net are not subject to discount, and cannot be bought at less than the published price. Books not marked net are subject to the discount which the bookseller allows.

Messrs. METHUEN's books are kept in stock by all good booksellers. If there is any difficulty in seeing copies, Messrs. Methuen will be very glad to have early information, and specimen copies of any books will be sent on receipt of the published price *plus* postage for net books, and of the published price for ordinary books.

This Catalogue contains only a selection of the more important books published by Messrs. Methuen. A complete and illustrated catalogue of their publications may be obtained on application.

Addleshaw (Percy). SIR PHILIP SIDNEY. Illustrated *Second Edition.* *Demy 8vo.* 10s 6d net

Adeney (W. F.), M.A. See Bennett (W H.).

Ady (Cecilia M.). A HISTORY OF MILAN UNDER THE SFORZA. Illustrated. *Demy 8vo* 10s. 6d. net

Aldis (Janet). THE QUEEN OF LETTER WRITERS, MARQUISE DE SÉVIGNÉ, DAME DE BOURBILLY, 1626–96. Illustrated *Second Edition. Demy 8vo.* 12s 6d net

Allen (M.). A HISTORY OF VERONA. Illustrated. *Demy 8vo.* 12s 6d. net.

Amherst (Lady). A SKETCH OF EGYPTIAN HISTORY FROM THE EARLIEST TIMES TO THE PRESENT DAY. Illustrated. *A New and Cheaper Issue. Demy 8vo.* 7s. 6d. net.

Andrewes (Amy G.) THE STORY OF BAYARD. Edited by A. G ANDREWES, *Cr 8vo.* 2s. 6d

Andrewes (Bishop). PRECES PRIVATAE. Translated and edited, with Notes, by F. E. BRIGHTMAN, M.A., of Pusey House, Oxford. *Cr. 8vo.* 6s

Anon. THE WESTMINSTER PROBLEMS BOOK. Prose and Verse. Compiled from *The Saturday Westminster Gazette* Competitions, 1904–1907 *Cr. 8vo* 3s. 6d net

VENICE AND HER TREASURES. Illustrated. *Round corners. Fcap. 8vo* 5s net

Aristotle. THE ETHICS OF Edited, with an Introduction and Notes, by JOHN BURNET, M A. *Cheaper issue. Demy 8vo* 10s. 6d. net).

Atkinson (C. T.), M A., Fellow of Exeter College, Oxford, sometime Demy of Magdalen College A HISTORY OF GERMANY, from 1715–1815 Illustrated. *Demy 8vo* 12s 6d net.

Atkinson (T. D). ENGLISH ARCHITECTURE Illustrated. *Fcap 8vo* 3s 6d net

A GLOSSARY OF TERMS USED IN ENGLISH ARCHITECTURE Illustrated. *Second Edition. Fcap 8vo* 3s 6d net.

Atteridge (A. H.). NAPOLEON'S BROTHERS Illustrated. *Demy 8vo* 18s net

Aves (Ernest) CO-OPERATIVE INDUSTRY. *Cr. 8vo.* 5s. net.

Bagot (Richard). THE LAKES OF NORTHERN ITALY. Illustrated. *Fcap 8vo.* 5s. net.

Bain (R. Nisbet), THE LAST KING OF POLAND AND, HIS CONTEMPORARIES. Illustrated *Demy 8vo.* *10s 6d. net.*

Balfour (Graham). THE LIFE OF ROBERT LOUIS STEVENSON Illustrated. *Fifth Edition in one Volume Cr 8vo. Buckram, 6s.*

Baring (The Hon. Maurice). WITH THE RUSSIANS IN MANCHURIA. *Third Edition. Demy 8vo 7s. 6d. net.*
A YEAR IN RUSSIA. *Second Edition. Demy 8vo. 10s. 6d. net.*
RUSSIAN ESSAYS AND STORIES. *Second Edition. Cr. 8vo. 5s. net.*
LANDMARKS IN RUSSIAN LITERATURE. *Cr. 8vo. 6s. net.*

Baring-Gould (S.). THE LIFE OF NAPOLEON BONAPARTE Illustrated *Second Edition. Wide Royal 8vo. 10s 6d. net.*
THE TRAGEDY OF THE CÆSARS: A STUDY OF THE CHARACTERS OF THE CÆSARS OF THE JULIAN AND CLAUDIAN HOUSES. Illustrated. *Seventh Edition. Royal 8vo 10s. 6d. net*
A BOOK OF FAIRY TALES. Illustrated *Second Edition Cr. 8vo Buckram. 6s.* Also *Medium 8vo. 6d*
OLD ENGLISH FAIRY TALES. Illustrated. *Third Edition Cr 8vo Buckram 6s.*
THE VICAR OF MORWENSTOW Revised Edition. With a Portrait. *Third Edition. Cr. 8vo. 3s. 6d*
OLD COUNTRY LIFE. Illustrated. *Fifth Edition Large Cr 8vo. 6s.*
A GARLAND OF COUNTRY SONG English Folk Songs with their Traditional Melodies Collected and arranged by S. BARING-GOULD and H F SHEPPARD *Demy 4to 6s*
SONGS OF THE WEST: Folk Songs of Devon and Cornwall. Collected from the Mouths of the People By S. BARING GOULD, M A , and H. FLEETWOOD SHEPPARD, M A. New and Revised Edition, under the musical editorship of CECIL J. SHARP. *Large Imperial 8vo. 5s. net*
STRANGE SURVIVALS : SOME CHAPTERS IN THE HISTORY OF MAN Illustrated. *Third Edition. Cr. 8vo. 2s. 6d. net.*
YORKSHIRE ODDITIES INCIDENTS AND STRANGE EVENTS. *Fifth Edition. Cr. 8vo 2s. net.*
A BOOK OF CORNWALL. Illustrated. *Second Edition Cr. 8vo. 6s.*
A BOOK OF DARTMOOR. Illustrated. *Second Edition. Cr 8vo. 6s.*
A BOOK OF DEVON. Illustrated. *Third Edition Cr. 8vo 6s.*
A BOOK OF NORTH WALES. Illustrated *Cr. 8vo. 6s.*
A BOOK OF SOUTH WALES Illustrated. *Cr 8vo. 6s*

A BOOK OF BRITTANY. Illustrated. *Second Edition. Cr 8vo. 6s*
A BOOK OF THE RHINE: From Cleve to Mainz. Illustrated. *Second Edition. Cr 8vo 6s*
A BOOK OF THE RIVIERA Illustrated. *Second Edition. Cr 8vo. 6s*
A BOOK OF THE PYRENEES Illustrated. *Cr. 8vo. 6s.*

Barker (E.), M.A , (Late) Fellow of Merton College, Oxford. THE POLITICAL THOUGHT OF PLATO AND ARISTOTLE. *Demy 8vo 10s. 6d net*

Baron (R. R. N.), M A. FRENCH PROSE COMPOSITION. *Fourth Edition. Cr. 8vo. 2s 6d Key, 3s. net*

Bartholomew (J. G.), F R S E. See Robertson (C G).

Bastable (C. F.), LL D THE COMMERCE OF NATIONS. *Fourth Edition Cr. 8vo. 2s. 6d.*

Bastian (H. Charlton), M A , M D , F.R S. THE EVOLUTION OF LIFE Illustrated. *Demy 8vo 7s. 6d. net.*

Batson (Mrs. Stephen). A CONCISE HANDBOOK OF GARDEN FLOWERS *Fcap 8vo 3s 6d net*
THE SUMMER GARDEN OF PLEASURE Illustrated. *Wide Demy 8vo. 15s. net.*

Beckett (Arthur). THE SPIRIT OF THE DOWNS. Impressions and Reminiscences of the Sussex Downs Illustrated *Second Edition. Demy 8vo. 10s 6d. net*

Beckford (Peter). THOUGHTS ON HUNTING. Edited by J OTHO PAGET Illustrated. *Second Edition. Demy 8vo. 6s*

Begbie (Harold). MASTER WORKERS Illustrated. *Demy 8vo. 7s. 6d. net*

Behmen (Jacob). DIALOGUES ON THE SUPERSENSUAL LIFE. Edited by BERNARD HOLLAND. *Fcap 8vo. 3s. 6d*

Bell (Mrs. Arthur G.). THE SKIRTS OF THE GREAT CITY. Illustrated. *Second Edition. Cr. 8vo. 6s.*

Belloc (H.), M.P PARIS. Illustrated. *Second Edition, Revised. Cr 8vo. 6s*
HILLS AND THE SEA. *Third Edition. Fcap 8vo. 5s*
ON NOTHING AND KINDRED SUBJECTS. *Third Edition. Fcap 8vo. 5s.*
ON EVERYTHING. *Second Edition. Fcap. 8vo 5s*
MARIE ANTOINETTE. Illustrated. *Third Edition. Demy 8vo 15s. net*
THE PYRENEES Illustrated. *Second Edition. Demy 8vo. 7s. 6d. net*

Bellot (H H. L.), M A. See Jones (L. A. A).

Bennett (Joseph). FORTY YEARS OF MUSIC, 1865-1905. Illustrated. *Demy 8vo.* 16s net

Bennett (W. H.), M A. A PRIMER OF THE BIBLE. *Fifth Edition. Cr. 8vo* 2s. 6d.

Bennett (W. H.) and Adeney (W. F.). A BIBLICAL INTRODUCTION. With a concise Bibliography. *Fifth Edition. Cr 8vo.* 7s. 6d

Benson (Archbishop). GOD'S BOARD. Communion Addresses. *Second Edition. Fcap 8vo.* 3s. 6d. net

Benson (R. M.). THE WAY OF HOLINESS. An Exposition of Psalm cxix Analytical and Devotional. *Cr 8vo* 5s

*Bensusan (Samuel L.). HOME LIFE IN SPAIN. Illustrated. *Demy 8vo.* 10s. 6d. net.

Berry (W. Grinton), M A. FRANCE SINCE WATERLOO Illustrated. *Cr 8vo.* 6s

Betham-Edwards (Miss). HOME LIFE IN FRANCE. Illustrated. *Fifth Edition. Cr 8vo* 6s.

Bindley (T. Herbert), B D. THE OECUMENICAL DOCUMENTS OF THE FAITH With Introductions and Notes. *Second Edition Cr. 8vo* 6s. net.

Binyon (Laurence). See Blake (William).

Blake (William). ILLUSTRATIONS OF THE BOOK OF JOB. With General Introduction by LAURENCE BINYON Illustrated. *Quarto* 21s. net.

Body (George), D.D. THE SOUL'S PILGRIMAGE : Devotional Readings from the Published and Unpublished writings of George Body, D.D Selected and arranged by J. H. BURN, D.D, F.R.S.E. *Demy 16mo.* 2s. 6d.

Boulting (W.). TASSO AND HIS TIMES. Illustrated. *Demy 8vo.* 10s. 6d net.

Bovill (W. B. Forster). HUNGARY AND THE HUNGARIANS. Illustrated. *Demy 8vo.* 7s. 6d net

Bowden (E. M.). THE IMITATION OF BUDDHA : Being Quotations from Buddhist Literature for each Day in the Year *Fifth Edition Cr. 16mo* 2s. 6d

Brabant (F. G.), M.A. RAMBLES IN SUSSEX. Illustrated. *Cr. 8vo.* 6s.

Bradley (A. G.). ROUND ABOUT WILTSHIRE. Illustrated. *Second Edition. Cr 8vo.* 6s.
THE ROMANCE OF NORTHUMBERLAND. Illustrated *Second Edition Demy 8vo.* 7s 6d net

Braid (James), Open Champion, 1901, 1905 and 1906. ADVANCED GOLF Illustrated *Fifth Edition. Demy 8vo* 10s. 6d net

Braid (James) and Others. GREAT GOLFERS IN THE MAKING. Edited by HENRY LEACH. Illustrated *Second Edition Demy 8vo* 7s. 6d. net

Brailsford (H. N.). MACEDONIA : Its RACES AND THEIR FUTURE. Illustrated *Demy 8vo* 12s 6d net.

Brodrick (Mary) and Morton (A. Anderson). A CONCISE DICTIONARY OF EGYPTIAN ARCHÆOLOGY. A Handbook for Students and Travellers. Illustrated. *Cr. 8vo.* 3s. 6d.

Brown (J Wood), M A THE BUILDERS OF FLORENCE. Illustrated. *Demy 4to* 18s. net

Browning (Robert). PARACELSUS Edited with Introduction, Notes, and Bibliography by MARGARET L. LEE and KATHARINE B LOCOCK. *Fcap 8vo.* 3s 6d net

Buckton (A M.). EAGER HEART. A Mystery Play. *Eighth Edition. Cr 8vo.* 1s net.

Budge (E. A. Wallis). THE GODS OF THE EGYPTIANS. Illustrated. *Two Volumes Royal 8vo.* £3 3s net

Bull (Paul), Army Chaplain GOD AND OUR SOLDIERS. *Second Edition. Cr. 8vo.* 6s.

Bulley (Miss). See Dilke (Lady)

Burns (Robert), THE POEMS. Edited by ANDREW LANG and W. A. CRAIGIE With Portrait. *Third Edition. Wide Demy 8vo, gilt top* 6s

Bussell (F. W.), D.D. CHRISTIAN THEOLOGY AND SOCIAL PROGRESS (The Bampton Lectures of 1905) *Demy 8vo.* 10s. 6d. net.

Butler (Sir William), Lieut -General, G C.B THE LIGHT OF THE WEST. With some other Wayside Thoughts, 1865-1908. *Cr. 8vo* 5s. net

Butlin (F M). AMONG THE DANES. Illustrated. *Demy 8vo.* 7s. 6d. net.

Cain (Georges), Curator of the Carnavalet Museum, Paris WALKS IN PARIS Translated by A R. ALLINSON, M.A Illustrated. *Demy 8vo* 7s 6d net

Cameron (Mary Lovett) OLD ETRURIA AND MODERN TUSCANY. Illustrated. *Second Edition. Cr 8vo.* 6s. net.

Carden (Robert W) THE CITY OF GENOA Illustrated *Demy 8vo.* 10s 6d net.

Carlyle (Thomas). THE FRENCH REVOLUTION. Edited by C. R L. FLETCHER, Fellow of Magdalen College, Oxford *Three Volumes Cr 8vo* 18s

THE LETTERS AND SPEECHES OF OLIVER CROMWELL With an Introduction by C. H. FIRTH, M A, and Notes and Appendices by Mrs S C LOMAS *Three Volumes Demy 8vo.* 18s net

Celano (Brother Thomas of). THE LIVES OF FRANCIS OF ASSISI. Translated by A G. FERRERS HOWELL. Illustrated. *Cr. 8vo* 5s *net.*

Chambers (Mrs. Lambert). Lawn Tennis for Ladies. Illustrated. *Crown 8vo* 2s. 6d. net.

Chandler (Arthur), Bishop of Bloemfontein. ARA CŒLI AN ESSAY IN MYSTICAL THEOLOGY *Third Edition. Cr. 8vo.* 3s. 6d. net.

Chesterfield (Lord). THE LETTERS OF THE EARL OF CHESTERFIELD TO HIS SON. Edited, with an Introduction by C. STRACHEY, with Notes by A CALTHROP. *Two Volumes Cr 8vo.* 12s

Chesterton (G K) CHARLES DICKENS With two Portraits in Photogravure *Sixth Edition. Cr 8vo* 6s.

ALL THINGS CONSIDERED. *Sixth Edition Fcap 8vo* 5s

TREMENDOUS TRIFLES *Fourth Edition Fcap. 8vo* 5s

Clausen (George), A R A., R.W.S. SIX LECTURES ON PAINTING. Illustrated. *Third Edition Large Post. 8vo.* 3s 6d net.

AIMS AND IDEALS IN ART. Eight Lectures delivered to the Students of the Royal Academy of Arts. Illustrated. *Second Edition. Large Post 8vo.* 5s. net.

Clutton-Brock (A.) SHELLEY : THE MAN AND THE POET. Illustrated. *Demy 8vo.* 7s 6d net

Cobb (W. F.), M A. THE BOOK OF PSALMS : with an Introduction and Notes *Demy 8vo* 10s 6d. net.

Cockshott (Winifred), St. Hilda's Hall, Oxford. THE PILGRIM FATHERS, THEIR CHURCH AND COLONY. Illustrated. *Demy 8vo.* 7s. 6d. net.

Collingwood (W. G), M.A. THE LIFE OF JOHN RUSKIN. With Portrait. *Sixth Edition. Cr. 8vo.* 2s. 6d. net.

Colvill (Helen H.). ST TERESA OF SPAIN. Illustrated. *Second Edition. Demy 8vo.* 7s. 6d. net.

Condamine (Robert de la) THE UPPER GARDEN *Fcap. 8vo* 5s. net.

Conrad (Joseph) THE MIRROR OF THE SEA : Memories and Impressions. *Third Edition. Cr. 8vo.* 6s.

Coolidge (W. A. B.), M.A. THE ALPS Illustrated. *Demy 8vo.* 7s 6d. net.

Cooper (C. S.),F.R.H S See Westell (W P)

Coulton (G. G.). CHAUCER AND HIS ENGLAND. Illustrated. *Second Edition Demy 8vo.* 10s 6d. net.

Cowper (William). THE POEMS Edited with an Introduction and Notes by J. C. BAILEY, M.A. Illustrated. *Demy 8vo* 10s. 6d. net.

Crane (Walter), R W S AN ARTIST'S REMINISCENCES Illustrated *Second Edition. Demy 8vo* 18s net.

INDIA IMPRESSIONS Illustrated. *Second Edition Demy 8vo.* 7s. 6d. net.

Crispe (T. E.). REMINISCENCES OF A K C With 2 Portraits. *Second Edition Demy 8vo* 10s 6d net

Crowley (Ralph H.). THE HYGIENE OF SCHOOL LIFE. Illustrated. *Cr. 8vo.* 3s 6d net

Dante (Alighieri). LA COMMEDIA DI DANTE The Italian Text edited by PAGET TOYNBEE, M A., D Litt. *Cr 8vo* 6s.

Davey (Richard). THE PAGEANT OF LONDON. Illustrated *In Two Volumes Demy 8vo.* 15s net

Davis (H. W. C.), M A., Fellow and Tutor of Balliol College. ENGLAND UNDER THE NORMANS AND ANGEVINS. 1066-1272 Illustrated. *Demy 8vo* 10s. 6d net.

Deans (R. Storry) THE TRIALS OF FIVE QUEENS : KATHARINE OF ARAGON, ANNE BOLEYN, MARY QUEEN OF SCOTS, MARIE ANTOINETTE and CAROLINE OF BRUNSWICK Illustrated. *Second Edition. Demy 8vo* 10s 6d. net.

Dearmer (Mabel) A CHILD'S LIFE OF CHRIST. Illustrated. *Large Cr. 8vo* 6s

D'Este (Margaret). IN THE CANARIES WITH A CAMERA. Illustrated. *Cr. 8vo.* 7s 6d. net.

Dickinson (G. L.), M.A., Fellow of King's College, Cambridge. THE GREEK VIEW OF LIFE. *Seventh and Revised Edition. Crown 8vo.* 2s 6d. net.

Ditchfield (P. H.), M A , F.S.A. THE PARISH CLERK. Illustrated *Third Edition. Demy 8vo.* 7s. 6d. net.

THE OLD-TIME PARSON Illustrated. *Second Edition. Demy 8vo* 7s. 6d. net.

Douglas (Hugh A.). VENICE ON FOOT With the Itinerary of the Grand Canal. Illustrated. *Second Edition. Fcap. 8vo* 5s. net.

Douglas (James) THE MAN IN THE PULPIT *Cr. 8vo. 2s. 6d. net.*

Dowden (J.), D D., Late Lord Bishop of Edinburgh. FURTHER STUDIES IN THE PRAYER BOOK. *Cr. 8vo. 6s.*

Driver (S. R.), D.D., D.C.L , Regius Professor of Hebrew in the University of Oxford. SERMONS ON SUBJECTS CONNECTED WITH THE OLD TESTAMENT *Cr 8vo. 6s.*

Duff (Nora). MATILDA OF TUSCANY. Illustrated *Demy 8vo. 10s 6d. net.*

Dumas (Alexandre). THE CRIMES OF THE BORGIAS AND OTHERS. With an Introduction by R. S. GARNETT Illustrated *Cr 8vo 6s*
THE CRIMES OF URBAIN GRAN DIER AND OTHERS. Illustrated. *Cr 8vo. 6s*
THE CRIMES OF THE MARQUISE DE BRINVILLIERS AND OTHERS Illustrated *Cr. 8vo 6s*
THE CRIMES OF ALI PACHA AND OTHERS Illustrated *Cr 8vo. 6s*
MY MEMOIRS. Translated by E M WALLER With an Introduction by ANDREW LANG With Frontispieces in Photogravure. In six Volumes. *Cr. 8vo 6s each volume*
VOL I 1802–1821. VOL. IV. 1830–1831
VOL II 1822–1825. VOL. V 1831–1832
VOL III 1826–1830. VOL VI 1832–1833.
MY PETS Newly translated by A R. ALLINSON, M.A. Illustrated. *Cr 8vo 6s.*

Duncan (David), D Sc., LL.D THE LIFE AND LETTERS OF HERBERT SPENCER. Illustrated *Demy 8vo. 15s*

Dunn-Pattison (R. P.). NAPOLEON'S MARSHALS. Illustrated *Demy 8vo Second Edition 12s 6d net*
THE BLACK PRINCE Illustrated *Second Edition. Demy 8vo. 7s. 6d. net.*

Durham (The Earl of). A REPORT ON CANADA With an Introductory Note. *Demy 8vo. 4s. 6d. net.*

Dutt (W. A.) THE NORFOLK BROADS Illustrated *Second Edition Cr 8vo 6s.*
WILD LIFE IN EAST ANGLIA. Illustrated. *Second Edition Demy 8vo 7s. 6d. net.*
SOME LITERARY ASSOCIATIONS OF EAST ANGLIA Illustrated. *Demy 8vo 10s 6d. net.*

Edmonds (Major J. E), R.E.; D A Q -M, G. See Wood (W. Birkbeck)

Edwardes (Tickner) THE LORE OF THE HONEY BEE. Illustrated. *Cr. 8vo 6s.*
LIFT-LUCK ON SOUTHERN ROADS. Illustrated *Cr 8vo. 6s*

Egerton (H E), M A. A HISTORY OF BRITISH COLONIAL POLICY *Third Edition. Demy 8vo 7s 6d. net*

Everett-Green (Mary Anne) ELIZA-BETH, ELECTRESS PALATINE AND QUEEN OF BOHEMIA. Revised by her Niece S. C. LOMAS. With a Prefatory Note by A. W WARD, Litt D *Demy 8vo 10s. 6d. net.*

Fairbrother (W. H.), M.A. THE PHILO-SOPHY OF T. H GREEN. *Second Edition Cr. 8vo, 3s 6d.*

Fea (Allan). THE FLIGHT OF THE KING Illustrated *New and Revised Edition Demy 8vo 7s 6d. net*
SECRET CHAMBERS AND HIDING-PLACES. Illustrated *New and Revised Edition. Demy 8vo 7s 6d. net*
JAMES II AND HIS WIVES Illustrated. *Demy 8vo. 10s. 6d. net.*

Fell (E F. B). THE FOUNDATIONS OF LIBERTY. *Cr. 8vo 5s net.*

Firth (C. H), M.A., Regius Professor of Modern History at Oxford CROM-WELL'S ARMY: A History of the English Soldier during the Civil Wars, the Commonwealth, and the Protectorate *Cr 8vo. 6s*

FitzGerald (Edward) THE RUBAÍYÁT OF OMAR KHAYYÁM. Printed from the Fifth and last Edition. With a Commentary by Mrs. STEPHEN BATSON, and a Biography of Omar by E. D. Ross. *Cr 8vo. 6s.*

*Fletcher (B F. and H. P.) THE ENGLISH HOME. Illustrated *Demy 8vo. 12s. 6d. net.*

Fletcher (J. S.). A BOOK OF YORK-SHIRE. Illustrated. *Demy 8vo. 7s 6d net.*

Flux (A W.), M.A , William Dow Professor of Political Economy in M'Gill University, Montreal ECONOMIC PRINCIPLES. *Demy 8vo 7s. 6d. net.*

Foot (Constance M). INSECT WON-DERLAND. Illustrated. *Second Edition. Cr 8vo. 3s. 6d net.*

Forel (A.). THE SENSES OF INSECTS. Translated by MACLEOD YEARSLEY. Illustrated. *Demy 8vo. 10s. 6d. net.*

Fouqué (La Motte) SINTRAM AND HIS COMPANIONS. Translated by A C. FARQUHARSON. Illustrated. *Demy 8vo. 7s. 6d. net Half White Vellum, 10s 6d. net.*

Fraser (J. F.) ROUND THE WORLD ON A WHEEL Illustrated. *Fifth Edition Cr 8vo 6s*

Galton (Sir Francis), F R.S ; D C L., Oxf.; Hon. Sc.D , Camb ; Hon. Fellow Trinity College, Cambridge. MEMORIES OF MY LIFE. Illustrated. *Third Edition Demy 8vo* 10s. 6d net.

Garnett (Lucy M. J.). THE TURKISH PEOPLE. THEIR SOCIAL LIFE, RELIGIOUS BELIEFS AND INSTITUTIONS, AND DOMESTIC LIFE. Illustrated. *Demy 8vo.* 10s. 6d net.

Gibbins (H. de B), Litt.D , M A INDUSTRY IN ENGLAND: HISTORICAL OUTLINES. With 5 Maps. *Fifth Edition Demy 8vo.* 10s 6d.
THE INDUSTRIAL HISTORY OF ENGLAND. Illustrated. *Fifteenth Edition Revised.* Cr. 8vo 3s
ENGLISH SOCIAL REFORMERS. *Second Edition.* Cr 8vo 2s 6d
See also Hadfield, R.A.

Gibbon (Edward) MEMOIRS OF THE LIFE OF EDWARD GIBBON Edited by G. BIRKBECK HILL, LL D Cr 8vo. 6s
*THE DECLINE AND FALL OF THE ROMAN EMPIRE. Edited, with Notes, Appendices, and Maps, by J. B BURY, M.A., Litt D , Regius Professor of Modern History at Cambridge. Illustrated. *In Seven Volumes. Demy 8vo. Gilt Top. Each* 10s. 6d net.

Gibbs (Philip) THE ROMANCE OF GEORGE VILLIERS: FIRST DUKE OF BUCKINGHAM, AND SOME MEN AND WOMEN OF THE STUART COURT. Illustrated. *Second Edition Demy 8vo* 15s. net.

Gloag (M. R.) and Wyatt (Kate M.) A BOOK OF ENGLISH GARDENS. Illustrated. *Demy 8vo.* 10s. 6d. net.

Glover (T. R.), M.A., Fellow and Classical Lecturer of St John's College, Cambridge. THE CONFLICT OF RELIGIONS IN THE EARLY ROMAN EMPIRE. *Fourth Edition. Demy 8vo.* 7s. 6d net

Godfrey (Elizabeth) A BOOK OF REMEMBRANCE. Being Lyrical Selections for every day in the Year Arranged by E. Godfrey *Second Edition Fcap. 8vo.* 2s. 6d net.
ENGLISH CHILDREN IN THE OLDEN TIME. Illustrated. *Second Edition. Demy 8vo* 7s. 6d net.

Godley (A. D.), M.A., Fellow of Magdalen College, Oxford. OXFORD IN THE EIGHTEENTH CENTURY. Illustrated. *Second Edition. Demy 8vo.* 7s. 6d. net.
LYRA FRIVOLA. *Fourth Edition. Fcap. 8vo.* 2s. 6d.
VERSES TO ORDER. *Second Edition. Fcap. 8vo.* 2s 6d.
SECOND STRINGS. *Fcap. 8vo.* 2s. 6d.

Goll (August). CRIMINAL TYPES IN SHAKESPEARE Authorised Translation from the Danish by Mrs. CHARLES WEEKES. Cr. 8vo. 5s net.

Gordon (Lina Duff) (Mrs. Aubrey Waterfield). HOME LIFE IN ITALY: LETTERS FROM THE APENNINES. Illustrated. *Second Edition. Demy 8vo.* 10s. 6d. net.

Gostling (Frances M.) THE BRETONS AT HOME. Illustrated. *Second Edition. Demy 8vo* 10s 6d. net

Graham (Harry). A GROUP OF SCOTTISH WOMEN Illustrated *Second Edition. Demy 8vo.* 10s 6d net.

Grahame (Kenneth). THE WIND IN THE WILLOWS. Illustrated. *Fourth Edition. Cr. 8vo.* 6s

Gwynn (Stephen), M.P A HOLIDAY IN CONNEMARA. Illustrated. *Demy 8vo* 10s 6d. net.

Hall (Cyril). THE YOUNG CARPENTER. Illustrated. Cr. 8vo. 5s

Hall (Hammond). THE YOUNG ENGINEER: or MODERN ENGINES AND THEIR MODELS. Illustrated. *Second Edition* Cr 8vo 5s

Hall (Mary) A WOMAN'S TREK FROM THE CAPE TO CAIRO. Illustrated *Second Edition. Demy 8vo.* 16s. net.

Hamel (Frank). FAMOUS FRENCH SALONS. Illustrated *Third Edition Demy 8vo.* 12s 6d. net.

Hannay (D.). A SHORT HISTORY OF THE ROYAL NAVY. Vol. I., 1217-1688. Vol II , 1689-1815. *Demy 8vo. Each* 7s. 6d. net.

Hannay (James O.), M.A. THE SPIRIT AND ORIGIN OF CHRISTIAN MONASTICISM. Cr. 8vo. 6s.
THE WISDOM OF THE DESERT. *Fcap 8vo.* 3s. 6d. net.

Harper (Charles G.). THE AUTOCAR ROAD-BOOK. Four Volumes with Maps Cr. 8vo Each 7s 6d. net.
Vol. I.—SOUTH OF THE THAMES.
Vol. II —NORTH AND SOUTH WALES AND WEST MIDLANDS.

Headley (F. W.) DARWINISM AND MODERN SOCIALISM. *Second Edition.* Cr 8vo 5s net.

Henderson (B. W.), Fellow of Exeter, College, Oxford. THE LIFE AND PRINCIPATE OF THE EMPEROR NERO Illustrated. *New and cheaper issue Demy 8vo* 7s. 6d net

Henderson (M. Sturge) GEORGE MEREDITH: NOVELIST, POET, REFORMER. Illustrated. *Second Edition.* Cr 8vo. 6s.

Henderson (T. F.) and Watt (Francis). SCOTLAND OF TO-DAY Illustrated *Second Edition.* Cr. 8vo. 6s.

Henley (W. E.). ENGLISH LYRICS CHAUCER TO POE, 1340-1849. *Second Edition.* Cr. 8vo. 2s. 6d. net

Heywood (W). A HISTORY OF PERUGIA. Illustrated. *Demy 8vo.* 12s. 6d. net.

Hill (George Francis) ONE HUNDRED MASTERPIECES OF SCULPTURE. Illustrated. *Demy 8vo.* 10s. 6d net

Hind (C Lewis) DAYS IN CORNWALL. Illustrated. *Second Edition.* Cr 8vo 6s.

Hobhouse (L. T.), late Fellow of C.C.C., Oxford THE THEORY OF KNOWLEDGE. *Demy 8vo* 10s. 6d. net.

Hodgetts (E A Brayley). THE COURT OF RUSSIA IN THE NINETEENTH CENTURY. Illustrated. *Two volumes.* Demy 8vo 24s net

Hodgson (Mrs W.). HOW TO IDENTIFY OLD CHINESE PORCELAIN. Illustrated. *Second Edition. Post 8vo.* 6s

Holdich (Sir T H), K C I E, C B, F S A. THE INDIAN BORDERLAND, 1880-1900. Illustrated. *Second Edition. Demy 8vo.* 10s. 6d. net

Holdsworth (W S), D C.L. A HISTORY OF ENGLISH LAW. *In Four Volumes.* Vols I, II., III. Demy 8vo. Each 10s. 6d. net

Holland (Clive). TYROL AND ITS PEOPLE. Illustrated. *Demy 8vo.* 10s. 6d. net.

Hollway-Calthrop (H C), late of Balliol College, Oxford; Bursar of Eton College. PETRARCH: HIS LIFE, WORK, AND TIMES. Illustrated. *Demy 8vo.* 12s 6d. net.

Horsburgh (E L S), M.A. LORENZO THE MAGNIFICENT. AND FLORENCE IN HER GOLDEN AGE. Illustrated *Second Edition. Demy 8vo* 15s. net.
WATERLOO; with Plans. *Second Edition.* Cr. 8vo. 5s.

Hosie (Alexander). MANCHURIA. Illustrated. *Second Edition. Demy 8vo* 7s. 6d. net.

Hulton (Samuel F.). THE CLERK OF OXFORD IN FICTION. Illustrated. *Demy 8vo* 10s. 6d. net.

*Humphreys (John H). PROPORTIONAL REPRESENTATION. *Cr. 8vo* 3s 6d net

Hutchinson (Horace G). THE NEW FOREST Illustrated. *Fourth Edition* Cr 8vo. 6s.

Hutton (Edward). THE CITIES OF UMBRIA. Illustrated *Fourth Edition* Cr 8vo 6s
THE CITIES OF SPAIN Illustrated. *Third Edition.* Cr 8vo 6s
FLORENCE AND THE CITIES OF NORTHERN TUSCANY, WITH GENOA Illustrated. *Second Edition. Crown 8vo.* 6s.
ENGLISH LOVE POEMS. Edited with an Introduction *Fcap 8vo* 3s 6d net
COUNTRY WALKS ABOUT FLORENCE. Illustrated. *Fcap 8vo* 5s net.
IN UNKNOWN TUSCANY With an Appendix by WILLIAM HEYWOOD Illustrated. *Second Edition. Demy 8vo* 7s. 6d net
ROME. Illustrated. *Second Edition* Cr. 8vo 6s.

Hyett (F A) FLORENCE: HER HISTORY AND ART TO THE FALL OF THE REPUBLIC. *Demy 8vo.* 7s 6d. net

Ibsen (Henrik) BRAND. A Drama Translated by WILLIAM WILSON. *Fourth Edition.* Cr. 8vo. 3s 6d.

Inge (W. R.), M A., Fellow and Tutor of Hertford College, Oxford. CHRISTIAN MYSTICISM (The Bampton Lectures of 1899) *Demy 8vo.* 12s. 6d. net.

Innes (A. D.), M A A HISTORY OF THE BRITISH IN INDIA. With Maps and Plans. Cr. 8vo. 6s.
ENGLAND UNDER THE TUDORS. With Maps. *Third Edition. Demy 8vo* 10s. 6d. net.

Innes (Mary). SCHOOLS OF PAINTING Illustrated. Cr 8vo 5s. net

James (Norman G. B.). THE CHARM OF SWITZERLAND. Cr. 8vo. 5s. net.

Jebb (Camilla). A STAR OF THE SALONS JULIE DE LESPINASSE. Illustrated. *Demy 8vo.* 10s. 6d net.

Jeffery (Reginald W.), M A THE HISTORY OF THE THIRTEEN COLONIES OF NORTH AMERICA, 1497-1763. Illustrated *Demy 8vo.* 7s. 6d. net

Jenks (E.), M.A., B.C.L. AN OUTLINE OF ENGLISH LOCAL GOVERNMENT. *Second Edition* Revised by R. C. K. ENSOR, M.A. Cr. 8vo. 2s. 6d.

Jennings (Oscar), M D. EARLY WOODCUT INITIALS. Illustrated. *Demy 4to* 21s. net.

Jerningham (Charles Edward). THE MAXIMS OF MARMADUKE. *Second Edition.* Cr. 8vo. 5s.

Johnston (Sir H. H.), K.C.B. BRITISH CENTRAL AFRICA. Illustrated. *Third Edition.* Cr. 4to. 18s. net

*THE NEGRO IN THE NEW WORLD. Illustrated. *Demy 8vo.* 16*s. net*

Jones (R. Crompton), M A POEMS OF THE INNER LIFE. Selected by R C JONES. *Thirteenth Edition Fcap 8vo.* 2*s 6d. net.*

Julian (Lady) of Norwich. REVELATIONS OF DIVINE LOVE. Edited by GRACE WARRACK. *Third Edition. Cr. 8vo.* 3*s 6d.*

'Kappa.' LET YOUTH BUT KNOW: A Plea for Reason in Education. *Second Edition Cr 8vo.* 3*s 6d net.*

Keats (John). THE POEMS Edited with Introduction and Notes by E. de SÉLINCOURT, M A. With a Frontispiece in Photogravure *Second Edition Revised Demy 8vo* 7*s 6d net.*

Keble (John). THE CHRISTIAN YEAR. With an Introduction and Notes by W. LOCK, D.D., Warden of Keble College. Illustrated. *Third Edition. Fcap 8vo.* 3*s. 6d.; padded morocco* 5*s.*

Kempis (Thomas à). THE IMITATION OF CHRIST. With an Introduction by DEAN FARRAR Illustrated. *Third Edition Fcap. 8vo.* 3*s. 6d, padded morocco,* 5*s.*
Also translated by C. BIGG, D.D. *Cr. 8vo.* 3*s. 6d.*

Kerr (S. Parnell). GEORGE SELWYN AND THE WITS. Illustrated. *Demy 8vo.* 12*s 6d net.*

Kipling (Rudyard). BARRACK-ROOM BALLADS. 96*th Thousand. Twenty-eighth Edition. Cr. 8vo.* 6*s.* Also *Fcap 8vo, Leather.* 5*s net*
THE SEVEN SEAS. 81*st Thousand. Sixteenth Edition. Cr. 8vo* 6*s.* Also *Fcap 8vo, Leather* 5*s net.*
THE FIVE NATIONS. 69*th Thousand. Seventh Edition Cr. 8vo* 6*s* Also *Fcap. 8vo, Leather.* 5*s. net*
DEPARTMENTAL DITTIES. *Eighteenth Edition. Cr. 8vo.* 6*s.* Also *Fcap 8vo, Leather.* 5*s. net*

Knox (Winifred F.). THE COURT OF A SAINT. Illustrated. *Demy 8vo.* 10*s. 6d. net.*

Lamb (Charles and Mary), THE WORKS. Edited by E V LUCAS. Illustrated. *In Seven Volumes. Demy 8vo.* 7*s 6d. each.*

Lane-Poole (Stanley). A HISTORY OF EGYPT IN THE MIDDLE AGES Illustrated. *Cr. 8vo* 6*s.*

Lankester (Sir Ray), K.C B, F.R S. SCIENCE FROM AN EASY CHAIR. Illustrated. *Fifth Edition. Cr. 8vo* 6*s.*

Leach (Henry). THE SPIRIT OF THE LINKS. *Cr. 8vo.* 6*s.*

Le Braz (Anatole). THE LAND OF PARDONS. Translated by FRANCES M GOSTLING Illustrated *Third Edition. Cr. 8vo.* 6*s.*

Lees (Frederick). A SUMMER IN TOURAINE Illustrated. *Second Edition. Demy 8vo.* 10*s 6d. net.*

Lindsay (Lady Mabel). ANNI DOMINI· A GOSPEL STUDY With Maps. *Two Volumes. Super Royal 8vo* 10*s net*

Llewellyn (Owen) and Raven-Hill (L.). THE SOUTH-BOUND CAR Illustrated. *Cr. 8vo* 6*s.*

Lock (Walter), D D, Warden of Keble College ST PAUL, THE MASTER-BUILDER *Second Edition. Cr. 8vo.* 3*s. 6d*
THE BIBLE AND CHRISTIAN LIFE. *Cr. 8vo* 6*s*

Lodge (Sir Oliver), F R.S. THE SUBSTANCE OF FAITH, ALLIED WITH SCIENCE A Catechism for Parents and Teachers. *Tenth Edition Cr 8vo* 2*s net*
MAN AND THE UNIVERSE. A STUDY OF THE INFLUENCE OF THE ADVANCE IN SCIENTIFIC KNOWLEDGE UPON OUR UNDERSTANDING OF CHRISTIANITY *Eighth and Cheaper Edition. Demy 8vo* 5*s net*
THE SURVIVAL OF MAN A STUDY IN UNRECOGNISED HUMAN FACULTY. *Fourth Edition. Demy 8vo.* 7*s. 6d. net*

Lofthouse (W. F.), M A. ETHICS AND ATONEMENT. With a Frontispiece *Demy 8vo.* 5*s. net.*

Lorimer (George Horace). LETTERS FROM A SELF-MADE MERCHANT TO HIS SON Illustrated *Eighteenth Edition Cr 8vo* 3*s 6d*
OLD GORGON GRAHAM Illustrated *Second Edition Cr. 8vo.* 6*s*

Lorimer (Norma). BY THE WATERS OF EGYPT. Illustrated *Demy 8vo.* 16*s net.*

Lucas (E. V.). THE LIFE OF CHARLES LAMB. Illustrated. *Fifth and Revised Edition in One Volume. Demy 8vo* 7*s 6d. net*
A WANDERER IN HOLLAND. Illustrated *Eleventh Edition Cr 8vo.* 6*s*
A WANDERER IN LONDON. Illustrated. *Ninth Edition Cr 8vo* 6*s.*
A WANDERER IN PARIS. Illustrated. *Fifth Edition Cr. 8vo.* 6*s.*

THE OPEN ROAD A Little Book for Wayfarers *Seventeenth Edition Fcp. 8vo. 5s , India Paper, 7s 6d*
THE FRIENDLY TOWN a Little Book for the Urbane *Sixth Edition Fcap 8vo 5s ; India Paper, 7s 6d.*
FIRESIDE AND SUNSHINE *Sixth Edition Fcap 8vo 5s*
CHARACTER AND COMEDY. *Sixth Edition Fcap 8vo. 5s*
THE GENTLEST ART. A Choice of Letters by Entertaining Hands. *Sixth Edition. Fcap 8vo.*
A SWAN AND HER FRIENDS Illustrated. *Demy 8vo. 12s 6d net.*
HER INFINITE VARIETY: A FEMININE PORTRAIT GALLERY. *Fifth Edition Fcap. 8vo 5s*
LISTENER'S LURE: AN OBLIQUE NARRATION. *Seventh Edition. Fcap. 8vo 5s.*
GOOD COMPANY: A RALLY OF MEN. *Second Edition Fcap 8vo. 5s.*
ONE DAY AND ANOTHER. *Fourth Edition. Fcap. 8vo 5s.*
OVER BEMERTON'S: AN EASY-GOING CHRONICLE. *Eighth Edition. Fcap. 8vo. 5s.*

M. (R.). THE THOUGHTS OF LUCIA HALLIDAY With some of her Letters Edited by R. M *Fcap. 8vo 2s 6d. net*

Macaulay (Lord). CRITICAL AND HISTORICAL ESSAYS Edited by F C MONTAGUE. M A. *Three Volumes. Cr. 8vo. 18s*

McCabe (Joseph) (formerly Very Rev. F ANTONY, O S F.). THE DECAY OF THE CHURCH OF ROME. *Second Edition. Demy 8vo 7s. 6d. net*

McCullagh (Francis). The Fall of Abd-ul-Hamid. Illustrated. *Demy 8vo. 10s. 6d. net.*

MacCunn (Florence A.). MARY STUART. Illustrated. *New and Cheaper Edition. Large Cr. 8vo. 6s*

McDougall (William), M A. (Oxon , M B (Cantab). AN INTRODUCTION TO SOCIAL PSYCHOLOGY. *Third Edition Cr 8vo. 5s. net*

'Mdlle Mori'(Author of). ST CATHERINE OF SIENA AND HER TIMES. Illustrated. *Second Edition. Demy 8vo. 7s 6d. net.*

Maeterlinck (Maurice). THE BLUE BIRD: A FAIRY PLAY IN FIVE ACTS. Translated by ALEXANDER TEIXEIRA DE MATTOS *Thirteenth Edition Fcap 8vo Deckle Edges 3s. 6d net. Also Fcap. 8vo. Paper covers, 1s net*

Mahaffy (J. P.), Litt D A HISTORY OF THE EGYPT OF THE PTOLEMIES Illustrated. *Cr. 8vo. 6s.*

Maitland (F. W.), M A., LL.D ROMAN CANON LAW IN THE CHURCH OF ENGLAND. *Royal 8vo. 7s. 6d.*

Marett (R. R.), M A., Fellow and Tutor of Exeter College, Oxford. THE THRESHOLD OF RELIGION. *Cr. 8vo 3s 6d. net.*

Marriott (Charles). A SPANISH HOLIDAY. Illustrated. *Demy 8vo. 7s. 6d. net.*

Marriott (J. A. R), M A. THE LIFE AND TIMES OF LORD FALKLAND Illustrated. *Second Edition. Demy 8vo 7s. 6d net.*

Masefield (John) SEA LIFE IN NELSON'S TIME. Illustrated. *Cr. 8vo. 3s 6d net*
A SAILOR'S GARLAND Selected and Edited. *Second Edition. Cr. 8vo. 3s. 6d net*
AN ENGLISH PROSE MISCELLANY Selected and Edited. *Cr. 8vo. 6s*

Masterman (C. F. G.), M A., M P TENNYSON AS A RELIGIOUS TEACHER. *Cr 8vo. 6s.*
THE CONDITION OF ENGLAND. *Fourth Edition Cr 8vo. 6s.*

Mayne (Ethel Colburn) ENCHANTERS OF MEN. Illustrated. *Demy 8vo. 10s 6d. net.*

Meakin (Annette M B), Fellow of the Anthropological Institute. WOMAN IN TRANSITION *Cr 8vo 6s.*
GALICIA: THE SWITZERLAND OF SPAIN. Illustrated. *Demy 8vo 12s. 6d. net.*

Medley (D J), M A , Professor of History in the University of Glasgow ORIGINAL ILLUSTRATIONS OF ENGLISH CONSTITUTIONAL HISTORY, COMPRISING A SELECTED NUMBER OF THE CHIEF CHARTERS AND STATUTES. *Cr. 8vo. 7s 6d net.*

Methuen (A M S), M A THE TRAGEDY OF SOUTH AFRICA. *Cr 8vo 2s net*
ENGLAND'S RUIN . DISCUSSED IN FOURTEEN LETTERS TO A PROTECTIONIST. *Ninth Edition Cr 8vo. 3d net*

Meynell (Everard) COROT AND HIS FRIENDS Illustrated *Demy 8vo. 10s 6d. net.*

Miles (Eustace), M A. LIFE AFTER LIFE. OR, THE THEORY OF REINCARNATION. *Cr 8vo 2s 6d net.*
THE POWER OF CONCENTRATION : How TO ACQUIRE IT *Third Edition. Cr. 8vo 3s 6d. net.*

Millais (J G). THE LIFE AND LETTERS OF SIR JOHN EVERETT MILLAIS, President of the Royal Academy Illustrated *New Edition Demy 8vo. 7s. 6d net*

Milne (J. G), M A A HISTORY OF EGYPT UNDER ROMAN RULE. Illustrated. *Cr. 8vo. 6s*

Mitton (G E), JANE AUSTEN AND HER TIMES Illustrated. *Second and Cheaper Edition. Large Cr 8vo. 6s.*

Moffat (Mary M). QUEEN LOUISA OF PRUSSIA Illustrated. *Fourth Edition. Cr. 8vo. 6s.*

Money (L G Chiozza). RICHES AND POVERTY *Ninth Edition. Cr 8vo. 1s. net* Also *Demy 8vo 5s. net*
MONEY'S FISCAL DICTIONARY, 1910 *Demy 8vo. Second Edition 5s net*

Moore (T Sturge). ART AND LIFE. Illustrated. *Cr. 8vo. 5s net*

Moorhouse (E Hallam). NELSON'S LADY HAMILTON. Illustrated. *Second Edition Demy 8vo 7s. 6d net.*

Morgan (J H), M.A THE HOUSE OF LORDS AND THE CONSTITUTION. With an Introduction by the LORD CHANCELLOR. *Cr. 8vo. 1s. net.*

Morton (A. Anderson). See Brodrick (M.).

Norway (A H). NAPLES. PAST AND PRESENT. Illustrated. *Third Edition. Cr. 8vo. 6s*

Oman (C. W C.), M A, Fellow of All Souls', Oxford A HISTORY OF THE ART OF WAR IN THE MIDDLE AGES. Illustrated. *Demy 8vo. 10s. 6d net*
ENGLAND BEFORE THE NORMAN CONQUEST. With Maps. *Second Edition. Demy 8vo. 10s 6d net.*

Oxford (M N.), of Guy's Hospital. A HANDBOOK OF NURSING. *Fifth Edition Cr 8vo 3s. 6d.*

Pakes (W. C. C.). THE SCIENCE OF HYGIENE Illustrated *Demy 8vo. 15s.*

Parker (Eric). THE BOOK OF THE ZOO; BY DAY AND NIGHT. Illustrated. *Second Edition. Cr. 8vo 6s.*

Parsons (Mrs. C.). THE INCOMPARABLE SIDDONS. Illustrated. *Demy 8vo 12s 6d net*

Patmore (K A.). THE COURT OF LOUIS XIII Illustrated. *Third Edition Demy 8vo. 10s. 6d. net.*

Patterson (A H) MAN AND NATURE ON TIDAL WATERS. Illustrated. *Cr. 8vo 6s.*

Petrie (W. M Flinders), D C L., LL.D., Professor of Egyptology at University College. A HISTORY OF EGYPT Illustrated. *In Six Volumes. Cr. 8vo. 6s. each.*

VOL. I. FROM THE EARLIEST KINGS TO XVITH DYNASTY. *Sixth Edition*
VOL. II. THE XVIITH AND XVIIITH DYNASTIES *Fourth Edition.*
VOL. III. XIXTH TO XXXTH DYNASTIES.
VOL. IV. EGYPT UNDER THE PTOLEMAIC DYNASTY. J P. MAHAFFY, Litt D
VOL. V. EGYPT UNDER ROMAN RULE. J G. MILNE, M A.
VOL. VI. EGYPT IN THE MIDDLE AGES. STANLEY LANE-POOLE, M A
RELIGION AND CONSCIENCE IN ANCIENT EGYPT. Lectures delivered at University College, London. Illustrated. *Cr 8vo. 2s 6d.*
SYRIA AND EGYPT, FROM THE TELL EL AMARNA LETTERS. *Cr 8vo. 2s 6d*
EGYPTIAN TALES. Translated from the Papyri. First Series, ivth to xiith Dynasty Edited by W M. FLINDERS PETRIE. Illustrated. *Second Edition Cr 8vo 3s 6d.*
EGYPTIAN TALES Translated from the Papyri Second Series, xviiith to xixth Dynasty. Illustrated. *Cr 8vo. 3s. 6d*
EGYPTIAN DECORATIVE ART. A Course of Lectures delivered at the Royal Institution. Illustrated. *Cr. 8vo, 3s. 6d.*

Phelps (Ruth S). SKIES ITALIAN A LITTLE BREVIARY FOR TRAVELLERS IN ITALY *Fcap. 8vo. 5s. net.*

Phythian (J. Ernest). TREES IN NATURE, MYTH, AND ART. Illustrated. *Cr. 8vo 6s.*

Podmore (Frank) MODERN SPIRITUALISM. *Two Volumes Demy 8vo 21s. net*
MESMERISM AND CHRISTIAN SCIENCE: A Short History of Mental Healing. *Second Edition. Demy 8vo 10s 6d. net.*

Pollard (Alfred W). SHAKESPEARE FOLIOS AND QUARTOS A Study in the Bibliography of Shakespeare's Plays, 1594–1685 Illustrated *Folio 21s. net.*

Powell (Arthur E.). FOOD AND HEALTH. *Cr. 8vo 3s. 6d. net.*

Power (J O'Connor) THE MAKING OF AN ORATOR. *Cr. 8vo 6s.*

Price (L L), M.A., Fellow of Oriel College, Oxon. A HISTORY OF ENGLISH POLITICAL ECONOMY FROM ADAM SMITH TO ARNOLD TOYNBEE. *Sixth Edition. Cr. 8vo. 2s. 6d.*

Pullen-Burry (B.). IN A GERMAN COLONY; or, FOUR WEEKS IN NEW BRITAIN. Illustrated. *Cr. 8vo 5s net*

Pycraft (W. P.). BIRD LIFE Illustrated. *Demy 8vo. 10s. 6d. net.*

Ragg (Lonsdale), B.D Oxon DANTE AND HIS ITALY Illustrated. *Demy 8vo 12s 6d. net.*

*__Rappoport (Angelo S)__ HOME LIFE IN RUSSIA. Illustrated. *Demy 8vo. 10s. 6d net*

Raven-Hill (L). See Llewellyn (Owen).

Rawlings (Gertrude) COINS AND HOW TO KNOW THEM Illustrated. *Second Edition Cr. 8vo 5s net*

Rea (Lilian). THE LIFE AND TIMES OF MARIE MADELEINE COUNTESS OF LA FAYETTE Illustrated *Demy 8vo 10s 6d. net.*

Read (C. Stanford), M.B. (Lond.), M R C.S, L.R.C.P. FADS AND FEEDING *Cr. 8vo 2s. 6d. net*

Rees (J D.), C I E , M P. THE REAL INDIA. *Second Edition. Demy 8vo. 10s 6d. net.*

Reich (Emil), Doctor Juris. WOMAN THROUGH THE AGES. Illustrated. *Two Volumes. Demy 8vo. 21s. net*

Reid (Archdall), M B THE LAWS OF HEREDITY. *Second Edition. Demy 8vo, 21s net*

Richmond (Wilfrid), Chaplain of Lincoln's Inn. THE CREED IN THE EPISTLES. *Cr. 8vo: 2s. 6d. net*

Roberts (M E.). See Channer (C.C.).

Robertson (A.), D D , Lord Bishop of Exeter. REGNUM DEI (The Bampton Lectures of 1901.) *A New and Cheaper Edition. Demy 8vo 7s 6d net.*

Robertson (C Grant), M.A., Fellow of All Souls' College, Oxford SELECT STATUTES, CASES, AND CONSTITUTIONAL DOCUMENTS, 1660-1832. *Demy 8vo. 10s. 6d. net*

Robertson (Sir G S), K C.S I CHITRAL: THE STORY OF A MINOR SIEGE Illustrated. *Third Edition. Demy 8vo 10s 6d. net*

Roe (Fred). OLD OAK FURNITURE. Illustrated. *Second Edition. Demy 8vo. 10s. 6d net.*

Royde-Smith (N G) THE PILLOW BOOK A GARNER OF MANY MOODS Collected *Second Edition Cr. 8vo. 4s 6d net*
POETS OF OUR DAY. Selected, with an Introduction. *Fcap. 8vo 5s.*

Rumbold (The Right Hon Sir Horace), Bart., G.C.B , G C M.G THE AUSTRIAN COURT IN THE NINETEENTH CENTURY Illustrated. *Second Edition Demy 8vo 18s net*

Russell (W. Clark). THE LIFE OF ADMIRAL LORD COLLINGWOOD. Illustrated *Fourth Edition Cr 8vo 6s.*

St. Francis of Assisi. THE LITTLE FLOWERS OF THE GLORIOUS MESSER, AND OF HIS FRIARS Done into English, with Notes by WILLIAM HEYWOOD. Illustrated. *Demy 8vo 5s net.*

'Saki' (H Munro) REGINALD. *Second Edition. Fcap 8vo 2s 6d. net*
REGINALD IN RUSSIA. *Fcap. 8vo 2s 6d. net.*

Sanders (Lloyd) THE HOLLAND HOUSE CIRCLE. Illustrated *Second Edition Demy 8vo 12s. 6d net.*

*__Scott (Ernest).__ TERRE NAPOLÉON, AND THE EXPEDITION OF DISCOVERY DESPATCHED TO AUSTRALIA BY ORDER OF BONAPARTE, 1800-1804 Illustrated. *Demy 8vo. 10s. 6d net*

Séllncourt (Hugh de) GREAT RALEGH Illustrated. *Demy 8vo. 10s 6d net*

Selous (Edmund) TOMMY SMITH'S ANIMALS Illustrated. *Eleventh Edition. Fcap 8vo 2s 6d*
TOMMY SMITH'S OTHER ANIMALS Illustrated. *Fifth Edition. Fcap. 8vo. 2s 6d.*

*__Shafer (Sara A.).__ A WHITE PAPER GARDEN. Illustrated. *Demy 8vo. 7s. 6d. net.*

Shakespeare (William).
THE FOUR FOLIOS, 1623; 1632; 1664, 1685 Each £4 4s. net, or a complete set, £12 12s net.
Folios 2, 3 and 4 are ready
THE POEMS OF WILLIAM SHAKESPEARE. With an Introduction and Notes by GEORGE WYNDHAM *Demy 8vo. Buckram, gilt top. 10s. 6d.*

Sharp (A). VICTORIAN POETS. *Cr. 8vo 2s 6d.*

Sidgwick (Mrs Alfred) HOME LIFE IN GERMANY. Illustrated *Second Edition. Demy 8vo. 10s. 6d. net.*

Sime (John). See Little Books on Art.

Sladen (Douglas) SICILY The New Winter Resort. Illustrated. *Second Edition Cr 8vo. 5s net.*

Smith (Adam). THE WEALTH OF NATIONS. Edited with an Introduction and numerous Notes by EDWIN CANNAN, M.A. *Two Volumes. Demy 8vo. 21s net*

Smith (Sophia S). DEAN SWIFT. Illustrated. *Demy 8vo. 10s 6d. net.*

Snell (F J). A BOOK OF EXMOOR Illustrated. *Cr. 8vo. 6s*

*'Stancliffe' GOLF DO'S AND DON'TS. *Second Edition. Fcap. 8vo. 1s*

Stead (Francis H), M.A. HOW OLD AGE PENSIONS BEGAN TO BE Illustrated *Demy 8vo 2s. 6d net.*

Stevenson (R L). THE LETTERS OF ROBERT LOUIS STEVENSON TO HIS FAMILY AND FRIENDS Selected and Edited by SIDNEY COLVIN. *Ninth Edition. Two Volumes. Cr. 8vo. 12s* VAILIMA LETTERS With an Etched Portrait by WILLIAM STRANG. *Eighth Edition. Cr 8vo Buckram 6s* THE LIFE OF R. L STEVENSON. See Balfour (G).

Stevenson (M. I). FROM SARANAC TO THE MARQUESAS. Being Letters written by Mrs. M. I STEVENSON during 1887-88. *Cr. 8vo 6s. net.* LETTERS FROM SAMOA, 1891-95. Edited and arranged by M C BALFOUR. Illustrated. *Second Edition. Cr. 8vo. 6s. net.*

Storr (Vernon F), M.A, Canon of Winchester DEVELOPMENT AND DIVINE PURPOSE. *Cr 8vo 5s net.*

Streatfeild (R A) MODERN MUSIC AND MUSICIANS. Illustrated. *Second Edition Demy 8vo. 7s. 6d. net.*

Swanton (E W). FUNGI AND HOW TO KNOW THEM. Illustrated. *Cr. 8vo. 6s net*

*Sykes (Ella C.). PERSIA AND ITS PEOPLE. Illustrated *Demy 8vo. 10s. 6d. net.*

Symes (J E). M A THE FRENCH REVOLUTION. *Second Edition Cr. 8vo. 2s. 6d*

Tabor (Margaret E) THE SAINTS IN ART. Illustrated. *Fcap. 8vo. 3s. 6d net*

Taylor (A E) THE ELEMENTS OF METAPHYSICS. *Second Edition Demy 8vo. 10s. 6d. net.*

Taylor (John W). THE COMING OF THE SAINTS. Illustrated. *Demy 8vo. 7s. 6d. net*

Thibaudeau (A C) BONAPARTE AND THE CONSULATE. Translated and Edited by G K FORTESCUE, LL.D Illustrated. *Demy 8vo. 10s 6d net.*

Thompson (Francis) SELECTED POEMS OF FRANCIS THOMPSON. With a Biographical Note by WILFRID MEYNELL. With a Portrait in Photogravure. *Second Edition. Fcap. 8vo. 5s net.*

Tileston (Mary W.). DAILY STRENGTH FOR DAILY NEEDS *Seventeenth Edition Medium 16mo. 2s 6d net.* Also an edition in superior binding, 6s.

Toynbee (Paget), M.A., D. Litt DANTE IN ENGLISH LITERATURE: FROM CHAUCER TO CARY. *Two Volumes Demy 8vo. 21s net* See also Oxford Biographies

Tozer (Basil) THE HORSE IN HISTORY Illustrated. *Cr 8vo 6s*

Trench (Herbert) DEIRDRE WEDDED, AND OTHER POEMS. *Second and Revised Edition. Large Post 8vo 6s* NEW POEMS. *Second Edition. Large Post 8vo. 6s.* APOLLO AND THE SEAMAN. *Large Post 8vo. Paper, 1s. 6d net; cloth, 2s. 6d net.*

Trevelyan (G M.), Fellow of Trinity College, Cambridge ENGLAND UNDER THE STUARTS With Maps and Plans *Fourth Edition Demy 8vo 10s 6d net*

Triggs (Inigo H), A R I B A. TOWN PLANNING: PAST, PRESENT, AND POSSIBLE. Illustrated. *Second Edition. Wide Royal 8vo. 15s net.*

Vaughan (Herbert M.), B A (Oxon), F.S.A THE LAST OF THE ROYAL STUARTS, HENRY STUART, CARDINAL, DUKE OF YORK. Illustrated. *Second Edition Demy 8vo. 10s 6d net* THE MEDICI POPES (LEO X. AND CLEMENT VII). Illustrated. *Demy 8vo 15s. net.* THE NAPLES RIVIERA. Illustrated. *Second Edition. Cr. 8vo 6s.* *FLORENCE AND HER TREASURES. Illustrated. *Fcap. 8vo. 5s. net.*

Vernon (Hon W. Warren), M A. READINGS ON THE INFERNO OF DANTE. With an Introduction by the REV. DR. MOORE. *Two Volumes. Second Edition. Cr 8vo. 15s. net.* READINGS ON THE PURGATORIO OF DANTE. With an Introduction by the late DEAN CHURCH. *Two Volumes. Third Edition. Cr. 8vo. 15s. net* READINGS ON THE PARADISO OF DANTE With an Introduction by the BISHOP OF RIPON. *Two Volumes Second Edition. Cr. 8vo. 15s net*

Vincent (J E) THROUGH EAST ANGLIA IN A MOTOR CAR. Illustrated. *Cr. 8vo. 6s*

Waddell (Col L A.), LL.D., C B LHASA AND ITS MYSTERIES With a Record of the Expedition of 1903-1904 Illustrated. *Third and Cheaper Edition. Medium 8vo. 7s. 6d net.*

Wagner (Richard). RICHARD WAGNER'S MUSIC DRAMAS Interpretations, embodying Wagner's own explanations. By ALICE LEIGHTON CLEATHER and BASIL CRUMP *In Three Volumes Fcap 8vo. 2s 6d each.*
    VOL I—THE RING OF THE NIBELUNG. *Third Edition.*

VOL. II.—PARSIFAL, LOHENGRIN, and THE HOLY GRAIL.
VOL. III.—TRISTAN AND ISOLDE.

Waineman (Paul). A SUMMER TOUR IN FINLAND. Illustrated. *Demy 8vo* 10s 6d net

Walkley (A. B.) DRAMA AND LIFE. *Cr. 8vo. 6s.*

Waterhouse (Elizabeth) WITH THE SIMPLE-HEARTED: Little Homilies to Women in Country Places. *Second Edition Small Pott 8vo 2s. net*
COMPANIONS OF THE WAY. Being Selections for Morning and Evening Reading. Chosen and arranged by ELIZABETH WATERHOUSE *Large Cr. 8vo. 5s net*
THOUGHTS OF A TERTIARY. *Second Edition Small Pott 8vo 1s net.*

Watt (Francis). See Henderson (T F.)

Weigall (Arthur E P). A GUIDE TO THE ANTIQUITIES OF UPPER EGYPT: From Abydos to the Sudan Frontier. Illustrated. *Cr. 8vo 7s 6d net.*

Welch (Catharine) THE LITTLE DAUPHIN. Illustrated. *Cr. 8vo 6s.*

Wells (J.), M.A., Fellow and Tutor of Wadham College. OXFORD AND OXFORD LIFE. *Third Edition. Cr. 8vo 3s. 6d.*
A SHORT HISTORY OF ROME. *Tenth Edition.* With 3 Maps. *Cr. 8vo. 3s. 6d*

Westell (W Percival) THE YOUNG NATURALIST. Illustrated. *Cr. 8vo. 6s.*

Westell (W. Percival), F.L.S., M.B.O.U., and **Cooper (C S.),** F R H S. THE YOUNG BOTANIST. Illustrated. *Cr, 8vo 3s. 6d. net.*

*•**Wheeler (Ethel R)** FAMOUS BLUE STOCKINGS. Illustrated. *Demy 8vo.* 10s 6d. net

Whibley (C.). See Henley (W. E.).

White (George F.), Lieut.-Col A CENTURY OF SPAIN AND PORTUGAL, 1788–1898 *Demy 8vo. 12s. 6d. net.*

Whitley (Miss). See Dilke (Lady).

Wilde (Oscar) DE PROFUNDIS. *Twelfth Edition. Cr 8vo 5s net.*

THE WORKS OF OSCAR WILDE. *In Twelve Volumes Fcap. 8vo. 5s. net each volume.*
I. LORD ARTHUR SAVILE'S CRIME AND THE PORTRAIT OF MR. W. H. II THE

DUCHESS OF PADUA. III POEMS IV LADY WINDERMERE'S FAN V A WOMAN OF NO IMPORTANCE. VI. AN IDEAL HUSBAND VII THE IMPORTANCE OF BEING EARNEST VIII A HOUSE OF POMEGRANATES. IX. INTENTIONS. X DE PROFUNDIS AND PRISON LETTERS XI ESSAYS XII SALOMÉ, A FLORENTINE TRAGEDY, and LA SAINTE COURTISANE.

Williams (H Noel) THE WOMEN BONAPARTES. The Mother and three Sisters of Napoleon. Illustrated *In Two Volumes Demy 8vo. 24s net*

A ROSE OF SAVOY : MARIE ADÉLAÏDE OF SAVOY, DUCHESSE DE BOURGOGNE, MOTHER OF LOUIS XV Illustrated. *Second Edition. Demy 8vo. 15s net.*

•THE FASCINATING DUC DE RICHELIEU : LOUIS FRANÇOIS ARMAND DU PLESSIS, MARÉCHAL DUC DE RICHELIEU. Illustrated. *Demy 8vo. 15s. net.*

Wood (Sir Evelyn), F.M., V.C, G C B., G C.M.G FROM MIDSHIPMAN TO FIELD-MARSHAL. Illustrated. *Fifth and Cheaper Edition. Demy 8vo. 7s 6d. net.*
THE REVOLT IN HINDUSTAN 1857–59. Illustrated. *Second Edition Cr 8vo 6s*

Wood (W. Birkbeck), M A, late Scholar of Worcester College, Oxford, and **Edmonds (Major J. E),** R E, D A Q M G A HISTORY OF THE CIVIL WAR IN THE UNITED STATES With an Introduction by H SPENSER WILKINSON. With 24 Maps and Plans *Second Edition Demy 8vo. 12s 6d net*

Wordsworth (W.). THE POEMS With an Introduction and Notes by NOWELL C. SMITH, late Fellow of New College, Oxford *In Three Volumes. Demy 8vo 15s. net*
POEMS BY WILLIAM WORDSWORTH. Selected with an Introduction by STOPFORD A. BROOKE. Illustrated. *Cr. 8vo. 7s. 6d. net*

Wyatt (Kate M.). See Gloag (M. R.).

Wyllie (M A). NORWAY AND ITS FJORDS. Illustrated. *Second Edition Cr. 8vo 6s.*

Yeats (W. B). A BOOK OF IRISH VERSE. *Revised and Enlarged Edition Cr. 8vo. 3s. 6d.*

Young (Filson). See The Complete Series.

PART II.—A SELECTION OF SERIES.

Ancient Cities.

General Editor, B. C. A. WINDLE, D.Sc., F.R S.

Cr. 8vo.   4s. 6d. net.

With Illustrations by E. H NEW, and other Artists

BRISTOL. By Alfred Harvey, M B
CANTERBURY By J. C Cox, LL D , F S A
CHESTER. By B. C. A Windle, D Sc., F.R.S
DUBLIN. By S A. O. Fitzpatrick

EDINBURGH By M. G Williamson, M.A
LINCOLN. By E Mansel Sympson, M A.
SHREWSBURY By T Auden, M.A , F S A.
WELLS and GLASTONBURY. By T S. Holmes

The Antiquary's Books.

General Editor, J. CHARLES COX, LL.D., F.S.A.

Demy 8vo.   7s. 6d. net.

With Numerous Illustrations.

ARCHÆOLOGY AND FALSE ANTIQUITIES By R Munro
BELLS OF ENGLAND, THE. By Canon J. J. Raven. *Second Edition*
BRASSES OF ENGLAND, THE. By Herbert W. Macklin *Second Edition*
CELTIC ART IN PAGAN AND CHRISTIAN TIMES. By J. Romilly Allen ⸸
DOMESDAY INQUEST, THE. By Adolphus Ballard.
ENGLISH CHURCH FURNITURE. By J C. Cox and A. Harvey. *Second Edition*
ENGLISH COSTUME. From Prehistoric Times to the End of the Eighteenth Century. By George Clinch
ENGLISH MONASTIC LIFE. By the Right Rev. Abbot Gasquet. *Fourth Edition.*
ENGLISH SEALS. By J Harvey Bloom.
FOLK-LORE AS AN HISTORICAL SCIENCE. By G L. Gomme.

GILDS AND COMPANIES OF LONDON, THE. By George Unwin.
MANOR AND MANORIAL RECORDS, THE. By Nathaniel J Hone.
MEDIÆVAL HOSPITALS OF ENGLAND, THE. By Rotha Mary Clay.
OLD SERVICE BOOKS OF THE ENGLISH CHURCH   By Christopher Wordsworth, M A , and Henry Littlehales
PARISH LIFE IN MEDIÆVAL ENGLAND   By the Right Rev. Abbot Gasquet. *Second Edition*
*PARISH REGISTERS OF ENGLAND, THE. By J. C. Cox
REMAINS OF THE PREHISTORIC AGE IN ENGLAND. By B C. A Windle *Second Edition.*
ROYAL FORESTS OF ENGLAND, THE. By J C Cox, LL D
SHRINES OF BRITISH SAINTS. By J. C. Wall.

The Arden Shakespeare.

Demy 8vo.   2s. 6d. net each volume.

An edition of Shakespeare in single Plays. Edited with a full Introduction, Textual Notes, and a Commentary at the foot of the page.

ALL'S WELL THAT ENDS WELL.
ANTONY AND CLEOPATRA.
CYMBELINE
COMEDY OF ERRORS, THE.
HAMLET. *Second Edition.*
JULIUS CAESAR
KING HENRY V
KING HENRY VI. PT. I.
KING HENRY VI PT. II.
KING HENRY VI. PT. III.
KING LEAR.
KING RICHARD III.
LIFE AND DEATH OF KING JOHN, THE.
LOVE'S LABOUR'S LOST.
MACBETH.

MEASURE FOR MEASURE.
MERCHANT OF VENICE, THE.
MERRY WIVES OF WINDSOR, THE.
MIDSUMMER NIGHT'S DREAM, A.
OTHELLO.
PERICLES.
ROMEO AND JULIET.
TAMING OF THE SHREW, THE.
TEMPEST, THE.
TIMON OF ATHENS.
TITUS ANDRONICUS.
TROILUS AND CRESSIDA.
TWO GENTLEMEN OF VERONA, THE.
TWELFTH NIGHT.

Classics of Art.

Edited by Dr. J. H. W. LAING.

With numerous Illustrations. Wide Royal 8vo Gilt top

THE ART OF THE GREEKS. By H. B Walters 12s. 6d net.

FIORENTINE SCULPTORS OF THE RENAISSANCE Wilhelm Bode, Ph.D Translated by Jessie Haynes 12s 6d net

*GEORGE ROMNEY By Arthur B. Chamberlain 12s 6d. net

GHIRLANDAIO. Gerald S. Davies Second Edition. 10s. 6d

MICHELANGELO By Gerald S. Davies 12s 6d. net.

RUBENS By Edward Dillon, M.A. 25s. net

RAPHAEL. By A. P. Oppé. 12s 6d. net

*TITIAN. By Charles Ricketts 12s 6d net

*TURNER'S SKETCHES AND DRAWINGS. By A. J FINBERG. 12s. 6d. net.

VELAZQUEZ. By A. de Beruete. 10s 6d. net.

The "Complete" Series.

Fully Illustrated. Demy 8vo.

THE COMPLETE COOK By Lilian Whitling 7s 6d. net

THE COMPLETE CRICKETER. By Albert E. KNIGHT. 7s. 6d net

THE COMPLETE FOXHUNTER. By Charles Richardson 12s. 6d. net Second Edition.

THE COMPLETE GOLFER By Harry Vardon. 10s 6d net Tenth Edition

THE COMPLETE HOCKEY-PLAYER. By Eustace E. White. 5s. net. Second Edition

THE COMPLETE LAWN TENNIS PLAYER By A. Wallace Myers. 10s 6d. net Second Edition.

THE COMPLETE MOTORIST. By Filson Young 12s. 6d. net New Edition (Seventh)

THE COMPLETE MOUNTAINEER. By G. D Abraham. 15s net. Second Edition.

THE COMPLETE OARSMAN By R C Lehmann, M P. 10s 6d. net.

THE COMPLETE PHOTOGRAPHER. By R Child Bayley. 10s. 6d net. Fourth Edition.

THE COMPLETE RUGBY FOOTBALLER, ON THE NEW ZEALAND SYSTEM By D Gallaher and W. J. Stead. 10s. 6d net Second Edition

THE COMPLETE SHOT. By G T. Teasdale Buckell. 12s 6d. net. Third Edition.

The Connoisseur's Library.

With numerous Illustrations. Wide Royal 8vo. Gilt top. 25s. net.

ENGLISH FURNITURE. By F. S Robinson. Second Edition.

ENGLISH COLOURED BOOKS By Martin Hardie.

EUROPEAN ENAMELS. By Henry H Cunynghame, C.B

GLASS. By Edward Dillon

GOLDSMITHS' AND SILVERSMITHS' WORK. By Nelson Dawson. Second Edition

*ILLUMINATED MANUSCRIPTS. By J A. Herbert.

IVORIES. By A. Maskell

JEWELLERY. By H Clifford Smith. Second Edition

MEZZOTINTS By Cyril Davenport

MINIATURES. By Dudley Heath

PORCELAIN. By Edward Dillon.

SEALS. By Walter de Gray Birch.

Handbooks of English Church History.

Edited by J. H. BURN, B.D. *Crown 8vo. 2s. 6d. net.*

THE FOUNDATIONS OF THE ENGLISH CHURCH. By J H. Maude.

THE SAXON CHURCH AND THE NORMAN CONQUEST. By C. T Cruttwell.

THE MEDIÆVAL CHURCH AND THE PAPACY By A. C. Jennings

THE REFORMATION PERIOD. By Henry Gee

THE STRUGGLE WITH PURITANISM By Bruce Blaxland.

THE CHURCH OF ENGLAND IN THE EIGHTEENTH CENTURY. By Alfred Plummer

The Illustrated Pocket Library of Plain and Coloured Books.

Fcap. 8vo 3s. 6d. net each volume.

WITH COLOURED ILLUSTRATIONS.

OLD COLOURED BOOKS By George Paston. 2s net

THE LIFE AND DEATH OF JOHN MYTTON, ESQ. By Nimrod. *Fifth Edition*

THE LIFE OF A SPORTSMAN By Nimrod

HANDLEY CROSS. By R. S. Surtees *Third Edition*

MR. SPONGE'S SPORTING TOUR. By R S. Surtees.

JORROCKS' JAUNTS AND JOLLITIES By R. S Surtees. *Third Edition*

ASK MAMMA. By R. S. Surtees.

THE ANALYSIS OF THE HUNTING FIELD. By R. S Surtees.

THE TOUR OF DR. SYNTAX IN SEARCH OF THE PICTURESQUE. By William Combe.

THE TOUR OF DR. SYNTAX IN SEARCH OF CONSOLATION. By William Combe.

THE THIRD TOUR OF DR. SYNTAX IN SEARCH OF A WIFE. By William Combe.

THE HISTORY OF JOHNNY QUAE GENUS. By the Author of 'The Three Tours.'

THE ENGLISH DANCE OF DEATH, from the Designs of T Rowlandson, with Metrical Illustrations by the Author of 'Doctor Syntax.' *Two Volumes.*

THE DANCE OF LIFE: A Poem By the Author of 'Dr. Syntax.'

LIFE IN LONDON. By Pierce Egan.

REAL LIFE IN LONDON By an Amateur (Pierce Egan) *Two Volumes*

THE LIFE OF AN ACTOR. By Pierce Egan.

THE VICAR OF WAKEFIELD. By Oliver Goldsmith.

THE MILITARY ADVENTURES OF JOHNNY NEWCOMBE By an Officer

THE NATIONAL SPORTS OF GREAT BRITAIN. With Descriptions and 50 Coloured Plates by Henry Alken.

THE ADVENTURES OF A POST CAPTAIN. By a Naval Officer.

GAMONIA. By Lawrence Rawstone, Esq.

AN ACADEMY FOR GROWN HORSEMEN. By Geoffrey Gambado, Esq.

REAL LIFE IN IRELAND By a Real Paddy

THE ADVENTURES OF JOHNNY NEWCOMBE IN THE NAVY By Alfred Burton

THE OLD ENGLISH SQUIRE. By John Careless, Esq

THE ENGLISH SPY By Bernard Blackmantle. *Two Volumes. 7s net.*

WITH PLAIN ILLUSTRATIONS.

THE GRAVE: A Poem By Robert Blair

ILLUSTRATIONS OF THE BOOK OF JOB. Invented and engraved by William Blake

WINDSOR CASTLE. By W. Harrison Ainsworth.

THE TOWER OF LONDON. By W. Harrison Ainsworth.

FRANK FAIRLEGH By F. E Smedley.

HANDY ANDY. By Samuel Lover.

THE COMPLEAT ANGLER. By Izaak Walton and Charles Cotton

THE PICKWICK PAPERS By Charles Dickens

Leaders of Religion.

Edited by H C. BEECHING, M.A., Canon of Westminster. *With Portraits.*

Crown 8vo.   2s. net.

CARDINAL NEWMAN. By R H Hutton.

JOHN WESLEY. By J. H. Overton, M.A.

BISHOP WILBERFORCE By G. W. Daniell, M.A.

CARDINAL MANNING   By A. W. Hutton, M.A.

CHARLES SIMEON. By H. C. G. Moule, D D.

JOHN KNOX. By F. MacCunn. *Second Edition.*

JOHN HOWE. By R. F. Horton, D.D.

THOMAS KEN. By F A Clarke, M.A.

GEORGE FOX, THE QUAKER. By T. Hodgkin, D.C.L. *Third Edition.*

JOHN KEBLE. By Walter Lock, D D

THOMAS CHALMERS. By Mrs. Oliphant.

LANCELOT ANDREWES. By R. L. Ottley, D D *Second Edition.*

AUGUSTINE OF CANTERBURY. By E. L Cutts, D.D.

WILLIAM LAUD. By W H Hutton, M A *Third Edition.*

JOHN DONNE. By Augustus Jessop, D.D.

THOMAS CRANMER. By A J. Mason, D.D.

BISHOP LATIMER. By R M. Carlyle and A J Carlyle, M A

BISHOP BUTLER. By W A Spooner, M.A.

The Library of Devotion.

With Introductions and (where necessary) Notes.

Small Pott 8vo, gilt top, cloth, 2s. ; leather, 2s. 6d. net

THE CONFESSIONS OF ST. AUGUSTINE. *Seventh Edition.*

THE IMITATION OF CHRIST. *Sixth Edition.*

THE CHRISTIAN YEAR. *Fourth Edition.*

LYRA INNOCENTIUM. *Second Edition.*

THE TEMPLE. *Second Edition.*

A BOOK OF DEVOTIONS. *Second Edition.*

A SERIOUS CALL TO A DEVOUT AND HOLY LIFE. *Fourth Edition*

A GUIDE TO ETERNITY.

THE INNER WAY *Second Edition.*

ON THE LOVE OF GOD.

THE PSALMS OF DAVID.

LYRA APOSTOLICA.

THE SONG OF SONGS.

THE THOUGHTS OF PASCAL. *Second Edition.*

A MANUAL OF CONSOLATION FROM THE SAINTS AND FATHERS.

DEVOTIONS FROM THE APOCRYPHA.

THE SPIRITUAL COMBAT.

THE DEVOTIONS OF ST. ANSELM.

BISHOP WILSON'S SACRA PRIVATA.

GRACE ABOUNDING TO THE CHIEF OF SINNERS.

LYRA SACRA · A Book of Sacred Verse. *Second Edition.*

A DAY BOOK FROM THE SAINTS AND FATHERS

A LITTLE BOOK OF HEAVENLY WISDOM. A Selection from the English Mystics

LIGHT, LIFE, and LOVE. A Selection from the German Mystics

AN INTRODUCTION TO THE DEVOUT LIFE.

THE LITTLE FLOWERS OF THE GLORIOUS MESSER ST. FRANCIS AND OF HIS FRIARS.

DEATH AND IMMORTALITY

THE SPIRITUAL GUIDE.

DEVOTIONS FOR EVERY DAY IN THE WEEK AND THE GREAT FESTIVALS.

PRECES PRIVATÆ

HORÆ MYSTICÆ: A Day Book from the Writings of Mystics of Many Nations.

Little Books on Art.

With many Illustrations. Demy 16mo. Gilt top. 2s. 6d. net

Each volume consists of about 200 pages, and contains from 30 to 40 Illustrations, including a Frontispiece in Photogravure.

ALBRECHT DURER. J. Allen.
ARTS OF JAPAN, THE. E Dillon.
BOOKPLATES E. Almack.
BOTTICELLI Mary L. Bloomer
BURNE-JONES F. de Lisle.
*CHRISTIAN SYMBOLISM. Mrs. H. Jenner.
CHRIST IN ART. Mrs H. Jenner.
CLAUDE E Dillon.
CONSTABLE. H. W. Tompkins
COROT. A. Pollard and E. Birnstingl
ENAMELS Mrs. N Dawson.
FREDERIC LEIGHTON A. Corkran.
GEORGE ROMNEY. G Paston.
GREEK ART. H. B Walters.
GREUZE AND BOUCHER E F. Pollard.

HOLBEIN. Mrs. G Fortescue.
ILLUMINATED MANUSCRIPTS. J W. Bradley
JEWELLERY. C. Davenport.
JOHN HOPPNER. H P. K. Skipton
SIR JOSHUA REYNOLDS J. Sime
MILLET. N. Peacock.
MINIATURES C Davenport.
OUR LADY IN ART Mrs. H Jenner.
RAPHAEL. A R. Dryhurst. *Second Edition*
REMBRANDT. Mrs E. A. Sharp
TURNER. F Tyrrell-Gill
VANDYCK. M. G. Smallwood
VELASQUEZ. W. Wilberforce and A. R. Gilbert
WATTS. R. E. D. Sketchley.

The Little Galleries.

Demy 16mo. 2s. 6d. net.

Each volume contains 20 plates in Photogravure, together with a short outline of the life and work of the master to whom the book is devoted.

A LITTLE GALLERY OF REYNOLDS.
A LITTLE GALLERY OF ROMNEY.
A LITTLE GALLERY OF HOPPNER

A LITTLE GALLERY OF MILLAIS.
A LITTLE GALLERY OF ENGLISH POETS

The Little Guides.

With many Illustrations by E. H. NEW and other artists, and from photographs.

Small Pott 8vo, gilt top, cloth, 2s. 6d. net; leather, 3s. 6d. net.

The main features of these Guides are (1) a handy and charming form; (2) illustrations from photographs and by well-known artists; (3) good plans and maps; (4) an adequate but compact presentation of everything that is interesting in the natural features, history, archæology, and architecture of the town or district treated.

CAMBRIDGE AND ITS COLLEGES. A. H. Thompson. *Second Edition*
ENGLISH LAKES, THE. F. G. Brabant.
ISLE OF WIGHT, THE. G. Clinch.
MALVERN COUNTRY, THE. B C. A. Windle
NORTH WALES. A. T Story.
OXFORD AND ITS COLLEGES. J Wells. *Ninth Edition.*

SHAKESPEARE'S COUNTRY. B C A. Windle *Third Edition.*
ST PAUL'S CATHEDRAL. G Clinch.
WESTMINSTER ABBEY. G. E. Troutbeck. *Second Edition.*

BUCKINGHAMSHIRE. E. S. Roscoe.
CHESHIRE. W. M. Gallichan.

THE LITTLE GUIDES—*continued.*

CORNWALL. A L. Salmon.
DERBYSHIRE J C. Cox.
DEVON. S. Baring-Gould.
DORSET. F. R. Heath. *Second Edition*
ESSEX. J. C. Cox.
HAMPSHIRE. J. C. Cox.
HERTFORDSHIRE H. W Tompkins
KENT. G. Clinch.
KERRY. C. P. Crane.
MIDDLESEX J B. Firth.
MONMOUTHSHIRE. G. W. Wade and J. H Wade.
NORFOLK W A Dutt *Second Edition, Revised.*
NORTHAMPTONSHIRE. W. Dry.
*NORTHUMBERLAND J E Morris.
NOTTINGHAMSHIRE. L. Guilford.

OXFORDSHIRE F G. Brabant
SOMERSET. G W. and J H Wade.
*STAFFORDSHIRE. C. E Masefield
SUFFOLK. W. A. Dutt.
SURREY. F. A. H. Lambert
SUSSEX F G Brabant *Second Edition*
*WILTSHIRE. F. R Heath.
YORKSHIRE, THE EAST RIDING. J E Morris.
YORKSHIRE, THE NORTH RIDING. J. E. Morris

———

BRITTANY S. Baring-Gould.
NORMANDY C. Scudamore.
ROME. C G Ellaby.
SICILY. F. H Jackson

The Little Library.

With Introductions, Notes, and Photogravure Frontispieces.

Small Pott 8vo. Gilt top. Each Volume, cloth, 1s. 6d. net ; leather, 2s 6d. net.

Anon. A LITTLE BOOK OF ENGLISH LYRICS. *Second Edition.*

Austen (Jane). PRIDE AND PREJUDICE *Two Volumes*
NORTHANGER ABBEY.

Bacon (Francis). THE ESSAYS OF LORD BACON.

Barham (R. H.). THE INGOLDSBY LEGENDS. *Two Volumes*

Barnet (Mrs. P. A.). A LITTLE BOOK OF ENGLISH PROSE.

Beckford (William). THE HISTORY OF THE CALIPH VATHEK

Blake (William) SELECTIONS FROM WILLIAM BLAKE.

Borrow (George). LAVENGRO. *Two Volumes*
THE ROMANY RYE

Browning (Robert). SELECTIONS FROM THE EARLY POEMS OF ROBERT BROWNING

Canning (George). SELECTIONS FROM THE ANTI-JACOBIN : with GEORGE CANNING's additional Poems.

Cowley (Abraham). THE ESSAYS OF ABRAHAM COWLEY.

Crabbe (George). SELECTIONS FROM GEORGE CRABBE

Craik (Mrs.). JOHN HALIFAX, GENTLEMAN. *Two Volumes.*

Crashaw (Richard). THE ENGLISH POEMS OF RICHARD CRASHAW.

Dante (Alighieri). THE INFERNO OF DANTE. Translated by H F. CARY.
THE PURGATORIO OF DANTE. Translated by H F CARY.
THE PARADISO OF DANTE. Translated by H. F. CARY.

Darley (George). SELECTIONS FROM THE POEMS OF GEORGE DARLEY.

Deane (A. C.). A LITTLE BOOK OF LIGHT VERSE.

Dickens(Charles). CHRISTMAS BOOKS. *Two Volumes.*

Ferrier (Susan). MARRIAGE. *Two Volumes*
THE INHERITANCE. *Two Volumes*

Gaskell (Mrs.). CRANFORD.

Hawthorne (Nathaniel) THE SCARLET LETTER.

Henderson (T. F.) A LITTLE BOOK OF SCOTTISH VERSE.

Keats (John). POEMS.

Kinglake (A. W.). EOTHEN. *Second Edition.*

Lamb (Charles). ELIA, AND THE LAST ESSAYS OF ELIA

Locker (F.). LONDON LYRICS

Longfellow (H. W.) SELECTIONS FROM LONGFELLOW.

THE LITTLE LIBRARY—*continued.*

Marvell (Andrew). THE POEMS OF ANDREW MARVELL.

Milton (John). THE MINOR POEMS OF JOHN MILTON

Moir (D. M.). MANSIE WAUCH.

Nichols (J. B. B.) A LITTLE BOOK OF ENGLISH SONNETS.

Rochefoucauld (La). THE MAXIMS OF LA ROCHEFOUCAULD.

Smith (Horace and James), REJECTED ADDRESSES.

Sterne (Laurence). A SENTIMENTAL JOURNEY.

Tennyson (Alfred, Lord). THE EARLY POEMS OF ALFRED, LORD TENNYSON
IN MEMORIAM.
THE PRINCESS.

MAUD.

Thackeray (W. M.). VANITY FAIR. *Three Volumes*
PENDENNIS *Three Volumes*
ESMOND
CHRISTMAS BOOKS.

Vaughan (Henry). THE POEMS OF HENRY VAUGHAN.

Walton (Izaak). THE COMPLEAT ANGLER.

Waterhouse (Elizabeth). A LITTLE BOOK OF LIFE AND DEATH. *Thirteenth Edition*

Wordsworth (W.). SELECTIONS FROM WORDSWORTH.

Wordsworth (W.) and Coleridge (S. T.) LYRICAL BALLADS.

The Little Quarto Shakespeare.

Edited by W J. CRAIG. With Introductions and Notes.

Pott 16mo. In 40 Volumes. Gilt top Leather, price 1s. net each volume.

Mahogany Revolving Book Case. 10s. net.

Miniature Library.

Gilt top.

EUPHRANOR : A Dialogue on Youth By Edward FitzGerald. *Demy 32mo Leather,* 2s net.

THE LIFE OF EDWARD, LORD HERBERT OF CHERBURY Written by himself. *Demy 32mo. Leather, 2s. net*

POLONIUS : or Wise Saws and Modern Instances. By Edward FitzGerald *Demy 32mo Leather, 2s. net.*

THE RUBÁIYÁT OF OMAR KHAYYÁM By Edward FitzGerald *Fourth Edition Leather, 1s. net.*

The New Library of Medicine.

Edited by C. W. SALEEBY, M.D., F.R.S. Edin. *Demy 8vo.*

CARE OF THE BODY, THE. By F. Cavanagh. *Second Edition.* 7s 6d. net.

CHILDREN OF THE NATION, THE. By the Right Hon Sir John Gorst. *Second Edition.* 7s 6d net.

CONTROL OF A SCOURGE, THE ; or, How Cancer is Curable By Chas. P. Childe. 7s 6d. net.

DISEASES OF OCCUPATION. By Sir Thomas Oliver 10s. 6d net

DRINK PROBLEM, THE, in its Medico-Sociological Aspects Edited by T N Kelynack. 7s 6d. net.

DRUGS AND THE DRUG HABIT. By H. Sainsbury.

FUNCTIONAL NERVE DISEASES. By A T Schofield. 7s. 6d. net.

*Heredity, THE LAWS OF By Archdall Reid 21s net.

HYGIENE OF MIND, THE By T. S. Clouston. *Fifth Edition.* 7s 6d. net.

INFANT MORTALITY By George Newman. 7s. 6d. net.

PREVENTION OF TUBERCULOSIS (CONSUMPTION), THE By Arthur Newsholme. 10s. 6d net

AIR AND HEALTH. By Ronald C. Macfie. 7s 6d. net. *Second Edition.*

The New Library of Music.

Edited by ERNEST NEWMAN. *Illustrated. Demy 8vo. 7s. 6d. net.*

HUGO WOLF. By Ernest Newman. Illustrated.

HANDEL. By R. A. Streatfeild. Illustrated. *Second Edition.*

Oxford Biographies.

Illustrated. Fcap 8vo. Gilt top. Each volume, cloth, 2s 6d net; leather, 3s 6d. net.

DANTE ALIGHIERI. By Paget Tonybee, M.A, D Litt. *Third Edition.*
GIROLAMO SAVONAROLA By E. L S Horsburgh, M A. *Second Edition.*
JOHN HOWARD. By E. C. S. Gibson, D D, Bishop of Gloucester
ALFRED TENNYSON. By A. C. Benson, M.A. *Second Edition*
SIR WALTER RALEIGH By I A Taylor.
ERASMUS. By E. F H. Capey.

THE YOUNG PRETENDER By C. S. Terry
ROBERT BURNS By T. F Henderson.
CHATHAM. By A S. M'Dowall.
FRANCIS OF ASSISI By Anna M Stoddart
CANNING By W. Alison Phillips.
BEACONSFIELD By Walter Sichel.
JOHANN WOLFGANG GOETHE. By H. G Atkins
FRANÇOIS FENELON. By Viscount St Cyres

Romantic History.

Edited by MARTIN HUME, M.A. *Illustrated. Demy 8vo.*

A series of attractive volumes in which the periods and personalities selected are such as afford romantic human interest, in addition to their historical importance.

THE FIRST GOVERNESS OF THE NETHERLANDS, MARGARET OF AUSTRIA. Eleanor E Tremayne. 10s. 6d. net.
TWO ENGLISH QUEENS AND PHILIP. Martin

Hume, M.A. 15s. net.
THE NINE DAYS' QUEEN Richard Davey With a Preface by Martin Hume, M A 10s 6d. net.

Handbooks of Theology.

THE DOCTRINE OF THE INCARNATION By R L Ottley, D D. *Fourth Edition revised.* Demy 8vo. 12s 6d
A HISTORY OF EARLY CHRISTIAN DOCTRINE. By J. F. Bethune-Baker, M.A. *Demy 8vo.* 10s. 6d.
AN INTRODUCTION TO THE HISTORY OF RELIGION By F B. Jevons M A Litt D *Fourth Edition. Demy 8vo.* 10s 6d.

AN INTRODUCTION TO THE HISTORY OF THE CREEDS By A. E Burn, D.D. *Demy 8vo* 10s 6d.
THE PHILOSOPHY OF RELIGION IN ENGLAND AND AMERICA. By Alfred Caldecott. D D. *Demy 8vo.* 10s. 6d.
THE XXXIX ARTICLES OF THE CHURCH OF ENGLAND Edited by E. C. S Gibson, D.D *Sixth Edition Demy 8vo.* 12s. 6d

The Westminster Commentaries.

General Editor, WALTER LOCK, D.D., Warden of Keble College.

Dean Ireland's Professor of Exegesis in the University of Oxford.

THE ACTS OF THE APOSTLES. Edited by R. B Rackham, M A. *Demy 8vo. Fourth Edition.* 10s- 6d.

THE FIRST EPISTLE OF PAUL THE APOSTLE TO THE CORINTHIANS. Edited by H. L. Goudge, M A. *Second Ed. Demy 8vo* 6s.

THE BOOK OF EXODUS. Edited by A H. M'Neile, B D With a Map and 3 Plans. *Demy 8vo* 10s. 6d.

THE BOOK OF EZEKIEL. Edited by H A. Redpath, M.A , D.Litt. *Demy 8vo.* 10s. 6d.

THE BOOK OF GENESIS. Edited with Introduction and Notes by S R. Driver, D.D. *Eighth Edition Demy 8vo.* 10s 6d.

ADDITIONS AND CORRECTIONS IN THE SEVENTH EDITION OF THE BOOK OF GENESIS. By S. R. Driver, D.D. *Demy 8vo.* 1s.

THE BOOK OF JOB Edited by E. C S. Gibson, D D *Second Edition Demy 8vo.* 6s

THE EPISTLE OF ST. JAMES Edited with Introduction and Notes by R. J. Knowling, D D. *Second Edition. Demy 8vo.* 6s.

PART III.—A SELECTION OF WORKS OF FICTION

Albanesi (E. Maria). SUSANNAH AND ONE OTHER. *Fourth Edition.* Cr. 8vo 6s
LOVE AND LOUISA. *Second Edition.* Cr. 8vo. 6s
THE BROWN EYES OF MARY. *Third Edition.* Cr. 8vo 6s
I KNOW A MAIDEN. *Third Edition* Cr. 8vo. 6s.
THE INVINCIBLE AMELIA. OR, THE POLITE ADVENTURESS. *Third Edition.* Cr. 8vo 3s. 6d.
*THE GLAD HEART. *Second Edition* Cr. 8vo. 6s.

Allerton (Mark). SUCH AND SUCH THINGS Cr. 8vo 6s

Annesley (Maude) THIS DAY'S MADNESS. *Second Edition* Cr. 8vo. 6s.

Bagot (Richard). A ROMAN MYSTERY *Third Edition* Cr. 8vo. 6s.
THE PASSPORT. *Fourth Edition.* Cr. 8vo. 6s.
TEMPTATION. *Fifth Edition.* Cr. 8vo. 6s
ANTHONY CUTHBERT. *Fourth Edition.* Cr. 8vo. 6s.
LOVE'S PROXY. Cr 8vo. 6s
DONNA DIANA. *Second Edition.* Cr. 8vo. 6s.
CASTING OF NETS. *Twelfth Edition.* Cr. 8vo. 6s.

Bailey (H. C.). STORM AND TREASURE *Second Edition.* Cr. 8vo. 6s.

Ball (Oona H) (Barbara Burke) THEIR OXFORD YEAR. Illustrated. Cr. 8vo. 6s.

BARBARA GOES TO OXFORD. Illustrated. *Third Edition.* Cr. 8vo. 6s

Baring-Gould (S). ARMINELL. *Fifth Edition* Cr 8vo. 6s
IN THE ROAR OF THE SEA. *Seventh Edition* Cr 8vo. 6s.
MARGERY OF QUETHER. *Third Edition.* Cr. 8vo. 6s.
THE QUEEN OF LOVE. *Fifth Edition.* Cr 8vo. 6s.
JACQUETTA *Third Edition.* Cr 8vo. 6s.
KITTY ALONE. *Fifth Edition* Cr 8vo 6s
NOÉMI Illustrated. *Fourth Edition.* Cr. 8vo. 6s
THE BROOM-SQUIRE. Illustrated. *Fifth Edition* Cr. 8vo. 6s.
DARTMOOR IDYLLS Cr 8vo 6s.
GUAVAS THE TINNER. Illustrated. *Second Edition.* Cr. 8vo 6s.
BLADYS OF THE STEWPONEY. Illustrated. *Second Edition.* Cr. 8vo. 6s.
PABO THE PRIEST Cr. 8vo. 6s.
WINEFRED. Illustrated. *Second Edition.* Cr. 8vo. 6s
ROYAL GEORGIE Illustrated. Cr. 8vo. 6s.
CHRIS OF ALL SORTS. Cr 8vo. 6s
IN DEWISLAND. *Second Edition.* Cr 8vo. 6s
THE FROBISHERS Cr 8vo. 6s
DOMITIA. Illustrated *Second Edition.* Cr 8vo. 6s
MRS CURGENVEN OF CURGENVEN. Cr. 8vo. 6s

Barr (Robert) IN THE MIDST OF ALARMS *Third Edition.* Cr. 8vo 6s.
THE COUNTESS TEKLA. *Fifth Edition.* Cr. 8vo. 6s.

THE MUTABLE MANY. *Third Edition.* Cr. 8vo 6s.

Begbie (Harold) THE CURIOUS AND DIVERTING ADVENTURES OF SIR JOHN SPARROW; or, THE PROGRESS OF AN OPEN MIND. *Second Edition.* Cr. 8vo 6s

Belloc (H). EMMANUEL BURDEN, MERCHANT. Illustrated. *Second Edition* Cr. 8vo. 6s.
A CHANGE IN THE CABINET. *Third Edition.* Cr. 8vo 6s

Benson (E F.). DODO: A DETAIL OF THE DAY. *Sixteenth Edition.* Cr. 8vo. 6s.

Birmingham (George A). THE BAD TIMES *Second Edition* Cr. 8vo. 6s
SPANISH GOLD. *Fifth Edition.* Cr. 8vo 6s
THE SEARCH PARTY. *Fourth Edition* Cr. 8vo. 6s.

Bowen (Marjorie). I WILL MAINTAIN. *Fourth Edition.* Cr. 8vo. 6s.

Bretherton (Ralph Harold). AN HONEST MAN. *Second Edition.* Cr. 8vo. 6s.

Capes (Bernard). WHY DID HE DO IT? *Third Edition.* Cr. 8vo. 6s

Castle (Agnes and Egerton). FLOWER O' THE ORANGE, and Other Tales. *Third Edition.* Cr. 8vo. 6s

Clifford (Mrs. W K) THE GETTING WELL OF DOROTHY Illustrated *Second Edition.* Cr 8vo. 3s. 6d

Conrad (Joseph). THE SECRET AGENT: A Simple Tale. *Fourth Ed* Cr 8vo. 6s.
A SET OF SIX. *Fourth Edition* Cr 8vo. 6s.

Corelli (Marie) A ROMANCE OF TWO WORLDS. *Thirtieth Ed.* Cr. 8vo. 6s
VENDETTA *Twenty-Eighth Edition* Cr. 8vo 6s.
THELMA. *Fortieth Ed.* Cr. 8vo. 6s
ARDATH: THE STORY OF A DEAD SELF. *Nineteenth Edition* Cr. 8vo 6s
THE SOUL OF LILITH. *Sixteenth Edition.* Cr. 8vo. 6s.
WORMWOOD. *Seventeenth Ed* Cr 8vo. 6s.
BARABBAS: A DREAM OF THE WORLD'S TRAGEDY. *Forty-Fourth Edition.* Cr. 8vo. 6s.
THE SORROWS OF SATAN. *Fifty-Sixth Edition.* Cr. 8vo. 6s
THE MASTER CHRISTIAN *Twelfth Edition.* 177th Thousand. Cr. 8vo. 6s
TEMPORAL POWER: A STUDY IN SUPREMACY. *Second Edition.* 150th Thousand. Cr 8vo 6s
GOD'S GOOD MAN: A SIMPLE LOVE STORY *Fourteenth Edition* 152nd Thousand. Cr. 8vo 6s
HOLY ORDERS: THE TRAGEDY OF A QUIET LIFE. *Second Edition* 120th Thousand Crown 8vo 6s
THE MIGHTY ATOM. *Twenty-eighth Edition.* Cr. 8vo. 6s

BOY: a Sketch. *Eleventh Edition.* Cr. 8vo 6s
CAMEOS. *Thirteenth Edition* Cr 8vo. 6s

Cotes (Mrs. Everard). See Duncan (Sara Jeannette).

Crockett (S. R). LOCHINVAR. Illustrated. *Third Edition* Cr 8vo. 6s.
THE STANDARD BEARER. *Second Edition.* Cr. 8vo. 6s.

Croker (Mrs B. M). THE OLD CANTONMENT. Cr. 8vo 6s.
JOHANNA. *Second Edition* Cr 8vo. 6s
THE HAPPY VALLEY. *Fourth Edition* Cr. 8vo 6s
A NINE DAYS' WONDER. *Third Edition.* Cr. 8vo. 6s
PEGGY OF THE BARTONS. *Seventh Edition* Cr 8vo 6s.
ANGEL *Fifth Edition.* Cr 8vo 6s.
A STATE SECRET. *Third Edition.* Cr. 8vo 3s. 6d
KATHERINE THE ARROGANT. *Sixth Edition* Cr 8vo. 6s.

Cuthell (Edith E) ONLY A GUARDROOM DOG Illustrated Cr. 8vo. 3s. 6d

Dawson (Warrington) THE SCAR. *Second Edition.* Cr. 8vo. 6s.
THE SCOURGE. Cr. 8vo. 6s.

Douglas (Theo.) COUSIN HUGH. *Second Edition* Cr 8vo. 6s.

Doyle (A Conan). ROUND THE RED LAMP. *Eleventh Edition.* Cr. 8vo. 6s.

Duncan (Sara Jeannette) (Mrs. Everard Cotes).
A VOYAGE OF CONSOLATION. Illustrated. *Third Edition* Cr 8vo. 6s
COUSIN CINDERELLA. *Second Edition* Cr 8vo 6s.
THE BURNT OFFERING. *Second Edition.* Cr 8vo. 6s

*Elliott (Robert). THE IMMORTAL CHARLATAN. *Crown 8vo.* 6s.

Fenn (G Manville). SYD BELTON, or, The Boy who would not go to Sea Illustrated. *Second Ed.* Cr 8vo. 3s. 6d

Findlater (J. H.). THE GREEN GRAVES OF BALGOWRIE. *Fifth Edition* Cr 8vo. 6s
THE LADDER TO THE STARS. *Second Edition.* Cr. 8vo. 6s.

Findlater (Mary). A NARROW WAY *Third Edition* Cr 8vo 6s
OVER THE HILLS. *Second Edition.* Cr 8vo. 6s
THE ROSE OF JOY *Third Edition* Cr 8vo 6s
A BLIND BIRD'S NEST Illustrated *Second Edition* Cr 8vo. 6s

Francis (M E). (Mrs. Francis Blundell) STEPPING WESTWARD. *Second Edition.* Cr. 8vo. 6s.

MARGERY O' THE MILL. *Third Edition. Cr. 8vo. 6s.*

HARDY-ON-THE-HILL. *Third Edition* Cr. 8vo. 6s

GALATEA OF THE WHEATFIELD. *Second Edition* Cr 8vo 6s.

Fraser (Mrs. Hugh). THE SLAKING OF THE SWORD. *Second Edition* Cr 8vo. 6s.

GIANNELLA *Second Edition* Cr 8vo 6s

IN THE SHADOW OF THE LORD. *Third Edition.* Cr. 8vo. 6s.

Fry (B and C. B) A MOTHER'S SON *Fifth Edition.* Cr. 8vo 6s.

Gerard (Louise). THE GOLDEN CEN-TIPEDE. *Third Edition.* Cr 8vo. 6s

Gibbs (Philip). THE SPIRIT OF RE-VOLT *Second Edition.* Cr. 8vo. 6s

Gissing (George) THE CROWN OF LIFE. Cr. 8vo 6s.

Glendon (George). THE EMPEROR OF THE AIR. Illustrated. Cr. 8vo. 6s

Hamilton (Cosmo). MRS. SKEFFING-TON *Second Edition.* Cr. 8vo 6s.

Harraden (Beatrice) IN VARYING MOODS. *Fourteenth Edition.* Cr. 8vo. 6s

THE SCHOLAR'S DAUGHTER. *Fourth Edition* Cr 8vo. 6s.

HILDA STRAFFORD and THE REMIT-TANCE MAN. *Twelfth Ed.* Cr. 8vo. 6s.

INTERPLAY. *Fifth Edition.* Cr. 8vo. 6s.

Hichens (Robert) THE PROPHET OF BERKELEY SQUARE. *Second Edition.* Cr. 8vo. 6s.

TONGUES OF CONSCIENCE. *Third Edition.* Cr. 8vo 6s.

FELIX. *Seventh Edition.* Cr. 8vo. 6s.

THE WOMAN WITH THE FAN *Eighth Edition.* Cr. 8vo 6s.

BYEWAYS Cr. 8vo 6s.

THE GARDEN OF ALLAH. *Nineteenth Edition.* Cr. 8vo 6s.

THE BLACK SPANIEL. Cr 8vo. 6s.

THE CALL OF THE BLOOD. *Seventh Edition.* Cr 8vo. 6s

BARBARY SHEEP. *Second Edition.* Cr. 8vo. 6s.

Hilliers (Ashton). THE MASTER-GIRL. Illustrated. *Second Edition.* Cr. 8vo. 6s.

Hope (Anthony) THE GOD IN THE CAR. *Eleventh Edition.* Cr. 8vo 6s

A CHANGE OF AIR. *Sixth Edition* Cr. 8vo. 6s

A MAN OF MARK. *Sixth Ed* Cr 8vo 6s

THE CHRONICLES OF COUNT AN-TONIO *Sixth Edition.* Cr. 8vo 6s

PHROSO. Illustrated. *Eighth Edition* Cr. 8vo 6s

SIMON DALE. Illustrated. *Eighth Edition* Cr 8vo 6s

THE KING'S MIRROR. *Fifth Edition.* Cr. 8vo. 6s.

QUISANTE. *Fourth Edition.* Cr. 8vo 6s

THE DOLLY DIALOGUES Cr 8vo 6s

A SERVANT OF THE PUBLIC. Illustrated. *Fourth Edition.* Cr. 8vo 6s

TALES OF TWO PEOPLE *Third Edition.* Cr. 8vo. 6s.

THE GREAT MISS DRIVER. *Fourth Edition.* Cr. 8vo 6s.

Hueffer (Ford Maddox). AN ENGLISH GIRL · A ROMANCE. *Second Edition* Cr 8vo. 6s

MR. APOLLO: A JUST POSSIBLE STORY *Second Edition.* Cr. 8vo. 6s.

Hutten (Baroness von). THE HALO. *Fifth Edition.* Cr. 8vo 6s.

Hyne (C. J. Cutcliffe). MR. HOR-ROCKS, PURSER. *Fifth Edition.* Cr. 8vo 6s

PRINCE RUPERT, THE BUCCANEER Illustrated. *Third Edition.* Cr. 8vo. 6s.

Jacobs (W. W.) MANY CARGOES. *Thirty-first Edition.* Cr. 8vo. 3s. 6d.

SEA URCHINS *Sixteenth Edition.* Cr. 8vo 3s. 6d.

A MASTER OF CRAFT Illustrated. *Ninth Edition.* Cr. 8vo. 3s. 6d

LIGHT FREIGHTS. Illustrated. *Eighth Edition.* Cr. 8vo 3s 6d

THE SKIPPER'S WOOING. *Ninth Edition.* Cr. 8vo 3s. 6d.

AT SUNWICH PORT Illustrated *Tenth Edition.* Cr. 8vo 3s. 6d.

DIALSTONE LANE. Illustrated. *Seventh Edition.* Cr. 8vo. 3s 6d.

ODD CRAFT Illustrated. *Fourth Edition* Cr 8vo 3s 6d.

THE LADY OF THE BARGE Illustrated *Eighth Edition* Cr. 8vo. 3s 6d

SALTHAVEN Illustrated. *Second Edition* Cr. 8vo. 3s. 6d.

SAILORS' KNOTS. Illustrated. *Fifth Edition* Cr 8vo 3s 6d.

James (Henry). THE SOFT SIDE. *Second Edition* Cr. 8vo. 6s.

THE BETTER SORT. Cr. 8vo. 6s

THE GOLDEN BOWL. *Third Edition* Cr. 8vo. 6s

Le Queux (William) THE HUNCHBACK OF WESTMINSTER. *Third Edition* Cr. 8vo. 6s.

THE CLOSED BOOK. *Third Edition* Cr. 8vo. 6s

THE VALLEY OF THE SHADOW. Illustrated *Third Edition* Cr. 8vo 6s

BEHIND THE THRONE *Third Edition* Cr. 8vo. 6s.

THE CROOKED WAY *Second Edition* Cr. 8vo 6s

Lindsey (William) THE SEVERED MANTLE. Cr. 8vo 6s.

London (Jack). WHITE FANG. *Seventh Edition.* Cr. 8vo 6s

Lubbock (Basil). DEEP SEA WARRIORS. Illustrated. *Third Edition.* Cr. 8vo. 6s.

Lucas (St John) THE FIRST ROUND Cr. 8vo 6s.

Lyall (Edna). DERRICK VAUGHAN, NOVELIST. 44th *Thousand. Cr 8vo* 3s. 6d.

Maartens (Maarten). THE NEW RELIGION: A MODERN NOVEL. *Third Edition.* Cr 8vo. 6s.
BROTHERS ALL; MORE STORIES OF DUTCH PEASANT LIFE. *Third Edition* Cr. 8vo 6s
THE PRICE OF LIS DORIS *Second Edition.* Cr. 8vo. 6s.

M'Carthy (Justin H.). THE DUKE'S MOTTO. *Fourth Edition.* Cr 8vo 6s

Macnaughtan (S.). THE FORTUNE OF CHRISTINA M'NAB. *Fifth Edition.* Cr. 8vo 6s.

Malet (Lucas). COLONEL ENDERBY'S WIFE. *Fourth Edition.* Cr. 8vo. 6s
A COUNSEL OF PERFECTION. *Second Edition.* Cr. 8vo 6s.
THE WAGES OF SIN. *Sixteenth Edition.* Cr. 8vo. 6s.
THE CARISSIMA. *Fifth Ed* Cr 8vo 6s
THE GATELESS BARRIER. *Fifth Edition* Cr 8vo 6s
THE HISTORY OF SIR RICHARD CALMADY. *Seventh Edition* Cr 8vo 6s.

Mann (Mrs. M E). THE PARISH NURSE. *Fourth Edition.* Cr 8vo 6s.
A SHEAF OF CORN. *Second Edition.* Cr 8vo 6s.
THE HEART-SMITER. *Second Edition* Cr 8vo. 6s.
AVENGING CHILDREN. *Second Edition.* Cr. 8vo. 6s.

Marsh (Richard). THE COWARD BEHIND THE CURTAIN. Cr. 8vo. 6s.
THE SURPRISING HUSBAND *Second Edition* Cr 8vo 6s
A ROYAL INDISCRETION *Second Edition.* Cr 8vo 6s.
LIVE MEN'S SHOES. *Second Edition.* Cr. 8vo. 6s.

Marshall (Archibald). MANY JUNES. *Second Edition* Cr. 8vo 6s
THE SQUIRE'S DAUGHTER. *Third Edition.* Cr. 8vo. 6s.

Mason (A. E. W.) CLEMENTINA. Illustrated. *Third Edition.* Cr 8vo. 6s.

Maud (Constance). A DAUGHTER OF FRANCE. *Second Edition.* Cr 8vo. 6s.

Maxwell (W B) VIVIEN. *Ninth Edition* Cr 8vo 6s.
THE RAGGED MESSENGER. *Third Edition* Cr. 8vo. 6s
FABULOUS FANCIES. Cr. 8vo. 6s.

THE GUARDED FLAME. *Seventh Edition* Cr. 8vo. 6s.
ODD LENGTHS *Second Ed.* Cr. 8vo. 6s.
HILL RISE. *Fourth Edition.* Cr. 8vo. 6s.
THE COUNTESS OF MAYBURY BETWEEN YOU AND I. *Fourth Edition* Cr. 8vo 6s.

Meade (L. T.) DRIFT. *Second Edition.* Cr. 8vo. 6s.
RESURGAM *Second Edition.* Cr. 8vo. 6s.
VICTORY. Cr. 8vo. 6s
A GIRL OF THE PEOPLE. Illustrated. *Fourth Edition* Cr. 8vo. 3s. 6d.
HEPSY GIPSY. Illustrated. Cr 8vo 2s 6d.
THE HONOURABLE MISS: A STORY OF AN OLD-FASHIONED TOWN Illustrated. *Second Edition.* Cr 8vo 3s 6d.

Mitford (Bertram). THE SIGN OF THE SPIDER. Illustrated. *Seventh Edition* Cr 8vo 3s 6d

Molesworth (Mrs.). THE RED GRANGE. Illustrated. *Second Edition.* Cr. 8vo. 3s 6d.

Montague (C. E). A HIND LET LOOSE *Third Edition.* Cr. 8vo 6s

Montgomery (K L). COLONEL KATE. *Second Edition.* Cr 8vo. 6s.

Morrison (Arthur). TALES OF MEAN STREETS *Seventh Edition.* Cr 8vo 6s.
A CHILD OF THE JAGO. *Fifth Edition* Cr 8vo. 6s.
THE HOLE IN THE WALL. *Fourth Edition.* Cr. 8vo. 6s.
DIVERS VANITIES Cr 8vo 6s

Nesbit (E), (Mrs H. Bland). THE RED HOUSE Illustrated *Fourth Edition* Cr. 8vo 6s

Noble (Edward) LORDS OF THE SEA. *Third Edition.* Cr. 8vo. 6s.

Ollivant (Alfred). OWD BOB, THE GREY DOG OF KENMUIR. With a Frontispiece. *Eleventh Ed* Cr. 8vo. 6s.

Oppenheim (E Phillips) MASTER OF MEN. *Fourth Edition* Cr 8vo 6s.

Oxenham (John) A WEAVER OF WEBS. Illustrated *Fourth Ed.* Cr. 8vo 6s
THE GATE OF THE DESERT. *Fourth Edition* Cr 8vo 6s
PROFIT AND LOSS *Fourth Edition.* Cr 8vo. 6s.
THE LONG ROAD. *Fourth Edition.* Cr 8vo 6s
THE SONG OF HYACINTH, AND OTHER STORIES. *Second Edition* Cr. 8vo. 6s.
MY LADY OF SHADOWS. *Fourth Edition* Cr 8vo 6s.

Pain (Barry) THE EXILES OF FALOO Crown 8vo 6s

Parker (Gilbert). PIERRE AND HIS PEOPLE. *Sixth Edition* Cr. 8vo. 6s

MRS FALCHION. *Fifth Edition. Cr 8vo 6s.*

THE TRANSLATION OF A SAVAGE *Third Edition Cr 8vo 6s*

THE TRAIL OF THE SWORD. Illustrated. *Tenth Edition Cr 8vo. 6s.*

WHEN VALMOND CAME TO PONTIAC The Story of a Lost Napoleon. *Sixth Edition Cr 8vo 6s.*

AN ADVENTURER OF THE NORTH The Last Adventures of 'Pretty Pierre.' *Fourth Edition. Cr 8vo 6s*

THE SEATS OF THE MIGHTY. Illustrated. *Sixteenth Edition Cr 8vo. 6s.*

THE BATTLE OF THE STRONG: a Romance of Two Kingdoms. Illustrated. *Sixth Edition. Cr. 8vo. 6s.*

THE POMP OF THE LAVILETTES. *Third Edition Cr 8vo 3s. 6d.*

NORTHERN LIGHTS. *Fourth Edition. Cr 8vo. 6s.*

Pasture (Mrs. Henry de la) THE TYRANT. *Fourth Edition Cr. 8vo. 6s*

Patterson (J. E). WATCHERS BY THE SHORE *Third Edition. Cr. 8vo. 6s.*

Pemberton (Max). THE FOOTSTEPS OF A THRONE. Illustrated. *Fourth Edition. Cr 8vo 6s.*

I CROWN THEE KING Illustrated *Cr. 8vo 6s.*

LOVE THE HARVESTER: A STORY OF THE SHIRES Illustrated *Third Edition. Cr. 8vo. 3s 6d*

THE MYSTERY OF THE GREEN HEART. *Second Edition Cr 8vo. 6s.*

Phillpotts (Eden). LYING PROPHETS *Third Edition Cr 8vo 6s*

CHILDREN OF THE MIST. *Fifth Edition. Cr. 8vo. 6s.*

THE HUMAN BOY. With a Frontispiece *Seventh Edition. Cr. 8vo 6s.*

SONS OF THE MORNING. *Second Edition Cr. 8vo. 6s.*

THE RIVER. *Third Edition. Cr. 8vo. 6s*

THE AMERICAN PRISONER. *Fourth Edition Cr 8vo 6s.*

THE SECRET WOMAN. *Fourth Edition Cr 8vo 6s.*

KNOCK AT A VENTURE *Third Edition. Cr 8vo 6s*

THE PORTREEVE. *Fourth Edition Cr 8vo. 6s*

THE POACHER'S WIFE *Second Edition Cr. 8vo. 6s*

THE STRIKING HOURS *Second Edition Cr 8vo. 6s*

THE FOLK AFIELD. *Crown 8vo. 6s.*

Pickthall (Marmaduke) SAÏD THE FISHERMAN. *Seventh Edition Cr 8vo. 6s.*

'Q' (A. T. Quiller Couch) THE WHITE WOLF. *Second Edition. Cr 8vo 6s.*

THE MAYOR OF TROY *Fourth Edition. Cr. 8vo 6s*

MERRY-GARDEN AND OTHER STORIES. *Cr. 8vo. 6s.*

MAJOR VIGOUREUX. *Third Edition. Cr. 8vo. 6s*

Querido (Israel) TOIL OF MEN. Translated by F S ARNOLD. *Cr 8vo 6s*

Rawson (Maud Stepney). THE ENCHANTED GARDEN. *Fourth Edition. Cr. 8vo. 6s.*

THE EASY GO LUCKIES OR, ONE WAY OF LIVING. *Second Edition. Cr. 8vo. 6s.*

HAPPINESS *Second Edition. Cr 8vo. 6s*

Rhys (Grace) THE BRIDE. *Second Edition Cr 8vo 6s*

Ridge (W. Pett). ERB. *Second Edition. Cr 8vo 6s*

A SON OF THE STATE. *Second Edition. Cr. 8vo. 3s 6d*

A BREAKER OF LAWS. *Cr. 8vo 3s. 6d.*

MRS. GALER'S BUSINESS Illustrated. *Second Edition. Cr. 8vo. 6s.*

THE WICKHAMSES *Fourth Edition Cr 8vo 6s*

NAME OF GARLAND. *Third Edition Cr 8vo 6s*

SPLENDID BROTHER. *Fourth Edition. Cr 8vo. 6s.*

Ritchie (Mrs. David G.) MAN AND THE CASSOCK. *Second Edition Cr 8vo. 6s.*

Roberts (C. G D) THE HEART OF THE ANCIENT WOOD. *Cr. 8vo. 3s 6d.*

Robins (Elizabeth). THE CONVERT. *Third Edition. Cr. 8vo. 6s.*

Rosenkrantz (Baron Palle). THE MAGISTRATE'S OWN CASE. *Cr. 8vo. 6s*

Russell (W. Clark). MY DANISH SWEETHEART. Illustrated *Fifth Edition Cr. 8vo 6s.*

HIS ISLAND PRINCESS. Illustrated. *Second Edition. Cr. 8vo. 6s*

ABANDONED. *Second Edition Cr 8vo 6s*

MASTER ROCKAFELLAR'S VOYAGE Illustrated *Fourth Edition. Cr. 8vo 3s 6d.*

Sandys (Sydney). JACK CARSTAIRS OF THE POWER HOUSE Illustrated. *Second Edition. Cr. 8vo. 6s*

Sergeant (Adeline) THE PASSION OF PAUL MARILLIER. *Cr 8vo 6s.*

*Shakespear (Olivia). UNCLE HILARY. *Cr. 8vo 6s*

Sidgwick (Mrs. Alfred) THE KINSMAN. Illustrated. *Third Edition. Cr. 8vo. 6s.*

THE SEVERINS. *Fourth Edition. Cr. 8vo 6s.*

Stewart (Newton V.) A SON OF THE EMPEROR.: BEING PASSAGES FROM THE LIFE OF ENZIO, KING OF SARDINIA AND CORSICA *Cr 8vo 6s*

Swayne (Martin Lutrell) THE BISHOP AND THE LADY. *Second Edition Cr 8vo 6s.*

Thurston (E Temple). MIRAGE *Fourth Edition. Cr. 8vo. 6s.*

Underhill (Evelyn). THE COLUMN OF DUST *Cr. 8vo 6s*

Vorst (Marie Van). THE SENTIMEN-TAL ADVENTURES OF JIMMY BUL-STRODE *Cr. 8vo 6s*
IN AMBUSH. *Second Edition. Cr. 8vo. 6s.*

Walneman (Paul). 'THE WIFE OF NICHOLAS FLEMING. *Cr. 8vo 6s*

Watson (H. B Marriott). TWISTED EGLANTINE. Illustrated *Third Edition. Cr 8vo. 6s.*
THE HIGH TOBY *Third Edition. Cr. 8vo 6s*
A MIDSUMMER DAY'S DREAM *Third Edition Cr 8vo 6s.*
THE CASTLE BY THE SEA *Third Edition Cr 8vo. 6s.*
THE PRIVATEERS. Illustrated *Second Edition Cr 8vo 6s*
A POPPY SHOW · BEING DIVERS AND DIVERSE TALES *Cr. 8vo 6s.*
THE FLOWER OF THE HEART. *Third Edition Cr. 8vo 6s*

Webling (Peggy) THE STORY OF VIRGINIA PERFECT. *Third Edition Cr 8vo. 6s*
•THE SPIRIT OF MIRTH. *Cr. 8vo. 6s*

Wells (H. G.). THE SEA LADY. *Cr 8vo. 6s.* Also *Medium 8vo. 6d.*

Weyman (Stanley). UNDER THE RED ROBE. Illustrated. *Twenty-Second Edition Cr 8vo 6s.*

Whitby (Beatrice). THE RESULT OF AN ACCIDENT. *Second Edition. Cr. 8vo. 6s.*

White (Edmund). THE HEART OF HINDUSTAN. *Cr. 8vo 6s*

White (Percy). LOVE AND THE WISE MEN *Third Edition. Cr. 8vo. 6s.*

Williamson (Mrs C. N). THE ADVEN-TURE OF PRINCESS SYLVIA *Second Edition. Cr 8vo 6s.*
THE WOMAN WHO DARED. *Cr. 8vo. 6s.*
THE SEA COULD TELL. *Second Edition. Cr 8vo 6s*
THE CASTLE OF THE SHADOWS. *Third Edition. Cr. 8vo. 6s.*
PAPA. *Cr 8vo. 6s.*

Williamson (C N and A M). THE LIGHTNING CONDUCTOR: The Strange Adventures of a Motor Car. Illustrated. *Seventeenth Edition Cr 8vo. 6s* Also *Cr 8vo. 1s net*
THE PRINCESS PASSES : A Romance of a Motor. Illustrated. *Ninth Edition Cr. 8vo 6s.*
MY FRIEND THE CHAUFFEUR. Illustrated *Tenth Edition Cr. 8vo 6s*
LADY BETTY ACROSS THE WATER. *Tenth Edition Cr 8vo 6s.*
THE CAR OF DESTINY AND ITS ERRAND IN SPAIN. Illustrated. *Fourth Edition Cr 8vo 6s.*
THE BOTOR CHAPERON. Illustrated. *Sixth Edition. Cr 8vo 6s.*
SCARLET RUNNER. Illustrated. *Third Edition. Cr. 8vo. 6s.*
SET IN SILVER. Illustrated. *Third Edition. Cr. 8vo 6s.*
LORD LOVELAND DISCOVERS AMERICA *Second Edition. Cr 8vo. 6s.*

Wyllarde (Dolf). THE PATHWAY OF THE PIONEER (Nous Autres). *Fourth Edition. Cr. 8vo. 6s.*

Books for Boys and Girls.

Illustrated. Crown 8vo. 3s. 6d.

THE GETTING WELL OF DOROTHY. By Mrs. W. K. Clifford. *Second Edition.*

ONLY A GUARD-ROOM DOG. By Edith E. Cuthell

MASTER ROCKAFELLAR'S VOYAGE By W. Clark Russell. *Fourth Edition.*

SYD BELTON : Or, the Boy who would not go to Sea. By G. Manville Fenn. *Second Edition.*

THE RED GRANGE. By Mrs Molesworth *Second Edition.*

A GIRL OF THE PEOPLE By L. T Meade. *Fourth Edition.*

HEPSY GIPSY. By L. T. Meade. *2s. 6d.*

THE HONOURABLE MISS. By L. T. Meade. *Second Edition*

THERE WAS ONCE A PRINCE. By Mrs. M E. Mann.

WHEN ARNOLD COMES HOME. By Mrs. M. E. Mann

The Novels of Alexandre Dumas.

Medium 8vo   Price 6d.   Double Volumes, 1s.

ACTÉ.

THE ADVENTURES OF CAPTAIN PAMPHILE.

AMAURY.

THE BIRD OF FATE.

THE BLACK TULIP.

THE CASTLE OF EPPSTEIN

CATHERINE BLUM.

CÉCILE.

THE CHATELET.

THE CHEVALIER D'HARMENTAL   (Double volume)

CHICOT THE JESTER.

THE COMTE DE MONTGOMERY

CONSCIENCE.

THE CONVICT'S SON.

THE CORSICAN BROTHERS; and OTHO THE ARCHER.

CROP-EARED JACQUOT.

DOM GORENFLOT.

THE FATAL COMBAT.

THE FENCING MASTER.

FERNANDE.

GABRIEL LAMBERT

GEORGES.

THE GREAT MASSACRE

HENRI DE NAVARRE

HÉLÈNE DE CHAVERNY

THE HOROSCOPE.

LOUISE DE LA VALLIÈRE. (Double volume.)

THE MAN IN THE IRON MASK. (Double volume.)

MAÎTRE ADAM.

THE MOUTH OF HELL.

NANON (Double volume.)

OLYMPIA.

PAULINE; PASCAL BRUNO; and BONTEKOR.

PÈRE LA RUINE.

THE PRINCE OF THIEVES.

THE REMINISCENCES OF ANTONY.

ROBIN HOOD.

SAMUEL GELB

THE SNOWBALL AND THE SULTANETTA

SYLVANDIRE.

THE TAKING OF CALAIS.

TALES OF THE SUPERNATURAL.

TALES OF STRANGE ADVENTURE.

TALES OF TERROR.

THE THREE MUSKETEERS (Double volume)

THE TRAGEDY OF NANTES.

TWENTY YEARS AFTER. (Double volume)

THE WILD-DUCK SHOOTER.

THE WOLF LEADER.

Methuen's Sixpenny Books.

Medium 8vo.

Albanesi (E Maria). LOVE AND LOUISA.

I KNOW A MAIDEN.

Anstey (F). A BAYARD OF BENGAL.

Austen (J). PRIDE AND PREJUDICE.

Bagot (Richard). A ROMAN MYSTERY.

CASTING OF NETS.

DONNA DIANA

Balfour (Andrew). BY STROKE OF SWORD.

Baring-Gould (S) FURZE BLOOM.

CHEAP JACK ZITA.

KITTY ALONE.

URITH.

THE BROOM SQUIRE.

IN THE ROAR OF THE SEA.

NOÉMI.

A BOOK OF FAIRY TALES. Illustrated.

LITTLE TU'PENNY

WINEFRED.

THE FROBISHERS.

THE QUEEN OF LOVE

ARMINELL.
BLADYS OF THE STEWPONEY.

Barr (Robert). JENNIE BAXTER.
IN THE MIDST OF ALARMS.
THE COUNTESS TEKLA.
THE MUTABLE MANY.

Benson (E F) DODO.
THE VINTAGE.

Brontë (Charlotte) SHIRLEY.

Brownell (C. L). THE HEART OF JAPAN.

Burton (J Bloundelle). ACROSS THE SALT SEAS.

Caffyn (Mrs). ANNE MAULEVERER.

Capes (Bernard) THE LAKE OF WINE.

Clifford (Mrs W K). A FLASH OF SUMMER.
MRS. KEITH'S CRIME.

Corbett (Julian) A BUSINESS IN GREAT WATERS.

Croker (Mrs B M) ANGEL.
A STATE SECRET.
PEGGY OF THE BARTONS
JOHANNA.

Dante (Alighieri) THE DIVINE COMEDY (Cary)

Doyle (A Conan). ROUND THE RED LAMP

Duncan (Sara Jeannette). A VOYAGE OF CONSOLATION
THOSE DELIGHTFUL AMERICANS

Eliot (George) THE MILL ON THE FLOSS.

Findlater (Jane H). THE GREEN GRAVES OF BALGOWRIE.

Gallon (Tom). RICKERBY'S FOLLY.

Gaskell (Mrs). CRANFORD.
MARY BARTON
NORTH AND SOUTH.

Gerard (Dorothea). HOLY MATRIMONY.
THE CONQUEST OF LONDON.
MADE OF MONEY.

Gissing (G.). THE TOWN TRAVELLER
THE CROWN OF LIFE.

Glanville (Ernest). THE INCA'S TREASURE.
THE KLOOF BRIDE.

Gleig (Charles). BUNTER'S CRUISE.

Grimm (The Brothers). GRIMM'S FAIRY TALES

Hope (Anthony). A MAN OF MARK.
A CHANGE OF AIR.
THE CHRONICLES OF COUNT ANTONIO.
PHROSO.
THE DOLLY DIALOGUES.

Hornung (E. W.). DEAD MEN TELL NO TALES.

Ingraham (J. H.). THE THRONE OF DAVID.

Le Queux (W.). THE HUNCHBACK OF WESTMINSTER.

Levett-Yeats (S. K.). THE TRAITOR'S WAY.
ORRAIN.

Linton (E. Lynn). THE TRUE HISTORY OF JOSHUA DAVIDSON.

Lyall (Edna). DERRICK VAUGHAN.

Malet (Lucas). THE CARISSIMA.
A COUNSEL OF PERFECTION

Mann (Mrs. M. E.). MRS PETER HOWARD.
A LOST ESTATE.
THE CEDAR STAR.
ONE ANOTHER'S BURDENS
THE PATTEN EXPERIMENT.
A WINTER'S TALE.

Marchmont (A. W.). MISER HOADLEY'S SECRET.
A MOMENT'S ERROR.

Marryat (Captain). PETER SIMPLE
JACOB FAITHFUL.

March (Richard). A METAMORPHOSIS
THE TWICKENHAM PEERAGE.
THE GODDESS.
THE JOSS.

Mason (A. E. W.). CLEMENTINA

Mathers (Helen). HONEY.
GRIFF OF GRIFFITHSCOURT.
SAM'S SWEETHEART.
THE FERRYMAN.

Meade (Mrs. L. T.). DRIFT.

Miller (Esther). LIVING LIES.

Mitford (Bertram). THE SIGN OF THE SPIDER.

Montresor (F. F.). THE ALIEN

Morrison (Arthur). THE HOLE IN THE WALL.

Nesbit (E.). THE RED HOUSE.

Norris (W. E.). HIS GRACE.
GILES INGILBY.
THE CREDIT OF THE COUNTY.
LORD LEONARD THE LUCKLESS.
MATTHEW AUSTEN
CLARISSA FURIOSA.

Oliphant (Mrs.). THE LADY'S WALK.
SIR ROBERT'S FORTUNE.
THE PRODIGALS
THE TWO MARYS

Oppenheim (E. P.). MASTER OF MEN.

Parker (Gilbert). THE POMP OF THE LAVILETTES.
WHEN VALMOND CAME TO PONTIAC.
THE TRAIL OF THE SWORD

Pemberton (Max). THE FOOTSTEPS OF A THRONE.
I CROWN THEE KING.

Phillpotts (Eden). THE HUMAN BOY
CHILDREN OF THE MIST.
THE POACHER'S WIFE.
THE RIVER.

'Q' (A. T. Quiller Couch). THE WHITE WOLF.

Ridge (W. Pett). A SON OF THE STATE.
LOST PROPERTY.
GEORGE and THE GENERAL.

ERB.

Russell (W. Clark). ABANDONED.
A MARRIAGE AT SEA.
MY DANISH SWEETHEART.
HIS ISLAND PRINCESS.

Sergeant (Adeline). THE MASTER OF BEECHWOOD
BALBARA'S MONEY
THE YELLOW DIAMOND
THE LOVE THAT OVERCAME.

Sidgwick (Mrs. Alfred). THE KINSMAN.

Surtees (R. S.). HANDLEY CROSS.
MR. SPONGE'S SPORTING TOUR
ASK MAMMA

Walford (Mrs. L. B.). MR. SMITH.
COUSINS.
THE BABY'S GRANDMOTHER.
TROUBLESOME DAUGHTERS.

Wallace (General Lew). BEN-HUR.
THE FAIR GOD.

Watson (H. B. Marriott). THE ADVENTURERS.
*CAPTAIN FORTUNE.

Weekes (A. B). PRISONERS OF WAR.

Wells (H. G.). THE SEA LADY.

White (Percy). A PASSIONATE PILGRIM.

PRINTED BY
WILLIAM CLOWES AND SONS, LIMITED,
LONDON AND BECCLES

Lightning Source UK Ltd.
Milton Keynes UK
UKOW021106270113

205403UK00006B/294/P